UFOS IN THE WHITE MOUNTAINS OF NEW HAMPSHIRE:

HIDING IN PLAIN SIGHT

FORMER LCDR JOHN SULLIVAN, USNR

This book is dedicated to Sydney Smith Sullivan, my wife, best friend, and partner, who saved my life when I had a vital equipment malfunction during a deep dive off the coast of Costa Rica. She was also a popular and respected Supervisory Senior Psychiatric Technician who served in private city jails via nursing services registry and the State of California's Departments of Developmental Services, Corrections, and Rehabilitation (with the criminally insane) for over 37 years prior to her retirement.

PREFACE

The intent of this book is to encourage people of the United States to look up into the clouds and skies above them. The truth is not "out there," as the Government and our media say, but in reality, it is "up there," hidden in plain sight. Another objective is also to advise the citizens of the United States directly (albeit through unofficial channels) that "We the People" have purportedly been notified by "other" entities that we must revisit—and perhaps reconsider—the actions of the U.S. Government and its "Military Technical/Industrial Complex" (MIC) first described by President Eisenhower in his farewell address in 1961. This includes all employees, agencies, and/or operatives of the Federal government of the United States of America regarding any criminal and/or legal responsibility that if it were known by the public, could be subject to prosecution. This, it has been said, must be done so the government will finally step up and reveal what they genuinely know about advanced alien civilizations and the treaties/agreements the Federal Government has made with them (past and/or present) in exchange for advanced technologies. To do this, it has been suggested, they must have complete immunity from legal action, because certain crimes may have been committed in violation of various international conventions.

Whatever one believes about this, there is evidence that much has been hidden about certain phenomena not just for decades—but for centuries. This book goes into the history of purported contact that has been reported on every continent and the purpose for such contact, including how the varying communities or civilizations reacted at the time. My desire here is to relay this kind of history as context for reported sightings and contact in the 20th and 21st centuries, including my sightings in my home in the White Mountains of New Hampshire. The subsequent photographs will be seen throughout this book.

I designed this book to serve as a primer to facilitate all U.S. citizens to conduct their own research to educate themselves about the possibility of such phenomena. Plus, I hope to encourage readers to investigate and demand Federal Government information about past and present reported UFO crashes and their retrieval by military and/or federal government authorities. The fact alone that the American public has been taxed to finance Black Operations' budgets is enough to be concerned about what *other* kinds of covert operations have been financed—and for what purpose. That the government has also covertly conducted and/or consented to human experiments is another aspect of the necessity of information regarding what might have been counter to international law via the Geneva Accords and Helsinki Protocols.

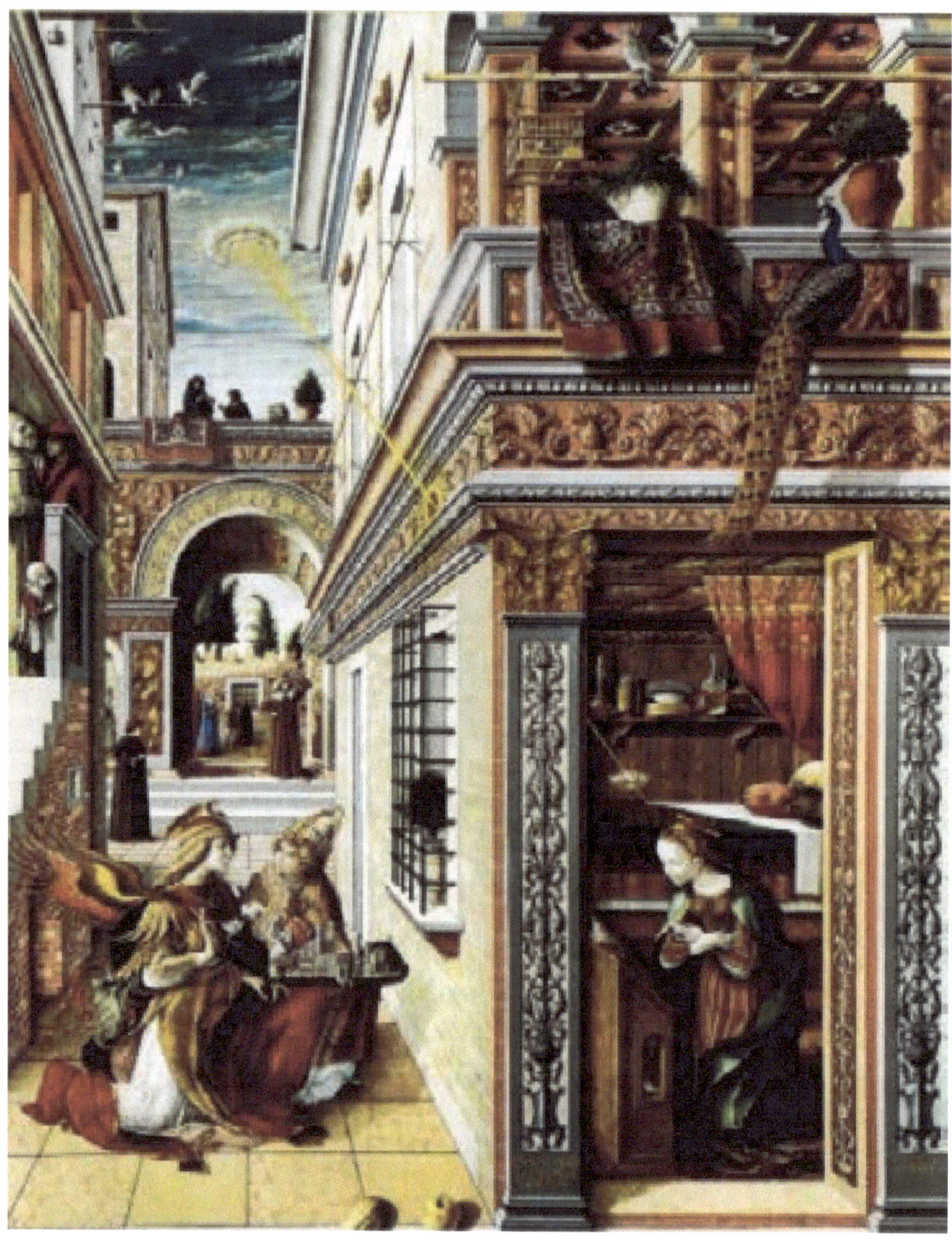

This work of art is titled The Annunciation with Saint Emidius created by the Artist Carlo Crivellis in 1486. It tells the story of the Archangel Gabriel who is distracted by the questions of a Bishop Saint named Emidius just before the Angel visits Mary to advise her of her pregnancy with the Christ Child Jesus. A cloud suggestive of a UFO is the apparent source of the Holy Spirit, which is coming down to Mary in the form of a dove. The painting is located in the town of Ascoli Piceno in the Italian Marches… UFOs have been seen by people throughout all humanity's ages of recorded time, and prior to it…

The position I take is that the time is long overdue for the government to come clean about its past and covert treaties/agreements etc. made with unidentified parties. This includes should any such treaties/agreements involve public health and experimentation to the detriment of individual liberties and our right to information. The government's usage of the "need to know," to use government-speak/military security parlance, seems to suggest government officials forget that the American people are sovereign, and that the government can only govern with our consent; this is especially important because through taxation, we are also footing the bills for certain actions that have a direct effect on our personal and collective sovereignty. We have the RIGHT to know about anything that directly affects us, and we have traditionally been far too patient in accepting distortion, red herrings, official denials, and silence of the U.S. Government and U.S. Military "for reasons of National Security." As someone who was an officer in the military with high-level security clearances—enough to also perform U.S. Congressional investigations—it is something I feel deeply for understandable reasons.

As a last note, the reader is free to accept, reject, or even ignore my research and theories, as a reader's own life experiences, research, and explorations may have already led them to alternate explanations. Again, my historical approach to purported UFO phenomena going back to prehistoric, ancient, and the colonial era of North America through to modern history are background to ask that we take our responsibility seriously in holding all of our governments accountable, whether it's about certain phenomena that has been kept secret—or even something much more obvious—how government has or has not acted when it has come to the imminent threats we have consistently experienced (climate change, unknown experimentation, covert agreements directly affecting the American public, etc.) in the name of government self-interest or willful disregard for the very people whom such governments are supposed to serve.

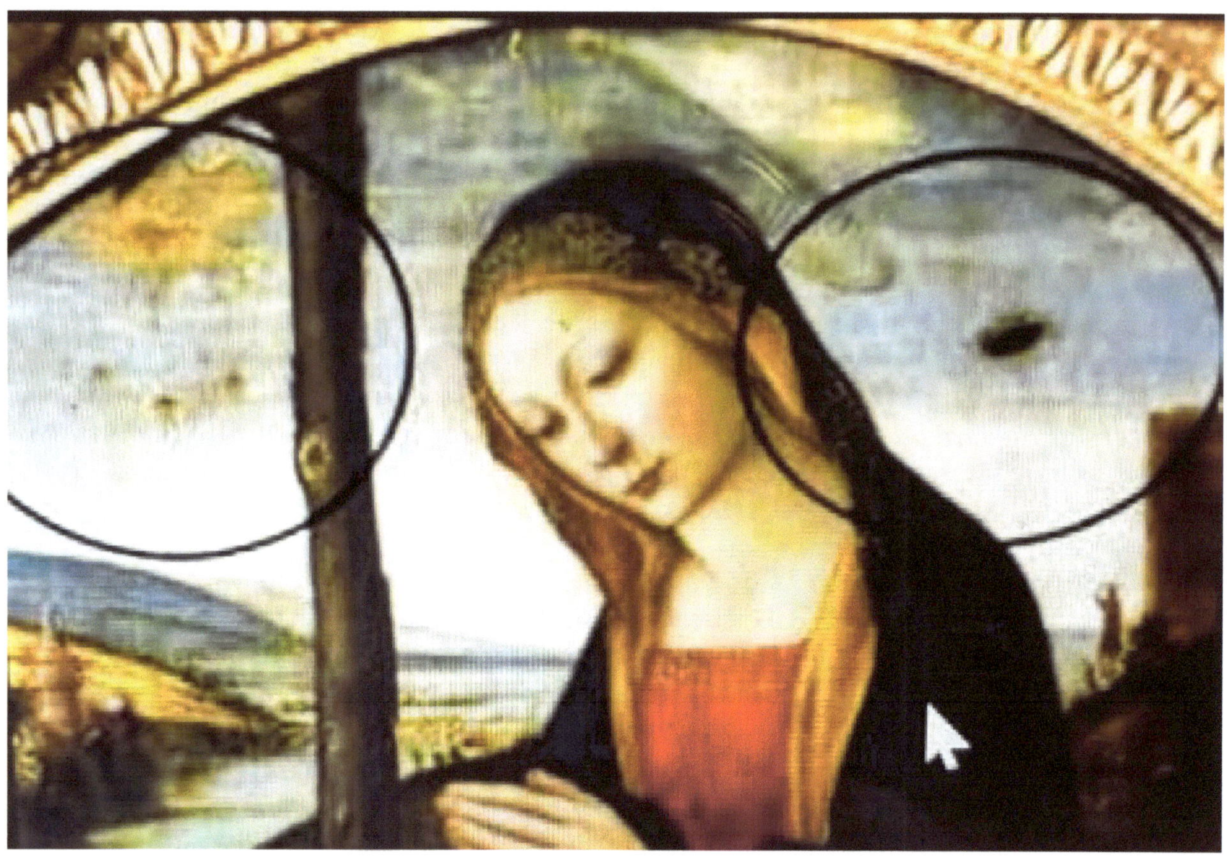

This Work of Art is titled The Madonna with Saint Giovannio but in modern times is called "Madonna of the UFO in Palazzio Vechio." It is located in the Hall of Hercules at the Vechio Palace in Florence Italy, and features what appear to be UFOs on the outer boundaries of the painting. It dates from the 1500s, or 16th Century. It is unknown for certain who painted it, as it was given to a nunnery. Credit for its creation is given by modern Scholars to Maestro del tondo Miller. Some disagree and believe it to be the work of Jacopo del Sellaio, or Sebastiano Maestro.

"There are more things in Heaven and Earth, Horatio, than are dreamt of in our Philosophy."

- Hamlet to Horatio in William Shakespeare's *Hamlet*

Chapter One

Native Americans and UFOs

The first inhabitants of Mount Washington and the White Mountains were Native Americans going back to Stone Age up to and after 10,000 BC. Paleo-Indian spear points, arrow heads, tomahawks, and other relics can often be found along streams, rivers, and lakes throughout the White Mountains and the Great North Woods.[1] In more recent history, the major Indian tribes who inhabited or hunted in the White Mountains included the Sokosis, Penacooks, Pequots, Penobscot, Pemigawasset, Coo-ash-aukes, Abenakis, St. Francis, Connecticut River, and Mohawk (Iroquois) Indians, the lattermost also called the "Five Nations."[2] The Mohawk's latter name was bestowed upon them by the British military and British colonists. It refers specifically to the Iroquois Confederacy (or League) of five tribes of which the Mohawks were a part. These five tribes held great councils in which intertribal matters including declarations of war, peace, and tribal cooperation on other matters were discussed. They would combine their resources and/or warriors as any challenge by enemy tribes or situational emergencies might require. The Five Nations were the Onondagas, Oneidas, Cayugas, Mohawk, and Senecas Tribes.[3] A historian could make a good argument that had the Iroquois Confederacy remained strong and intact, they may have kept the white colonists and later pioneers (or invaders), from taking over their lands. This, however, is speculation best left to historians, including Native American historians who have not had nearly enough of a presence in history books.

It is with the Native Americans that this story of certain phenomena, including what have been popularly known as Unidentified Flying Objects (UFOs) in the White Mountains, begins. The time period just after the year 1600 was the period when the French and English peoples began to explore (or invade) and establish their respective early settlements upon tribal lands that would later become the United States and Canada. From the most ancient times, the Native Americans associated the highest mountains of their lands with the Great Spirit, or a Manitou. A Manitou was the manifestation of the spiritual life force present in all living things and the environment. If not personifying as the Great Spirit, a Manitou could also be a good or evil spirit, either male or female.[4]

---

[1] Note: Please mark where found on a map *and* make sure these are not legally protected; always check with park rangers and any local tribes before taking home.

[2] Bisbee, 2-6.

[3] Radin, 276 -280

[4] Mount Rainier in the state of Washington, for example, was and is sacred to the Native Americans of the Northwest. It is also the same case with Mount Washington in New Hampshire. Mount Rainier's original Native American name came from the Puyallup tribe whose name for it was Tacoma, Tahoma, or Taquoma.

In the case of Mount Washington, its original ancient Native American name came down from the Algonquins as "Waumbik," meaning "White Rocks," whereas more local tribes like the Penacook, Abenakis, and others called the mountain "Angiochook" and "Angiocochook." Angiochook means "The Place of the Concealed One," and Angiocochook meant both "Home of the Great Spirit," and "Mother [of the] Storm."[5]

The connection of the White Mountains of New Hampshire with UFOs begins with the story of a famous chief of New England named Chief Passaconaway. His name in Penacook means "Child of the Bear."[6] While a young man, he already achieved a reputation as a war chief and shaman, or medicine man. A shaman was a holy man with a unique connection to the Great Spirit (what colonists would consider to be God). A shaman had the power to commune with the Great Spirit while in a state of trance, use spiritual healing ways for curing the sick, divining whatever is hidden, and discerning future events. He was so renowned for his strong connection to the Great Spirit and the Great Mystery not only with the tribe but among the earliest white colonists. These new arrivals to North America exhibited a certain ignorance as they thoroughly believed these powers were bestowed upon Chief Passaconaway by the Devil himself. This included their belief in his prowess in the "Dark Arts," which included the power to make water burn with fire, make rocks move, trees dance, and to turn himself into a human torch of flaming fire without either being burned or consumed. He could also reportedly transform a dead snake's skin into a living snake, which onlookers could see, handle physically, and hear as it slithered away.[7] More importantly, early historians describe his possession of extraordinary leadership skills, which led to his selection as the Supreme Chief of the Eastern Indian Confederacy, which combined all the warriors and resources of the tribes living in what are now the states of Maine, New Hampshire, and Massachusetts. Such unity was needed so they could fight and defend themselves against their most dangerous enemy tribe at the time, the Mohawks.[8]

In the year 1620, the English ship Mayflower landed at Plymouth, Massachusetts. Chief Passaconaway and three other shamans were thought to have spent three days in a nearby swamp close to the Plymouth settlement, attempting to invoke the wrath of a manitou upon

---

The Indian tribes living near it believe this mountain is the abode of a female manitou named "Tacoma" whose name means "She who gives us the Waters." (Ruppenstein, 1). Mount Tacoma (Rainier) is significant because it is the place where the first fleet of UFOs flying in formation were thought to have been sighted in modern times by a civilian pilot and businessman named Kenneth Arnold. He was flying a private plane near this mountain in June of 1947 when he spotted the UFOs, and afterwards while being interviewed by the news media described these vehicles as "Flying Saucers." The name has been commonly used ever since for UFOs (Time-Life Books, 36).

[5] Piotrowski, 182.

[6] Bisbee, 53.

[7] *Ibid.*, 4.

[8] *Ibid.*

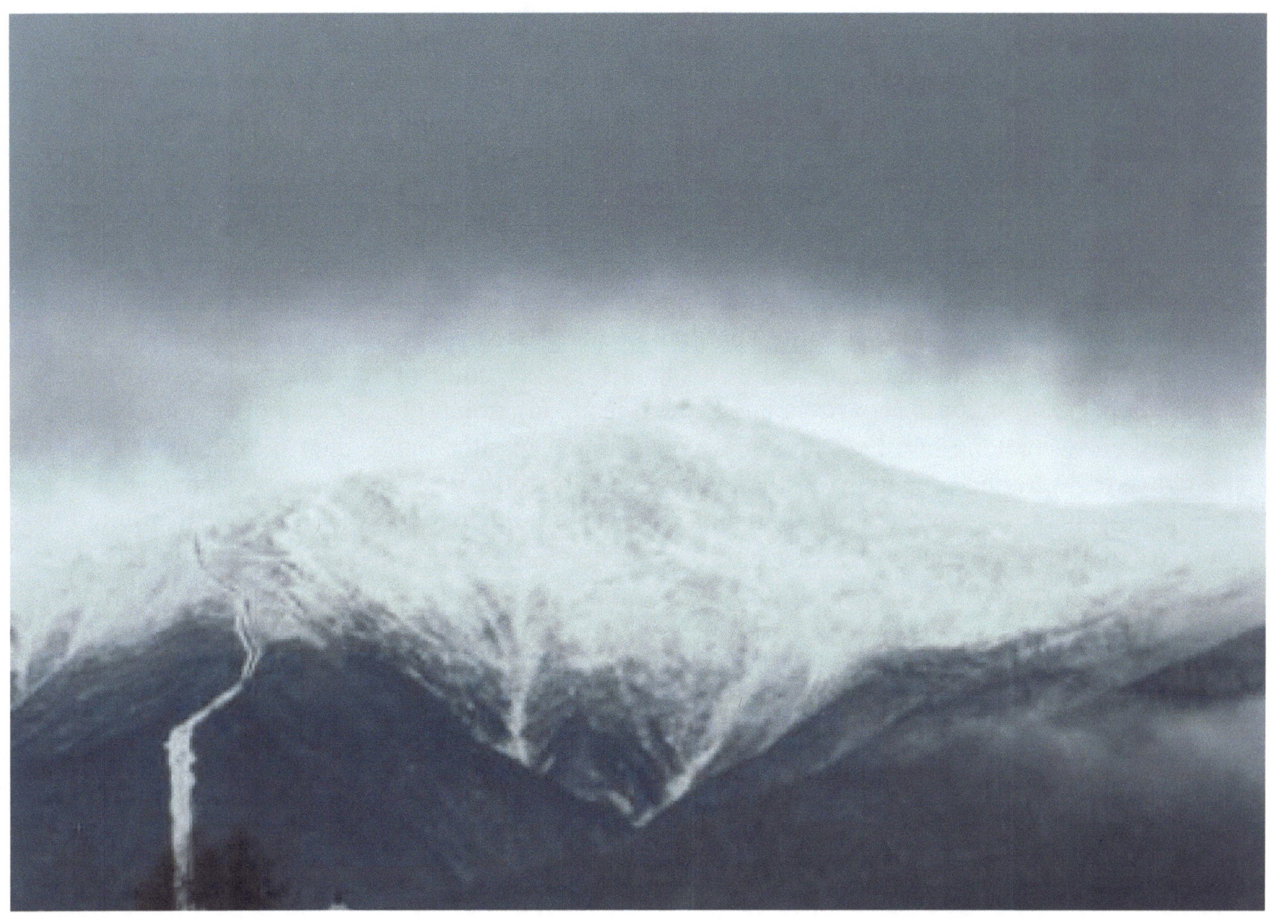

Mount Washington in New Hampshire during the winter. It is the highest Mountain in the northeast, standing at 6,288 feet or 1,916.6 meters high. Named for George Washington, First President of the United States, 6 Star Commanding General of the American Continental Army during the Revolutionary War (1775 to 1789). It was previously named, and remains so by the original resident Native Americans as "Angiocochook," which means "Home of the Great Spirit" and/or "Mother Goddess of Storm."

the white invaders.[9] It was thought[10] that when their repeated attempts to bring down lightening to start fires to burn up the Mayflower and Plymouth settlement failed, Passaconaway was supposed to have figured the white men's magic must be stronger than the Indians'. Given most historians' perspective, he was thought to have considered discretion to be the better part of valor at this point, seeing that the tribes had no weapons to counter the white men's weaponry.

What has been "historically" described as "Fire and Thunder Sticks" by Native Americans were the Puritan English colonists' and soldiers' blunderbusses and muskets. Blunderbusses were short fowling shotguns with a flared muzzle, versatile and designed not to miss by spreading out up to nine lead balls, gravel, nails, or anything else loaded into it when shot.[11] It could also fire a large round lead ball, about the size of a ping-pong ball. Muskets were long-barreled firearms with a much greater range then the blunderbuss. (Muskets were the precursors to the even longer-ranged rifle.) Both these weapons could only discharge one shot at a time and took at least a minute to reload. During such a minute, a tribal warrior frequently could close the distance between himself and a musketeer, engaged in reloading. Hence, the time to reload was most disadvantageous in frontier battle, such that a colonist's versatility and skill with sword, bayonet, or knife were vital for survival during this period if there was a conflict. Rifles are so named because they have circular machining within the insides of their barrels (as opposed to the musket's smooth bore barrel's metal insides), called "rifling," which makes the bullet spin as it proceeds upon being shot through the rifle barrel, providing for a much longer range (or distance the bullet will travel, before it loses energy and drops) after being shot.

Soon after their attack failed, Chief Passaconaway and the other tribes made overtures of peace to these English Puritans, commonly referred to as Pilgrims. (Puritans were English Colonists that elected to take the dangerous journey across the Atlantic to what they believed to be the "New World" (though for the First Nations, it had always existed) in order to obtain religious freedom. They left during the reigns of Queen Elizabeth I and the subsequent two kings of England, James I and James II. Puritans rejected both the Roman Catholic Church and the Protestant Church of England, both of which they thought taught too many superstitions or doctrines that they considered human inventions instead of the "Word of God." Puritans made up most of the English colonists to settle in New England during the early part of the 17th Century. Chief Passaconaway and the tribes, after

---

[9] *Ibid.*

[10] Note: there needs to be the recognition that most historians of colonial history for the United States are still often seeing from a colonialist's lens of perception. Several centuries of a particular perspective has infiltrated history for generations of students and their parents. Only more recently—from the later part of the 20th Century to today—has the indigenous perspective of North American tribes and their history finally entered the discourse.

[11] https://www.nrablog.com/articles/2016/9/the-blunderbuss-roar-of-the-high-seas/

their failed attempts to dissuade the white invaders, nevertheless brought the Puritans corn, plants, edible roots, and game meat. It was this event that American citizens in future years monumentalized as the "Thanksgiving" holiday, celebrated every November. (This is despite Native Americans feeling differently about the holiday—and certainly for understandable reasons).

The Pilgrims never could have imagined Chief Passaconaway's attempts to get rid of them, instead thinking it surely must have been God's intervention to make such a powerful chief desirous of peace, rather than war.[12] Unfortunately, in less than a decade (in or about 1629), the growing English settlements no longer enjoyed certain instances of peace experienced while Puritans made up most of the English colonies' populations. Historians before the 20th century indigenous movements suggested that the Puritans believed in God and the Bible and purported to dedicate their lives to following the moral code proclaimed by Jesus Christ, which prescribed that they love their neighbors as themselves. Unfortunately, this became less the case as increasing amounts of new colonists arrived who neither shared nor observed these tenets. It didn't take long for there to be increasing conflicts with the local tribes as contact between the two peoples steadily grew on tribal lands. To maintain the peace, and prevent worse conflict and war, Passaconaway decided to grant the English colonists the gift of a large tract of land that stretched from the Piscataqua River on New Hampshire's boundary with Maine to the mouth of the Merrimac River.[13] It is possible that one motive for Passaconaway's generosity was to get the English colonists' help in his conflict with the Mohawk tribe. Historians have suggested his rationale was that if the English were settled near or among the Penacooks, they would then fight with him and his people against the Mohawks if only to save their own hides.

Regrettably, Chief Passaconaway, his tribe, and the other tribes of his confederacy were rewarded for this by insults, robbing, and other abuses by the English colonists. One of the many examples of such abuse during this period includes the incident of a Native American mother carrying her baby in a papoose secured inside of her canoe, while paddling to a trading post. On arrival she was pulling her canoe into a berthing area near the post when three colonial sailors approached her canoe and purposefully upset the canoe, sending the baby to the bottom. The mother immediately dove in and retrieved and saved her baby. The motivation for these ignorant and cruel men was having heard a tale that Indian babies could "swim from birth" and "needed no swimming instruction," so they decided to put the matter to the test. Unfortunately, the infant also got ill and died shortly after this incident.[14] The father, who in this case was a tribal chief, naturally blamed the white colonists, rallied his warriors, and two major massacres of white settlements soon

---

[12] Bisbee, 2.
[13] Belknapp, 7-9.
[14] Bisbee, 5.

followed. As time went on, instead of joining with the Penacooks to fight the Mohawks, the English colonists paid the Mohawks gold to raid Penacook settlements.

Chief Passaconaway would be famous alone for just achieving one of his many life accomplishments such as being a shaman, also a major northeast tribal chief, and finally Sachem of the Northeast Indian Confederacy. Although he was a famous chief and leader, Chief Passaconaway's death is not considered unique among those of other famous tribal chiefs, warriors, and frontier heroes in terms of his past exploits and his passage from the world. Many stories of famous chiefs and great warriors include making pilgrimage to the top of the highest mountain in their respective lands when death was thought to be near. There, at those mountain summits, they would meet a manitou or the Great Spirit. When Chief Passaconaway was, according to legend, 120 years old, he heard the cries of a pack of wild wolves being carried ahead of them by the north wind echoing against the hills as they strongly drove towards his village.[15] It was a clear and frigid winter's night, with a ghostly, gibbous moon lighting up the snow like a giant's lantern. Wild furry creatures large and small sounded an alarm and dove back into their respective dens and caves, as the pack of wolves coursed by, and the frigid winds of the Quebec northlands blew over and past them. They became as one with the wind in speed, as they charged into a kaleida-scoping panorama of vast lakes, rivers, moose bogs, endless tracts of forests—all almost as visible as if it were day.

Many Penacook villagers the following morning testified to seeing a pack of yelping wild wolves harnessed to a hickory wood snow sled containing a beautifully carved wooden seat draped with fine furs. The sled stopped at Chief Passaconaway's door, and the old man immediately mounted the sled and sped off in this obviously supernatural carriage. The growling and yelping wolves speedily carried Chief Passaconaway across the frozen surface of Lake Winnipesaukee and upwards into the hills and highlands. Lonely night-time hunters heard the heralding wolf pack's barks and cries as the death song of Passaconaway echoed amidst the snow-laden and majestic walls of the White Mountains. With ever increasing speed, the sled and old man were propelled like a cannon shot up the side and soon to the top regions of Agiocochook (Mount Washington). Upon reaching the summit, the sled immediately burst into flames, and the wolves were released from their harnesses, howling and bounding off together, soon to disappear amidst the snow drifts down the mountain.[16] Simultaneously, Chief Passaconaway was lifted by invisible means into the sky itself and soon disappeared among the moon and stars. The legend claims the Great Spirit took him, but it could have also been Extraterrestrial Biological Entities ("EBEs" in military parlance).

[15] Ibid., 3.
[16] Ibid.

In the year 1600, the Mohawks attacked a fortified hill the Penacooks held as a stronghold in what is now the state capital of New Hampshire, the city of Concord.[17] The Mohawks early on in this battle managed to strategically divide the Penacook's army of warriors, and both sides fought desperately with arrows, spears, knives, and tomahawks, making such a mutual slaughter that only a few warriors from each side remained standing. The Penacook warriors fell back to their fort as a last resort to defend their women and children, their corn stores, as well as themselves; no Penacook warrior surviving ever forgot the destruction and horror of this desperate battle. This was because both sides lost too many warriors, and although the Penacooks technically won the battle, it was a pyrrhic victory. Most significantly, it's thought that it was during this period, that the Mohawks established their reputation among the Northeast tribes as "man eaters."[18]

The Mohawks are not unique among North American tribes, according to white historians, in the practice of war-associated cannibalism. Also mentioned for doing so were the Canadian and Great Lakes Indians, notably the Ottawas, Chippewas, Menominies, and Patawatomis.[19] During the French and Indian War, these Canadian and Great Lakes area tribes fought the English army and English colonists on the side of France. They were then under the command of the brilliant French General and Marquis Louis-Joseph de Montcalm. In 1756, Montcalm soundly defeated the British Army and their Colonial militia at Fort William Henry, beside Lake George, in what is now New York state. This was the same battle that author James Fenimore Cooper records in his classic novel, *Last of the Mohicans.* A Hollywood movie based on Cooper's novel of the same name, released in 1992, directed by Michael Mann and starring Daniel Day-Lewis as Hawkeye, was for the most part in alignment with the history of this battle. Specifically, where the victorious French General Montcalm allows the surviving English army, its commanding officer Lieutenant-Colonel George Monro, and his colonial militia soldiers to honorably surrender with full military honors for his week-long and steadfast defense. Monro and his Army left Fort William Henry with their colors (flags) and arms (rifles and swords). What isn't true,

---

[17] Ibid., 2-3.

[18] Note: there are many such accounts that have been proffered by white historians, and it is incumbent upon the reader to weigh these against the tribes' own histories. It is also important to note that there is significant self-interest in such historians using such "histories" as justification for the atrocities committed first by the colonists and later additional settlers including treaty violations, ethnic cleansing, and genocide. To present "evidence" of First Nation "savagery" mitigated any sense of responsibility to accurately reflect an honest historical record. Such accounts present Mohawks and other Indian Tribes after capturing their tribal enemies or white colonial prisoners, not only torturing them, but roasting them alive after tying them to wooden stakes or spits and eating them (Northrup, 155-91). The accounts then continue, including cutting out and eating various organs, like the heart, fingers, or other portions of their prisoners' bodies (Again, it is always incumbent on the reader to evaluate different histories and perspectives—not just one— in determining a balanced view, rather than that of the "conqueror," whose word is often not challenged immediately.

[19] Jacobs, 250-1.

however, is that any of them were allowed to keep their gun powder, without which they couldn't fire their flint-lock muskets and pistols. Shortly after leaving the fort, Colonel Monro and his army, colonial militia, and civilian followers were all ambushed, mostly massacred, and only some taken as prisoners (or booty) by the tribes who had fought under the French General Montcalm. Colonel Monro did in fact survive this massacre.

One mitigating circumstance concerning French General Montcalm's role in the matter, was although he had dispatched a company of 400 French soldiers fully armed to escort the English away from the fort, there was little they could do to prevent thousands of Indians from killing the English and taking anything of value from the dead bodies they might find. The Indians, whether they assisted the French or the English in battle, proved themselves as not being very subject to the command or control of white military officers on the battlefield. The Indians would attack, or not do so, as their interests (chances for booty), a war chiefs' direction, or as opportunities presented themselves on the battlefield.

The importance for recounting some of the early history of the White Mountains region is because we are only a mere 300 years separated in time from our country's earliest frontiers and pioneering days. Our human species—whatever its location or history—has had wars and killed each other given sufficient reasons, notably self-defense, war, or criminal activity fostered by need for survival or self-interest. This is significant, because, as we'll later learn, some advanced civilizations, despite any technological progress over the last 300 years, continue to describe our human species as "primitive and dangerous." This is in large part from our ongoing capacity to not only kill each other individually, but in mass amounts. It is also exemplified by periods of genocide and ethnic cleansing that came from the "discovery" of new lands to conquer by various civilizations over hundreds of years. Worse still, our species turned the murder of millions of people into a science in the 20th Century. This was not just true during the end of the colonial era, but as amply recorded and occurring in the millions by Nazi Germany, the USSR under Stalin, and in Communist China. Under Truman during WWII, and thanks to weapons of mass destruction such as the development of nuclear and thermo-nuclear weapons, our species now has the capability to massively kill billions of people within a split second.

Chapter Two

First Contact—or Something Else?

In addition to indigenous peoples' sightings and experience with certain phenomena, history has perhaps always shown that our human species has been watched—and visited— by non-human intelligence for many thousands of years. While this book emphasizes the Northeast's Native American tribes—and the colonists—of the White Mountains of New Hampshire's geographical area, holy books going back to ancient times, such as the Bible, Bhagavad-Gita, and others describe God(s), angels, and other supernatural beings, often including flying vehicles that these either piloted or used.

One example (of many) in the Bible occurs in the Old Testament (here, the King James Version) in Book of Ezekiel for the entire first chapter. In this case, Ezekiel observed winged beings and a flying vehicle with four wheels. The Old Testament (KJV) Book of Exodus 13:18-22 provides yet another example about God Almighty providing a "Pillar of Cloud" by day and "Pillar of Fire" by night which guided and led the people of Israel out of bondage from Egypt. In the New Testament (KJV) of the Bible's Book, The Acts of the Apostles 1:9-11, tells of the final time Jesus Christ met with his disciples after his resurrection from the dead. After giving all of them his final blessings, Jesus Christ rose into the air right in front of his disciples and disappeared into a cloud above them. While the Disciples were watching this, "two men in white apparel" suddenly appear in their midst declaring, "You Men of Galilee, why do you stand gazing up into Heaven? This same Jesus, which is taken up from you into heaven, shall so come in like manner as you have seen him go into heaven." Via a few choice references to the most ancient scriptures from India, The God of the Sun is described as a "Golden Being of Energy" with "golden beard and brown eyes like a kapyasa flower, Lord of the high worlds of beyond, where the desires of the gods' are fulfilled." (Chandogya Upanishad 1.6.6-8)[20] And another wherein the Sun's chariot is described as a vehicle with one wheel. "The Resplendent-One moves in his orbit in a one-wheeled car" (Mahabharata 12.362.1).[21] This subject alone, our species' quest for spiritual answers, whereby a guru, prophet, leader, saint, warrior, or hero, climbs a mountain and meets God and other spiritual beings, goes far beyond the limit of this book or that of the religious books mentioned. Yet, it would be remiss not to provide some other major examples herein.

Besides the ancient written accounts, we have photographs, sculptures, paintings, and even Stone Age glyphs and drawings readily available to tell us about our species' story.

[20] Danielou, 94-5.
[21] Ibid., 95.

It is self-evident that most of humanity's cultures during their early history and religious development associated their god(s) with their highest mountains. The original Mount Sinai is today called Jabal Maqla ("the Burned Mountain" in Arabic), and is 7,631 feet—or 2,326 meters—high and located in Northwest Saudi Arabia.[22] This is the mountain where the Hebrew prophet Moses received the Ten Commandments from God Almighty. It's located in an area that in ancient times was called Midian. Here, archeologists have found the site of the altar Moses built and the split rock from where Moses brought water for the thirsting Jewish People through the power of God. Mount Olympus in Greece is 9,570 feet—or 2,917 meters—high, located between Thessaly and Macedonia.[23] This was the abode of the ancient king of the Greek gods, Zeus and his associated pantheon of less powerful, subordinate gods. These included the Greek god of war Ares; Poseidon, the brother of Zeus and Greek god of the seas; and Hades, Greek god of the underworld. Then one may look at the Hill of Tara in Ireland, which was once an ancient royal center of power. Celtic kings from Neolithic times (2500 BC) to the Middle Ages are said to have reigned from there. Additionally, these ancient Celts believed Tara was a sacred place of dwelling for their gods, notably Cernunnos, the ancient Celtic god of fertility.[24]

Mount Fuji, the highest mountain in Japan, is a sleeping but potentially active volcano located on Honshu Island in Japan. It has been considered sacred since the most ancient times. It is 12,360 feet—or 3,776 meters—high. Japanese of both Buddhist and Shinto faiths consider it "The Abode of the Immortals."[25] A primary example of one of these "Immortals" is the ancient Japanese god of lightning, thunder, and agriculture named Raijin. Shinto Shrines are located at the mountain's base and along a pilgrimage trail that honors the Kami, the supernatural deities of the Shinto Faith. The Chief Kami is the Princess Konohanasakuya, whose symbol is the Cherry Blossom.[26] Likewise, Mont St. Michel, located beside the ocean in northern France, has a circumference of 3,150 feet—or 960 meters—which provided a great foundation for building. Its highest point is 302 feet—or 92 meters—above sea-level. Mont St. Michel received its current name when the Archangel St. Michael appeared to Aubert, the Catholic Bishop of Avranches on top of this mountain in the year 708 AD.[27] Consequently, it was soon crowned with a Roman Catholic Church, which eventually grew into a Benedictine monastery and medieval fortress. Prior to this, for thousands of years the ancient French People called "Gauls" by the Romans, worshipped their god(s) on top of this same mountain, which rises from a tidal island base. The Gauls also believed the mountain was the gateway to other dimensions—and to the Land of the Dead.

[22] Mauro (Vid.)
[23] New Columbia Encyclopedia, 2002.
[24] Murphy, 1-4.
[25] Sutherland, 1-4.
[26] Wikipedia, Mount Fuji.
[27] Fleurisson, www.france.fr/en/normandy/article/mont-saint-michel-0

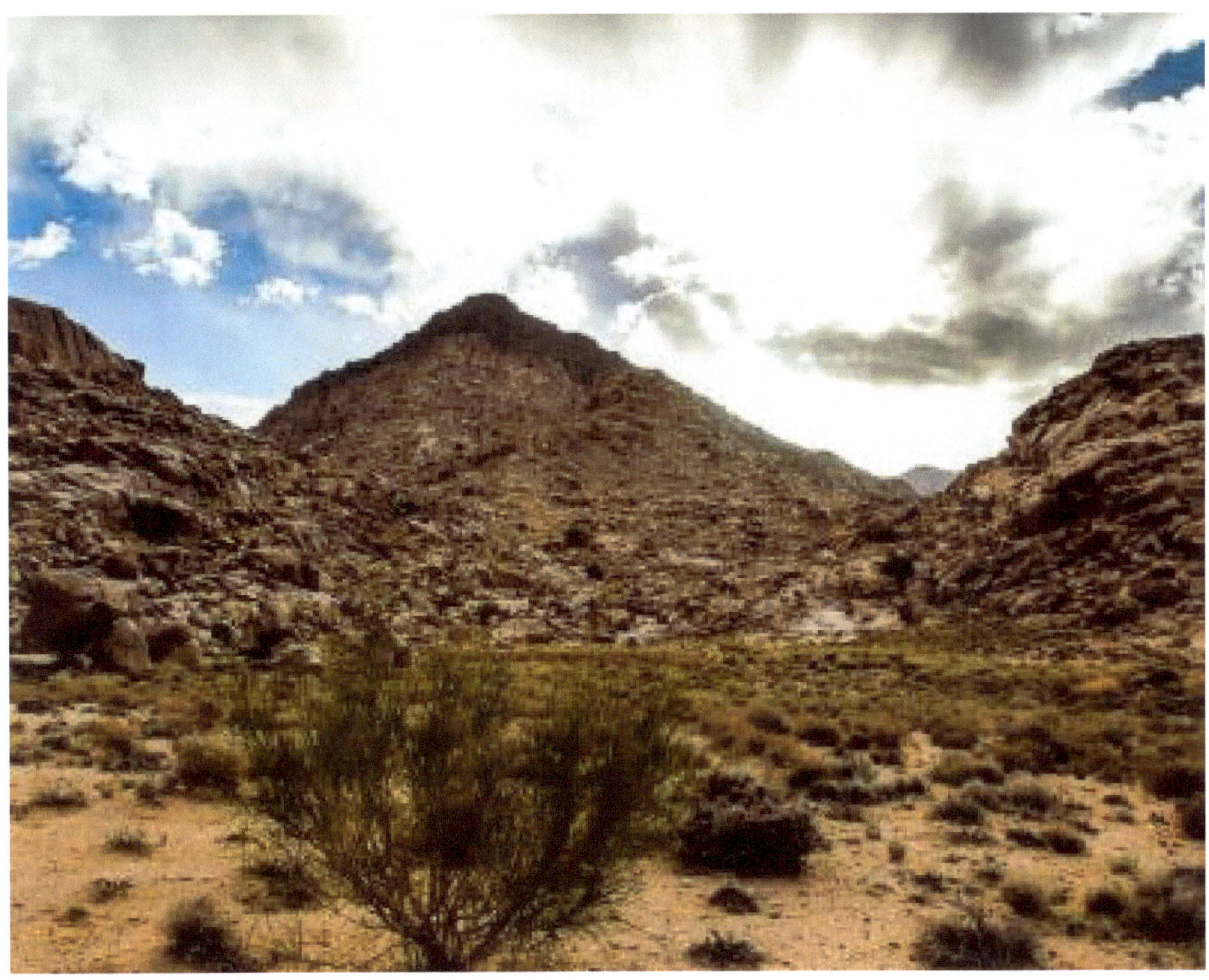

This is the real Mount Sinai, located in Saudi Arabia. It is called "The Burned Mountain" or "Jabal Maqla" by Saudi Arabians. This is where the Hebrew prophet Moses received the Ten Commandments from God Almighty.

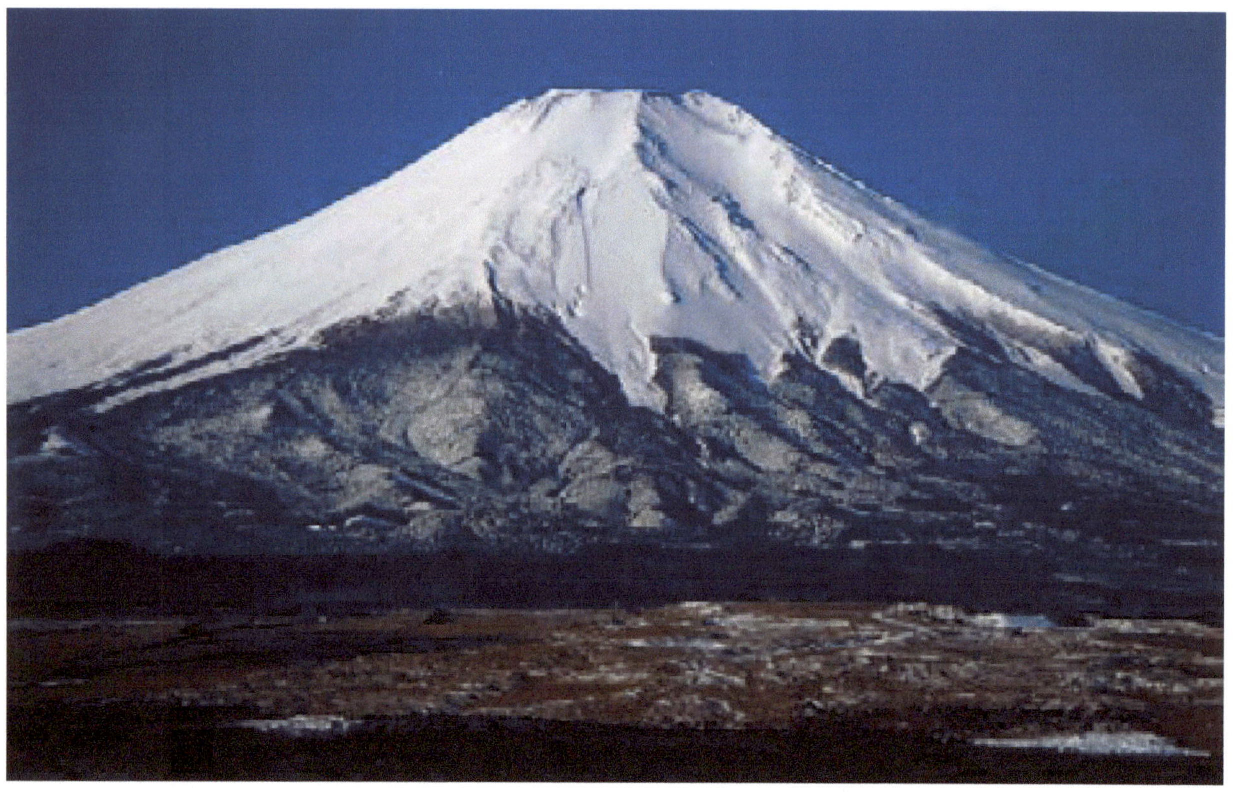

Mount Fuji in Japan is 12,395 feet high, located on Honshu Island Japan. It is considered "The Abode of the Immortals" like the Japanese God of Lightning and Storm, named Raigin.

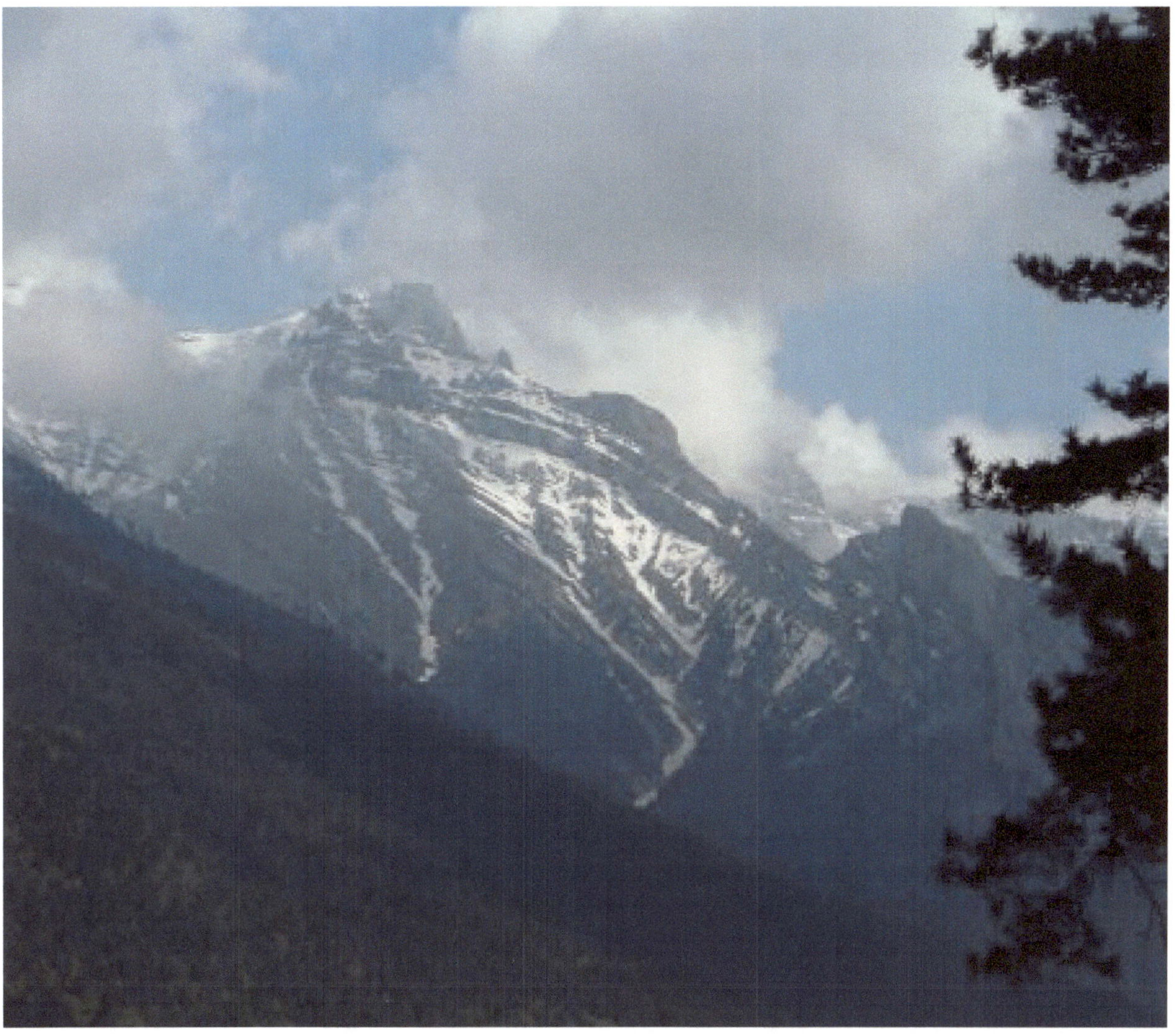

Mount Olympus in Greece is 9,570 feet high, located between Thessaly and Macedonia, where the Ancient Greek God Zeus lived and his Pantheon of subordinate Greek Gods.

Other major examples include Saint Francis of Assisi, who on September 17th, 1224, AD scaled Monte Penna (called *La Verna* in his time), 9,554 feet high. This mountain is in the center of the Tuscan Apennines Mountains of Italy. Saint Francis alone and in deep prayer wished in mind and body to always be an instrument of Jesus Christ, the Son of God. For his chastity, founding of the Franciscan Order, and life-long dedication to Christ, he was given the gift to feel in body and spirit what Jesus Christ felt during the Passion and to know in his heart the love Jesus felt for humanity.[28] In answer to his prayer, a six-winged Seraph Angel appeared and bestowed upon Saint Francis the Stigmata, or the wounds of Jesus Christ caused after Jesus Christ's hands and feet were nailed down upon an execution cross by Roman Soldiers, under the authority of Rome in what was then Roman-Occupied Jerusalem.[29] Before the time of St. Francis, the mountain was named for the female patron pagan Goddess of Thieves, Laverna, for the robbers and thieves who at one time inhabited this mountain's caves. Prior to that, the ancient Italians' pagan god, Pan (or "Pen") was worshiped there. The numbers of similar examples are immeasurable. Yet, the oldest major example is Ayers Rock, located near the city of Alice Springs in Australia. In terms of the vast distances of the Australian Outback, the 280-mile drive from Alice Springs to what may be considered the largest monolith in the world is apparently considered "near" Alice Springs, by many Australians. It is red sandstone 348 meters—or 1,044 feet—high (higher than the Eiffel Tower in France), surrounded by other huge rocks and boulders.[30] Ayers Rock is of oval shape 2.2 miles long by 1.5 miles wide. It was formed over 500 million years ago during the Cambrian prehistoric period when the land and rocks there were beneath the ocean.[31] The Aboriginal tribes of Australia's original name for this sacred rock is "Uluru." It is currently a major national park of Australia but remains under the care and supervision of perhaps the oldest culture known of on our planet, the Anangu aboriginal tribe. (Some suggest the oldest culture is instead the San—once called "Bushmen"—in Africa, but this is still being debated.) Uluru contains caves and Stone Age pictures and glyphs going back to between 30,000 to 60,000 years. Uluru dates to the time the Aboriginal people of Australia call "The Dreamtime" and "Time Before Time."[32] "Uluru" therefore appears to signify the original location where the creation of all things occurred. The creation they believe was performed by their ancestor spirits, which sometimes assumed the form of snakes.[33] There are Stone Age glyphs and paintings that some modern UFO researchers believe are Stone Age portraits of EBEs. Religious prayers, chants, and rites are still regularly performed here by the indigenous Australians. Uluru,

---

[28] Cuthbert, 407-9.

[29] Website: https://parksaustralia.gov.au/uluru/discover/highlights/amazing facts/

[30] Website: https://www.ayersrockresort.com.au/our-story/anangu-culture

[31] Ibid.

[32] Ibid.

[33] Time-Life Books, 36-40.

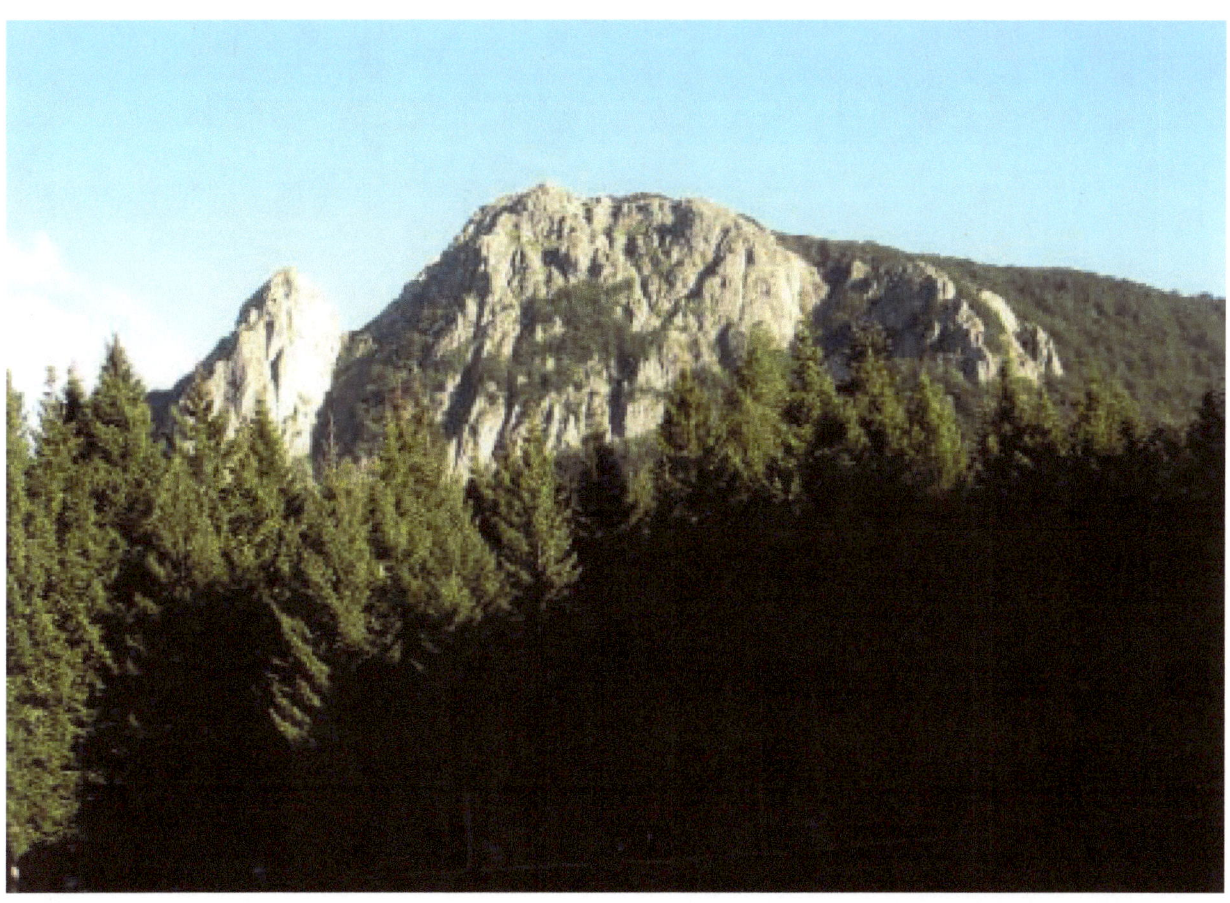

Monte Penna, known as La Verna during the Middle Ages was scaled by Saint Francis of Assisi on September 17th, 1224 AD in the Tuscan Apennines Mountains of Italy. Here, he received the Stigmata, (the wounds of Jesus Christ) on this hands and feet from a six-winged Seraph angel. The mountain is 9,554 feet high.

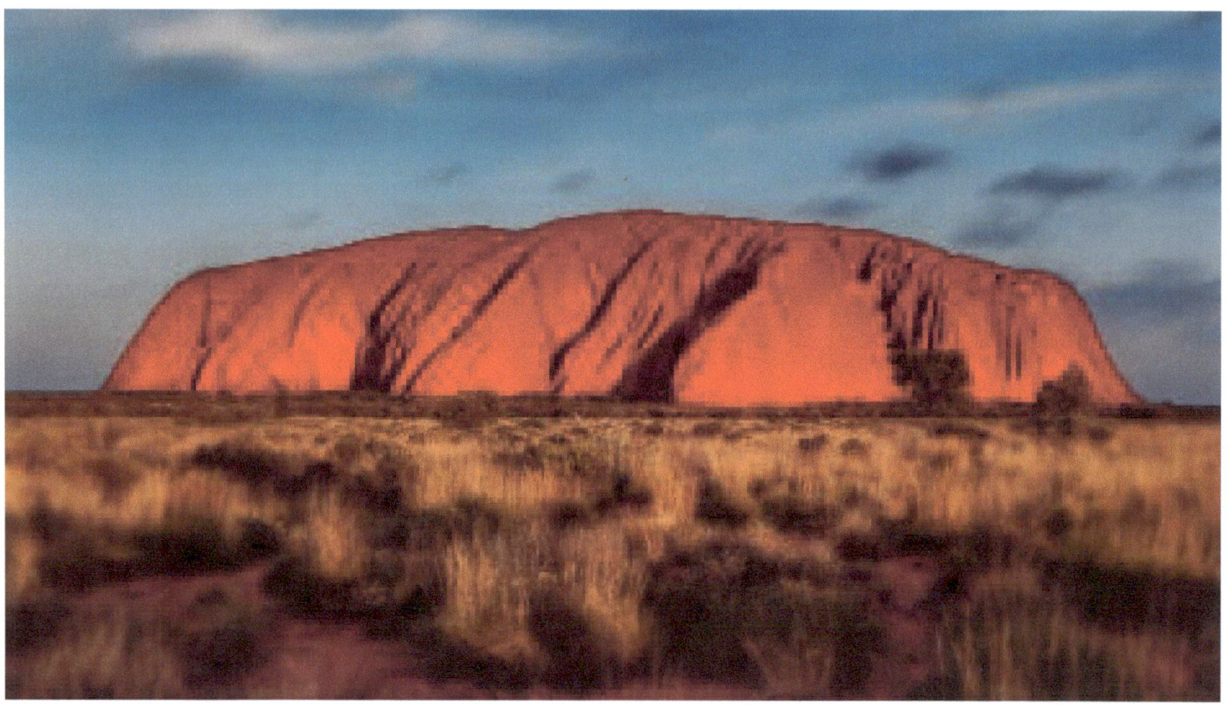

"Uluru" Prehistoric (Cambrian Era 500 million years ago) red sandstone formation near city of Alice Springs, Australia, where Aboriginal tribes of Australia believe their Ancestor Spirits created all things. Commonly called "Ayers Rock" in modern times.

they believe, is now the "Resting Place of the Ancestral Spirits" which created the rocks, rivers, hills, and people.

In North America, in addition to the White Mountains of New Hampshire, Mount Rainier, or "Tacoma," is significant because it's the very place in modern times (24th of June 1947) that a civilian pilot and businessman named Kenneth Arnold, while flying his private plane at an altitude of 9,200 feet, was the first person to spot a group of nine UFOs near Mount Rainier.[34] One of them was crescent shaped and the others shaped like discs, or teacup plates or saucers. These UFOs were flying in an echelon formation (diagonally in a long chain) at supersonic speed. Using his plane's control panel clock, Arnold timed how long it took the UFO fleet to pass Mount Rainier and continue to pass the nearby Mount Adams. It was one minute and 42 seconds. He then checked out his map for the distance between these two mountains as 47 miles, at over 1600 mph (e.g. convert one minute and 42 seconds to minutes, then divide 1.6 minutes into 60 minutes to get factor 37.5 minutes for (time) and multiply these times 47 miles (distance traveled) to get Miles Per Hour (mph) = 1,762.5 mph).[35] Mr. Arnold, when he was questioned by newspaper reporters, described these phenomena for the first-time as "Flying Saucers," and his name for them was generally adopted and has carried on ever since.[36]

Shortly after this, during the same year on July 2, 1947, two UFO crashes simultaneously occurred in the city of Roswell, New Mexico. Significant to this development, was that on July 2nd there was a massive thunder and lightning storm system over the entire Roswell area. There were some reports that people of the area, watching the storm's lightning and thunder displays from their house windows, had, at around 10pm, observed a large oval and white glowing object flying at high speed amidst the storm clouds. A sheep rancher named Mac Brazel, living northwest of the city of Roswell, reported hearing a terrific explosive detonation in the sky right above his house's ceiling—much louder than the thunderbolts otherwise booming all around him.[37] In the morning he inspected his property and found a metallic debris field extending over a quarter of a mile. According to his account, this debris was metal-like, or like aluminum foil in appearance, but upon handling this debris, he found it to be very thin metal which was flexible and pliable. However, he found it too strong for his hands alone to tear open or break. Looking beyond the debris field, he found a disk-shaped object that had crashed hard, partially buried right into the ground. About a quarter of the craft had penetrated the desert's sandy soil, whereas about three quarters of the craft was readily visible. Brazel quickly reported

---

[34] Ibid., 14.
[35] Ibid., 39.
[36] Ibid.
[37] Ibid.

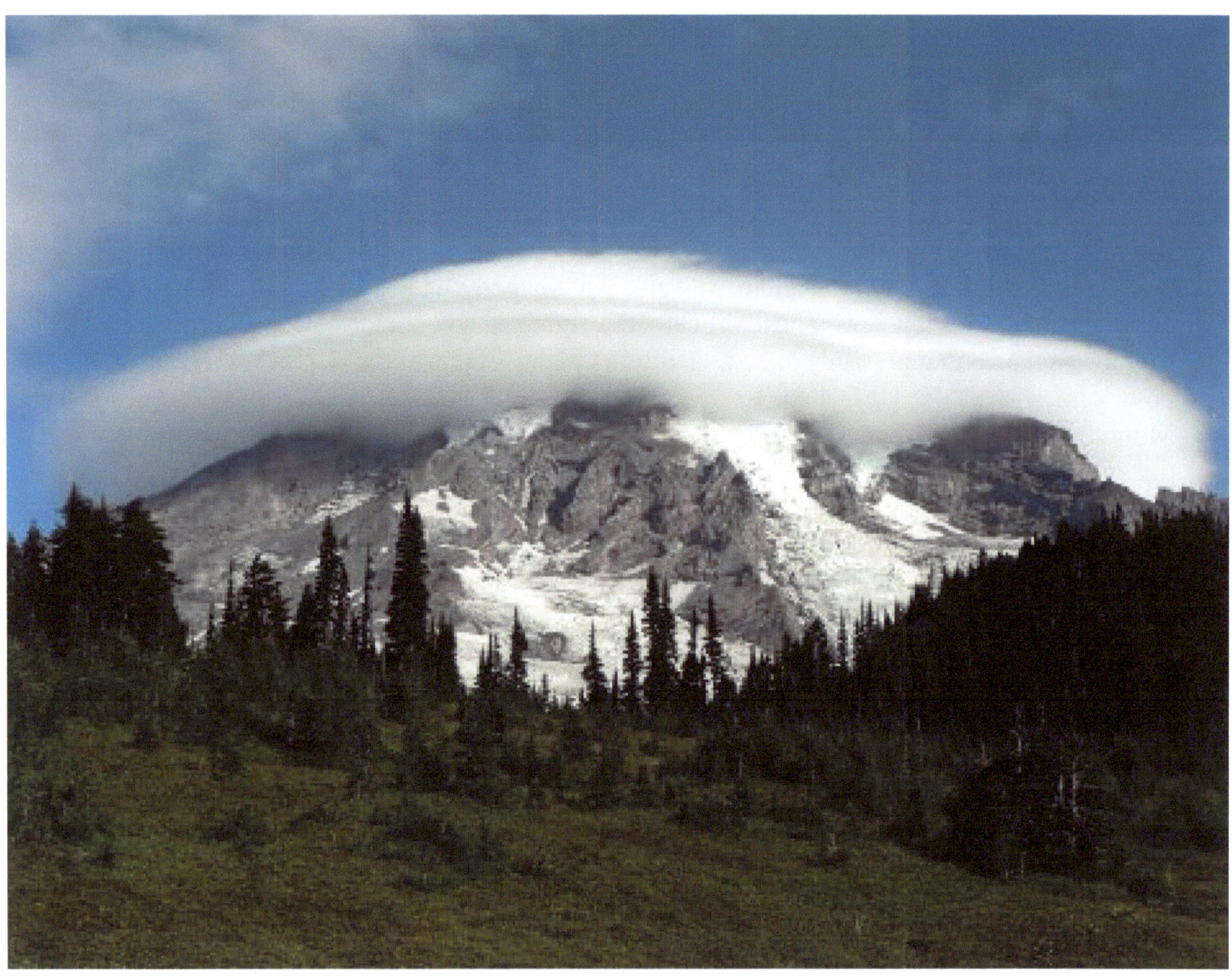

Mount Rainier in Washington State. This mountain is called "Tacoma" by Native Americans living near it, meaning "She who gives us the Waters." It is considered the abode of a female Manitou whose name is also "Tacoma." It was by this mountain that a civilian pilot, Ken Arnold, in a private plane spotted a formation of UFOs in June of 1947. While describing what he saw to newspaper reporters, he referred to the UFOs as "Flying Saucers." That name has been commonly adopted by people to describe UFOs ever since.

the whole matter to a military officer of the day (or Command Watch Officer) at the nearby Roswell Army Airfield.[38]

Shortly afterward, Military Police, trucks, utility vehicles and armed soldiers arrived at the crash sites and debris field, ordering local law enforcement and civilians out of the area. Once the area was cordoned off, they proceeded to collect and remove both the alien crafts and any of their debris completely. These "materials" were draped and sent off by night covertly to military bases (including Wright-Patterson near Dayton, Ohio). On July 8th, 1947, the local paper, the *Roswell Daily Record*, printed a statement by the public affairs officer of the local military base, Lieutenant Warren Haught, as follows:

> The many rumors regarding the flying disk became a reality yesterday when the Intelligence Office of the 509th Bomb Group of the Eighth Air Force, Roswell Army Air Field, was fortunate enough to gain possession of a disk through the cooperation of one of the local ranchers and the sheriff's office of Chaves County.[39]

Soon after, Brigadier General Roger Ramey (who inspected some of these "Disk Fragments" which earlier had been sent to 8th Air Force Headquarters in Fort Worth Texas) shut down both the disk story and the civilian press. He also got on the radio (as television was not yet the major form of immediate news communications until the early 1950s) to declare the entire matter was a mistake. He said that what had been found was no flying disk but rather the wreckage of a weather device.[40]

However, the civilian newspaper reporters, their photographers, and many other people didn't believe the General's story. Neither did they buy his official press conference featuring a photo exhibit, with two Air Force officers displaying a torn-up weather balloon and related debris.[41] The U.S. Government has kept this information secret in addition to what the military recovered from these (and other crash sites) from the American people for now 75 years at the time of this writing. For those wanting more information about what genuinely happened there, now deceased Army Colonel Philip J. Corso's 1997 book, *The Day after Roswell*, is an account of events. Corso was a WWII Army Intelligence Officer who as a Captain went after Nazi Gestapo and other Nazi operatives in Italy. He rose to serve under the Supreme Commander of Allied Forces Europe, General Dwight D. Eisenhower, who soon afterward became President of the United States.

After the War, Colonel Corso worked for a top Lieutenant General (Nathan F. Twining) at the Pentagon and in 1961, he was given responsibility for—and custody of—the Roswell

---

[38] Ibid.
[39] Ibid.
[40] Ibid., 39-40.
[41] Ibid.

alien crafts' artifacts recovered by the U.S. Army Air Force in 1947.[42] (Note: The Air Force was part of the U.S. Army until September 18, 1947, when it became its own branch.) He also was given the same responsibilities for the official Top Secret Reports and photographs associated with the artifacts and Roswell crafts. It has been reported that one of the craft inhabitants had survived but was injured and tried to escape from the crash area as military vehicles approached. Unfortunately, a few of the UFO Recovery Team soldiers with M1 Rifles panicked and fired at the small four foot or less humanoid figure, killing it.[43] Bodies of the other dead beings operating the crafts were also said to have been recovered and examined.

There is plenty of evidence indicating humanity has been visited by such beings, or EBEs, for many thousands of years. After such books as the Bible, Bhagavad Gita and artwork from cave paintings to the Renaissance, reports of unidentified object (hereafter called UFO) sightings, including people observing formations of them flying together, started most significantly in the 1940s, especially during World War II. During the air battles and dog fights over Europe in WWII, both American and German airmen reported being chased by fireballs of energy colored red, orange, green, and white. These UFOs would dart in between the United States, British, and German warplanes at tremendous velocities, far beyond the capacity of either side's aircraft. The UFOs would also follow human-piloted aircraft with sometimes as many as a half-dozen or more surrounding an airplane, but all would turn away after a few minutes and speed off to disappear within seconds. American pilots of the time called these UFOs "foo fighters" or "kraut balls," but none of them were recorded to have harmed any United States aircraft.[44] It appears the technological developments associated with this war, like radar, war rockets, jets, and missiles like the German V2, must have attracted the interest of these EBEs, whom many believe flew in to check on the human airborne capabilities.

It's unfortunate that the recent interests of EBEs in our planet have not come about as dramatized in a popular 1960s *Star Trek* television and movie franchises; in *Star Trek: First Contact* (1996), the fictitious Vulcan species decide to make "First Contact" with humans as a newly discovered intelligent species when one of their science starships observed that humans had successfully developed "warp" space travel capacity. Such a capacity, in this case, referred to the scientific and technological development of engaging energy to safely travel through space at the speed of light and beyond. In looking for a major event in modern times signifying an advanced technological accomplishment which could in like manner trigger an advanced civilization to initiate a "First Contact" with humanity, the author and many other UFO researchers believe it occurred during the World War II era. Specifically, the United States made the world's first atomic bomb, and shortly

---

[42] Ibid.
[43] Corso, 42.
[44] Ibid., 24.

after its development, successfully performed the world's first atomic bomb test detonation at Trinity Station, New Mexico on July 17th, 1945.[45] Shortly afterwards, the United States' wartime dropping of two atomic bombs on Japan in early August 1945 not only effectively ended World War II, but simultaneously was said to really get EBE attention!

In any event, their vehicles began showing up not only individually but in entire groups flying in formation within two years of these atomic bombs being detonated. These UFOs were first observed (as earlier described), by a private pilot, Kenneth Arnold, who first sighted a formation of UFOs near Mount Rainier in Washington State on the 24th of June 1947, and as stated, fewer than two weeks after this event two of these UFOs crashed in Roswell, New Mexico in early July 1947. UFOs from that time forward have been observed hovering near military bases where nuclear weapons are stored, including outside and above U.S. Air Force nuclear aircraft bases and intercontinental ballistic missile (ICBM) silos.[46] UFOs have also been documented turning United States and Russian missiles "on" to launch, or "off" when the missiles were previously turned on to a "launch mode" for testing purposes.

Incidentally, the United States military has a film of a UFO intercepting one of their test ICBMs off the coast of California. This test missile was going at supersonic speed over the Pacific Ocean when a military tracking camera filmed a UFO literally flying in circles around the missile in 1964.[47] Next, this same UFO seems to hit the missile with an energized force or particle beam, and the missile immediately tumbled out of control into the ocean. This information was revealed to a news reporter in 1982 by a former U.S. Air Force First Lieutenant who oversaw the filming of this specific Atlas Missile Test. This former officer Robert Jacobs was by 1982 an Assistant Professor of Radio-Film TV at the University of Wisconsin, who stated, "The UFOs are real. I know they're real. The Air Force knows they're real. And the U.S. Government knows they are real. I reckon it's high time that the American Public knows it too." Further, during the nuclear test detonations by the United States in the late 1940s to the late 1950s, U.S. Air Force jets filming the mushroom clouds of detonated nuclear bombs tests have picked up UFOs flying through and around these toxic and deadly super-heated exploded nuclear clouds. On the 26th of July 1952, at about 11pm according to a United States Air Force intelligence report, up to 12 UFOs hovered over and performed aerial maneuvers in formation around the dome of the nation's Capital Building. These UFOs buzzing the nation's Capital in Washington D.C. were also picked up and tracked on radar by the Washington National Airport and Andrews Air Force Base (the latter Base is responsible for defending the airspace both of, and around the Capital). The Air Force dispatched two night-time/all-weather Lockheed F-94 Jet Interceptors to check out the "Radar Contacts" who reported 7 "solid targets" and

---

[45] Goodchild, 160-61.
[46] Good, 300-1.
[47] Ibid., 292.

one pilot seeing "4 lights" at one time and "one light" to his front which went out when he attempted to close in for a better view. The best "Official Explanation" the Military Public Affairs Officers could come up with at the time to explain these UFOs' solid radar contacts were that they were caused by "Air Temperature Inversions." Additionally, United States astronauts have reported electrical instrument malfunctions, communications jamming, and being "buzzed" by UFOs. What do you suppose are the EBEs trying to tell us? Or is there more than one group of them? The belief among UFO proponents is that some are benevolent, and others appear quite the opposite towards our species. The question remains: Are aliens always benevolent? What about marauders, rogue criminal aliens, or space travelers harboring germs and disease deadly to humans? There are no ends to the types of beings and UFO designs and sizes being sighted by people today—not just in the near and distant past and especially at the present time (2022) thanks to the easy availability of smartphone cameras.

What is the basis for the increased cases of UFOs being sighted since 1947? Many believe it was the initial Trinity Station New Mexico's Atomic Bomb Test on July 16, 1945, and the close following WWII atomic bomb explosions in August 1945, that piqued the possible interest of advanced civilizations. Even now, the "nuclear nations'" test detonations of atomic and hydrogen bombs (and associated nuclear missile, artillery, rocket, and nuclear tank-shell weapons tests) released deadly radiation and nuclear waste openly into the planet's atmosphere and environment between 1946 and 1963. It was upon discovering that these nuclear tests produced deadly radioactive isotopes which were entering the planet's food crops by the United States and other nuclear powers (during the late 1950s), which led to the October 1963 Partial Limited Test Ban Treaty negotiated by President John F. Kennedy.[48] During this period, prior to this Test Ban Treaty, these five countries were the only ones possessing nuclear weapons and conducting nuclear tests into the planet's atmosphere and oceans. In short, the nitrogen oxides produced by such massive nuclear explosions destroyed major portions of the planet's protective Ozone layer and thinned out that remaining.[49] These nations' armed forces and associated atomic scientists wanted to measure the effects of surface nuclear detonations, air bursts (or exploding nuclear bombs above a target), and sub-surface bursts beneath the oceans (measured metrically in kilotons or megatons). The major public reason for the Test Ban Treaty was because radioactive isotopes were showing up in the U.S.A.'s milk and other agribusiness areas of the Midwest in wheat, corn, and other major food crops despite these being many thousands of miles away from the nuclear test sites. The same was the case in all countries throughout the world, so the agreement was made only to test nuclear weapons deep underground. The USSR, England, and the United States all signed the treaty, but the remaining nuclear powers of that time, China and France, refrained, claiming the Treaty

---

[48] Website: https://www.jfklibrary.org/learn/about-jfk/jfk-in-history/nuclear-test-ban-treaty
[49] Hoerlin, 1-57.

was discriminatory because the Treaty placed limits on how many and what types of nuclear weapons France and China would be allowed to produce.

(For some Metric System context: One megaton is the equivalent in nuclear explosive power to one million tons of TNT (dynamite). A kiloton is the equivalent in nuclear explosive power to one thousand tons of TNT. The first war-time atomic bomb, named "Little Boy" dropped on the city of Hiroshima, Japan on the morning of the 6th of August 1945, was between 4 and 13 kilotons, or between 4000 and 13,000 tons of TNT in detonative force (depending upon the informational source). It also killed over 200,000 people immediately, counting both military and civilian casualties, according to the Japanese estimates.[50] The second WWII atomic bomb was dubbed "Fat Man" and was dropped on the Japanese city of Nagasaki on the morning of the 9th of August 1945, measuring 21 kilotons, dispersing the energy of 21 thousand tons of TNT. It immediately killed over 100,000 Japanese, both military and civilians.)[51]

These WWII nuclear bombs are now considered small especially when compared to the explosive power of the nuclear weapons of our own time. The largest unclassified nuclear test between 1945 and 1963 per author sources was the "Tsar H-Bomb" test on October 30, 1961, performed by the USSR (now the Russian Federation).[52] This H-Bomb detonation was (depending on the informational source) between 50, 57, or 64 megatons. Imagine 60 million tons of TNT detonating at one time. This bomb was dropped in the Russian Arctic Ocean area of the Island named Novaya Zemlya and was detonated close to and into the Ozone Layer and was thought to destroy 6% of the Planet's Ozone at that time.[53] The nuclear cloud from that explosion alone was over 40 miles high. The world's first H (Hydrogen) bomb was invented by the United States, which also conducted the first H-Bomb test detonation in 1952, code named "Ivy-Mike" or "Mike." Its explosive force was estimated at between 10 million to 13 million tons (or 13 megatons) as compared to the atomic bomb dropped on Hiroshima, Japan (13 thousand tons of TNT, or 13 kilotons of explosive force) in 1945 during WWII.[54]

The first Partial Limited Nuclear Test Ban Treaty[55] was signed and specified that nuclear tests in the open atmosphere, beneath the oceans, or in outer space would not occur. It further directed that any future nuclear weapons tests would only be performed underground. President John F. Kennedy hoped that having the countries with the most nuclear weapons sign the treaty (USSR, England, and the United States) would set into

---

[50] Ibid., 167.
[51] Ibid., 168.
[52] Lengel, 1.
[53] Ibid.
[54] Ibid.
[55] Encyclopedia Britannica, 820.

motion an example and an ongoing negotiation process that would eventually result in the complete banning of all nuclear weapons throughout the world.

Since 1963, more countries became nuclear powers (including via testing), notably North Korea, Israel, Pakistan, India, and Japan, with Iran pending, and South Africa having once been a nuclear power only to later disarm. Much more powerful nuclear bombs and missiles with nuclear warheads have been developed since 1963 including initial Inter-Continental-Ballistic Missiles (ICBMs), called "unitary," with a single warhead (bomb) on a single individual missile. Today, these singular ICBMs have Multiple Independently Targetable Reentry Vehicles (MIRVs), containing between 3 and up to 16 nuclear warheads, or bombs.[56] Once a launched individual missile begins its descent toward a primary target, the nose (front) of the ICBM pops open and shoots between 3 to 16 smaller delivery missiles, all carrying an atomic or hydrogen bomb (warhead), thereby capable of destroying any primary and between 3 to 16 additional targets. Target examples could be enemy naval fleets, land armies, military bases or silos, nuclear submarines, and cities.

Since 1963, nearly all the countries with nuclear weapons have informally agreed to only conduct underground nuclear weapons test detonations to avoid poisoning the entire planet and making it lifeless. Unfortunately, no such restrictions have been placed on the nuclear power industry. Since March 11th of 2011, Fukushima Japan's three destroyed nuclear power plants' melted down radioactive fuel slags continue to mix daily with underground streaming fresh water from the nearby highlands above these plants. This underground river now transformed into radiated fresh water containing unknown to infinite amounts of deadly radioactive isotopes (just one example is plutonium with a half-life of between 100,000 to 200,000 years) that will continue to leak (via underground channels) 300 tons or more of nuclear contaminated water daily into the Pacific Ocean.[57] The crops, farm animals, and plants of California exposed to the open environment are receiving radio-active rain, yet the band plays on.[58] While the US government has assured that any Fukushima radioactive contamination are within "safe limits," scientific studies long ago revealed the impact of repetitive consumption or exposure to radioactive items leads to building up of a cumulative negative impact to bodily health often leading to cancers, heart defects, etc. months to years later. Advances in robotics are the means being planned to resolve the Fukushima Nuclear Disaster's situation, although futurists predict it will be 30 to 40 more years for a technological resolution of Fukushima's problems. Fukushima will subsequently continue to change the Pacific Ocean into a radioactive lake with long-term effects on both flora and fauna. Yet, despite all the nuclear accidents and incidents in recent history, multi-national nuclear power corporations continue to profit, fully supported by their governments.

---

[56] Boyer, 356-7.

[57] Housley, February 8, 2017.

[58] Website: coupmedia.org Tuesday, April 3, 2012.

Some UFO researchers believe these kinds of accidents and use of nuclear material in weapons and for other purposes are part of the reason for their appearance since the nuclear age began. Those who believe their purported purpose to be benevolent suggest they are here to either prevent WWIII or similar technological extinction event including any human action that will render the planet lifeless. Given humanity's overall incapacity to be good planetary stewards when it comes to controlling over-population, pollution, and the on-going nuclear and chemical contaminative destruction of their own living environment, it seems this is indeed a "Hail Mary" conclusion that we cannot count on.

Chapter Three

A Tale of Two Bombs and Two Brilliant Men

It is important to reveal why the 1963 Test Ban Treaty came about to begin with given nuclear bomb and nuclear missile warhead testing in the planet's open atmosphere. As mentioned in the previous chapter, atomic bomb and thermo-nuclear (H-Bomb) explosions (all of which the United States and other nuclear states' atomic scientists eventually discovered) had unwittingly distributed radioactive fallout throughout the world. Dangerous levels of fallout were found thousands of miles away from the purposefully isolated test sites where these nuclear detonations occurred.[59] In the latter 1950s, birth defects, thyroid cancers, heart problems, and other maladies were affecting people all over the world because of the fallout (dust, dirt, and ash from nuclear detonations containing radioactive (gamma ray emitting) isotopes.[60] These early nuclear bomb test explosions into the planet's open atmosphere always carried radioactively contaminated particles miles up into the high stratosphere in a mushroom-looking type of cloud. Then in an hour or so, the fallout in the form of dust, ash, and dirt particulates slowly descend back down to the planet's surface where people breathe it in and are either killed immediately or suffered horrible disfigurement: loss of hair, fevers and infections, and chronic sickness often leading to death. Additionally, such fallout, given enough exposure to it, would cause people to succumb to radiation sickness and nuclear dysentery, leading inevitably to death. Fallout also includes the gaseous products of nitric oxide and superheated oxygen which are both unstable gas molecules (or "Free Radicals" in Health Care terminology), which are always produced by nuclear detonations and will cause damage to human body cells along with the forementioned gamma-ray emitting particulates that will also change and/or damage human DNA.[61]

The other factor, although not commonly known back then (and still debated among some scientists today) was that these 1940s through 1962 atomic bomb and thermal-nuclear (H-Bomb) tests were the primary and initial cause of measurable climate effects. As mentioned, the military's top officers, federal atomic scientist employees, and civilian (under federal contract) atomic scientists had by the late 1950s determined that all the nuclear test explosions into the planet's atmosphere had resulted in significant destruction to the planet's ozone layer.[62] This has more recently been borne out by atomic scientists and Pentagon military authorities who estimate that 50% to 70% of the planet's ozone

---

[59] Hodge, *The Sun*, June 26, 2018.
[60] MacDonald. Website: DailyMail.com, December 22, 2017.
[61] Glasstone, April 1962.
[62] Bauer & Gilmore, 451.

could be destroyed in the event of a nuclear war with 500 megatons nuclear capacity.[63] They also estimated in that event that the greatest reduction of ozone would occur in the northern hemisphere, where most the nuclear weapons would detonate. During the top-secret Manhattan Project of World War II, the American and Allied countries' atomic scientists at Los Alamos, New Mexico (including the historical "Father of the Atomic Bomb," J. Robert Oppenheimer, and mutually historical "Father of the Hydrogen Bomb," Edward Teller) for all their combined intelligence and education were not aware that climate impacts were even a potential outcome, let alone a problem. Rather, the pressures of budgetary considerations, top-down military pressure, and under highly stressful wartime working conditions, these civilian scientists were tasked during WWII to produce an atomic bomb before Nazi Germany did. Many people alive today don't realize that Germany had the technological edge over the United States and its allies at WWII's beginning, and that Nazi German scientists were who developed the world's first guided missiles (the V1 and V2 rockets) that the English referred to as "Buzz Bombs." Each V1 or V2 rocket (missile) carried a warhead packed with conventional high explosives which killed many British civilians and destroyed major portions of England's capital city (London).

Even as late as 1979, during my first trip to London England, I could see the WWII Era's Nazi Bomb scarring and associated black carbon and fire stains from explosions along the right-side of Westminster Cathedral's front entrance's outside walls. Towards the end of WWII, Nazi German scientists had also invented the world's first jet-fighter aircraft and were making significant progress towards making the world's first atomic bomb. The Nazis occupied Norway in June of 1940 in large part because of the traitorous actions of a former Norwegian Army Officer and Norwegian Government Agricultural Minister by the name of Vidkun Quisling. He left the Government in 1933 to form the fascist National Union Party of Norway. After meeting and collaborating with Adolph Hitler in 1939, Quisling proclaimed himself head of the Norwegian Government after the German Military's invasion of Norway in April 1940.[64] Telemark Norway shortly afterwards became the major research and development location for the Nazi's Atomic Bomb Program. In February of 1943, "Operation Gunnerside" was the code name for a team of 6 British-led Office of Strategic Service (OSS) Commandos, including a heroic Norwegian Resistance Army lieutenant named Knut Haugland, who waded through a freezing river, got through the German sentries, mines, and floodlights to enter the Nordsk Hydro Plant.[65] They next planted explosives that blew up the heavy water producing cells and reactor machinery in which plutonium could be bred from natural uranium. The heroic action of these brave men gave the United States and its allied scientists the time to invent

[63] Williams, December 16, 2020.
[64] Encyclopedia Britannica, 865.
[65] PaperlessArchives.com DVD 2010 and Website: http://www.paperlessarchives.com.

and produce the world's first atomic bomb ahead of Nazi Germany. The Nazi atomic bomb was the one weapon (had the Germans successfully developed it before the Western Alliance), with which they could have won World War II even had it been near the end of the war.

This concern to beat the Nazis in creating an atomic bomb was why U.S. President Franklin Delano Roosevelt and the United States military and its allied scientists started the above Top-Secret Manhattan Project in the first place. Unlike scientists of today in knowing more about nuclear chemistry, at the time their major concern was the Atomic Bomb's potential upon its detonation to set the planet's atmosphere itself on fire. It wasn't until early 1945 that Edward Teller, a top atomic scientist at the Los Alamos Manhattan Project in New Mexico had "theoretically" ruled out this major concern. Teller reported that he'd tested all the calculations to determine the specifics pertaining to the character of the atomic bomb's fission detonation, claiming there was "no possibility" of igniting the planet's atmosphere.[66] Eventually, about a decade later, they discovered that all the atomic bomb and hydrogen bomb tests detonations had destroyed major portions of the planet's stratospheric ozone layer at both the North and South poles. Atomic scientists and military top brass not only detected large holes in the ozone layer at both the planet's poles, but that the remaining ozone layer covering the rest of the planet had been thinned as well.

Again, in the declining 1950s, the nuclear scientists "theoretically" made a convenient determination, namely that the planet would eventually repair the problem itself if given enough time. 70+ years later, the nations that did these tests are still "Waiting for Godot" when it comes to the planet producing more ozone to repair the damage. In fact, a National Ocean and Atmospheric Administration (NOAA) Report dated October 27th, 2021 determined in concert with the National Aeronautics and Space Administration (NASA) that the Ozone hole above Antarctica currently ranks as the 13th largest and deepest on record since 1979. It covers 9.6 million square miles per satellite imagery. Ozone is the Earth's natural sunscreen in the upper atmosphere with its building block an inorganic molecule containing three oxygen atoms. It is formed in the lower atmosphere by the action of Ultra-Violet (UV) light and electrical discharges within the planet's atmosphere. This action produces ozone in the form of a pale blue gas that rises and becomes a beneficial component of the upper atmosphere. This is because ozone absorbs most of the sun's UV light, so it doesn't reach the Earth's surface. It also absorbs excessive heat energies also radiated by the sun.

The problem with detonating nuclear weapons into the Earth's atmosphere is that these nuclear explosions always produce high levels of nitrogen oxides. In short, nitrogen oxides are gases produced by nuclear explosions which destroy the stratospheric ozone layer.

---

[66] NOAA Report, October 27, 2021.

Thanks to my past military background, I procured some recently unclassified reports about the atmospheric nuclear tests done by the United States government from the 1945 through 1962 period addressed in this book. Additional valuable information was also provided by copies of the original unclassified reports directly from the Los Alamos Scientific Laboratory of the University of California in Los Alamos, New Mexico. For a fee, many of these reports are available by contacting the Los Alamos Scientific Laboratory. One of the reports most helpful in my research which itself references related additional reports was: "UNITED STATES HIGH-ALTITUDE TEST EXPERIENCES: A Review Emphasizing the Impact on the Environment" by Herman Hoerlin PhD, issued in October 1976. Another significant report with references that the author found helpful was "PHOTOCHEMISTRY IN THE STRATOSPHERE—WITH APPLICATIONS TO SUPERSONIC TRANSPORTS Prepared for the U.S. Atomic Energy Commission" by Harold S. Johnston PhD issued in September 1973 under the auspices of the Lawrence Berkeley National Laboratory, of the University of California, Berkeley, California.[67]

My review of the data from Doctor Hoerlin's Report revealed only one report indicative of the United States government's specific contribution to the reduction of the Earth's ozone because of its atmospheric nuclear tests. This was for the period of 1952 to 1962 in which it was determined that these nuclear tests had resulted in the reduction of more than 10% of the Earth's total ozone layer. Anything post-1962 is apparently still classified information. In any case, it does not provide ozone loss calculations for the calendar years 1945 through 1951, or for the first nine months of 1963 prior to President John F. Kennedy's signing of the Limited Test Ban Treaty in October of 1963. Neither was there any speculation, or valid information (except for one, the previously-mentioned 1961 Russian Tsar H-Bomb Test) available about Russia, China, France, or England's contributions to ozone layer loss in association with their respective early atmospheric nuclear tests. I will conclude with an insertion here of the last sentence from one of these reports that was left unsigned by the nuclear scientist writing it: "It is evident that the consequences of massive military operations in the upper atmosphere would be grave." That is, were a great number of nuclear bombs or missiles to detonate, as in a major nuclear exchange in a nuclear war, or ongoing atmospheric nuclear tests with large yields (as in higher kiloton or megaton-level nuclear explosions), the ozone layer protecting life on this planet would be destroyed. In short, life on the surface of this planet would soon cease to exist.

However, it wasn't the atomic and hydrogen bomb atmospheric tests alone that destroyed major portions of the planet's ozone layer, but in our own time we must now include the ongoing massive amounts of commercial airline jet exhausts regularly released into the planet's stratosphere. I explored how these millions of flights (both subsonic and

---

[67] Goodchild, 146-7.

supersonic), might impact the ozone layer and discovered some of the major works of now deceased University of California Berkeley's Emeritus Professor, Harold S. Johnston. He worked for the Federal Government in classified operations as a young graduate student, (likely at the Manhattan Project) during WWII. After the war in 1945, he returned to his studies at the California Institute of Technology to complete his PhD in Chemistry, with a minor in Physics.[68] He initially taught at Stanford University and the California Institute of Technology respectively; prior to being selected for his post at University of California Berkeley. He was awarded the National Medal of Science, and many other awards of highest scientific prestige, too numerous to list here, but all culminated in his appointment as a member of the National Academy of Science.[69]

Johnston was a pioneer Atmospheric Chemist and UC Berkeley Emeritus Professor from 1957 through 1991. He additionally was the Dean of UC Berkeley's College of Chemistry from 1966 to 1970. He did extensive research in and specialized his career around the fundamental kinetics of nitrogen oxides in the atmosphere. He wrote groundbreaking scientific papers and books implicating the airline corporations' subsonic and supersonic jets (like France's supersonic Concordes) collectively negative impact on the stratosphere from these jets' fuel exhausts which contain nitrous oxides; again, these, like in the aftermath of nuclear detonation, destroy ozone the same as the atomic and yydrogen bombs testing in the open atmosphere originally did from 1946 through 1963.[70]

He went on to reveal that aviation fuel exhausts also released sulfur dioxide into the stratosphere which ultimately condense to become fine droplets of sulfuric acid which in turn comes down to the surface as acidic rain. He presented his own and some of his professional colleagues' research models of the stratosphere in which experiments could be performed simulating the global ozone shield and projecting the distribution and effects of the exhaust gases of groups of subsonic and supersonic commercial jet transports. Further, the release of nitrous oxides into the stratosphere not only reduce the ozone layer but cause a consequential increase in the intensity of ultraviolet (uv) radiation reaching the earth's surface.[71]

One dimensional (vertical) models of the stratosphere consider turbulent diffusion, in some cases a vertical wind, and large sets of chemical reactions. Two dimensional models add a substantial set of chemical reactions and both vertical and horizontal stratospheric simulations in response to jet fuel effluents released at greater or lesser amounts. These can be partially calibrated against observed stratospheric data following the atmospheric

---

[68] Goodchild, 9-21.
[69] Ibid.
[70] Ibid.
[71] Ibid.

nuclear bomb testing between 1952 to 1962, which there are reliable records for, as their mushroom clouds transported nitrous oxides many miles high into the stratosphere.

These laboratory models also readily permit the simulation of jet exhausts of subsonic and supersonic flight gases, including chemical and photo-chemical reactions. One three-dimensional model of the atmosphere, for example, has 11 layers simulating altitudes up to 31 kilometers (or 19.3 miles). It includes oceans and continents, evaporation and condensation of moisture, seasonally varying radiation, and both absorption and condensation of radiant energy.[72] These models through their determination of ozone depletion, allowed atmospheric scientists to calculate the amount of the sun's harmful ultra-violet (UV) and heat radiations reaching and impacting the Earth's surface, causing atmospheric warming and increasing skin cancers among human and animal species on land or in oceans.

I used one of these models to calculate the impact of jet fuel exhausts into the stratosphere upon the ozone layer of 16 million subsonic jet flights over a one year time span (the figure in 2021 was higher: 22.2 million). "Subsonic" means that these jets' traveling speeds were all less than 767 miles per hour. United States commercial jet flights, and that of other nations for that matter, mainly fly in the Northern Hemisphere. I set some of the calculation's factors for all these jets being used 7 hours a day and flying at a routine stratospheric altitude between 33,000 to 39,000 feet (or 10 to 12 kilometers, or between 6 and a quarter mile, and 7 and a half miles high). It was interesting to find out too, that such jets not flying at stratospheric altitudes have no impact upon the planet's ozone level. Using the graphic table on page 17 of the National Academy of Sciences book, titled "Environmental Impact of Stratospheric Flight: Biological and Climatic Effects of Aircraft Emissions in the Stratosphere" revealed that a projected 32% loss of Stratospheric Ozone will occur in one year's time. A similar model also simultaneously determines the amount of skin cancer which can be anticipated, as each 1% reduction in ozone will lead to an increase of 2% increase in the intensity of ultraviolet light at the ground level. Hence, there will be 6,400 new case of serious skin burning or skin cancers.

With the use of such models supported by advanced computers, balloon atmospheric gas sampling, and associated satellite monitoring and scanning, Johnston and his colleagues influenced the federal government to pass laws in 1973 that prevented the Concorde or any other commercial supersonic aircraft from flying over U.S. soil. These factors along with the sonic booms these craft produced, shattering the windows of the houses below their flight paths, deterred federal government authorities and the American commercial airline industry from creating new fleets of supersonic jet transports capable of reaching Europe from the United States' East Coast in under 4 hours.

[72] Ibid.

This may now be upon the verge of changing, as while doing research, I found a sea-change in the Federal Aviation Administration's (FAA) outlook, as recently as 2020, openly saying that the federal government was now favorably inclined towards developing supersonic jet transport. The claim was also made at that time that Congress was planning to change these laws to facilitate the development of supersonic commercial airline fleets. I found after reviewing the documentation that there was much talk about how technological progress could reduce or remove the sonic boom outburst, which was thought to be the major problem. Other limiting factors mentioned were the increased expenses of fuel, equipment, new designs for more passenger space, and increased pilot education and specialized training expenses. I found no mention of any environmental concerns such as ozone depletion from jet fuel exhausts in any of these reports.

In any case, Johnston's presentations to federal government authorities, research publications and books produced so much consternation among the commercial airline corporations that the President or another higher-up Executive from Boeing came to UC Berkeley and met with the Chancellor of the University to fire the professor. According to Johnston's account of the matter, and much to the credit of the University, instead of being fired he was given a salary increase.[73]

All of this is context is necessary, as the effects of scientific research are not produced in a vacuum. They are led by prominent figures whose work is the basis for other advancements—which also can produce unintended consequences. These are supported by governments either in concert with or followed by corporate interests. (Indeed, nuclear technology first for use in weapons would later be used for power sources of whole geographic areas by corporations.) What may start as a military and/or government project eventually becomes a boon to commercial and industrial interests. When such interests become endemic internationally, with equally far-reaching consequences, it is here that other parties, as it were, seem to take an interest.

Because this tendency of EBEs (and UFOs) to be spotted in conjunction to major human events, it is important to look more deeply into the origin of the 20th Century's most famous initial contact and the reason behind it. This, for me, begins with the "Father of the Atomic Bomb," J. Robert Oppenheimer. The son of German Jewish parents, his father (Julius) did very well after leaving Germany for New York City in the late 19th Century, taking a position in his extended family's previously established and highly successful clothing industry. His mother (Ella Friedman) was a well-known painter in New York (having received an education in Paris) teaching art in NYC when she met Julius Oppenheimer.[74]

---

[73] Ibid.
[74] Ibid.

J. Robert Oppenheimer was born on the 22nd of April 1904, where he grew up in a first-rate apartment with his parents, their maid, and house servants on Riverside Drive in New York City. At age five he was taken to visit the ancestral family home in Germany where his grandfather gave him a rock and mineral collection. That gift started a hobby that not only interested the young Oppenheimer but lasted for years into his early adult life: mineralogy.[75]

At the age of 11, J. Robert Oppenheimer was a member of the New York Mineralogical Club, and shortly after joining, he presented his first paper and public address. Oppenheimer also attended a private elementary school administered by the New York Society for Ethical Culture.[76] His parents had as adults rejected traditional Orthodox Jewish society and culture, preferring this school which offered studies in ethical humanism rather than any religious faith for constructing a system of values as well as moral and philosophical development. Oppenheimer was taught principally that a man should form his own attitudes independently towards the unknown and the mysteries of life. Here he excelled in reading and speaking Greek, read the Classics like Homer and Plato, and soon demonstrated similar excellence in chemistry. Robert Oppenheimer was also encouraged by his parents and school faculty to play outdoor sports as a child, but he lacked physical coordination. He made a serious attempt at tennis, but in the final analysis played too badly to seriously continue.

Astutely perceiving his son's preference for independent-type sports, and possessing the finances for doing so, he provided the teenage Robert Oppenheimer with a 28-foot sloop, and Robert soon rose to become an expert sailor and yachtsman.[77] A testimony to his seamanship was his parents allowing Robert to take his younger brother Frank sailing with him. Graduating after his last year of high school with straight A's, he was known among other students for being polite, bookish, goal-driven, yet at times arrogant and a snob. His profound seriousness of mind and habit of goal setting, combined with steadfast follow-through, were firmly implanted at an early age. He hardly ever laughed, and his need for academic knowledge-building activity, love of the classics and other fine literature set him apart from his student peers. His intellectual brilliance and psychological isolationism often resulted in his rejection by other students. My review of available information indicates that Oppenheimer befriended his teachers more than his student peers. Oppenheimer's snobbishness and "teacher's pet" type behaviors were resented and resulted in counter-rejection and ongoing insulting remarks from other students. This was amply demonstrated while attending summer camp at age 14, when a group of teens there stripped him naked and locked him in the Camp's icehouse all night.[78] After graduating

---

[75] Ibid.

[76] Ibid.

[77] Ibid.

[78] Ibid.

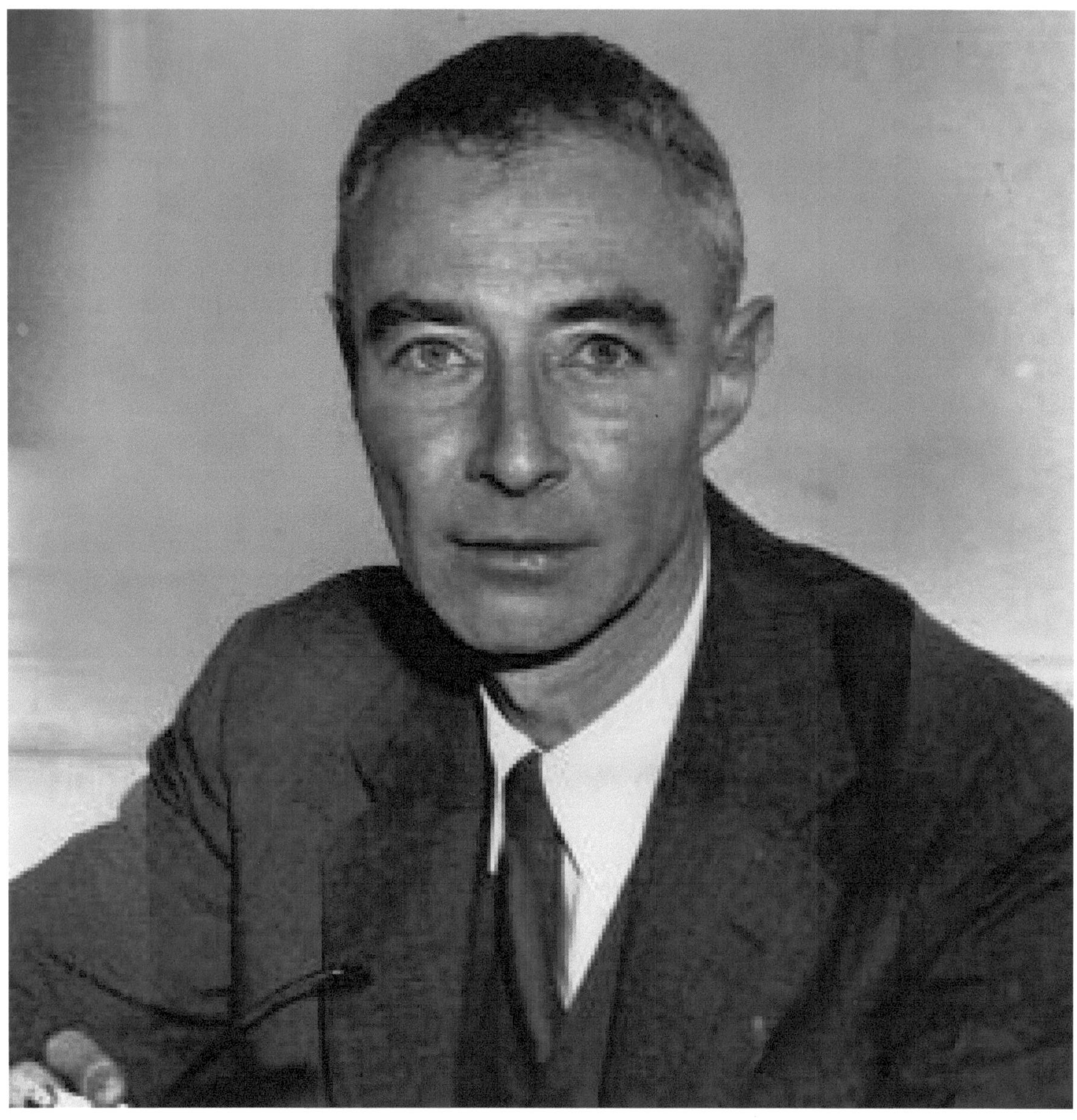

This is a photograph of the brilliant Julius Robert Oppenheimer, nuclear physicist, atomic sciences director of the above top secret World War II "Manhattan Project," ordered by President of the United States Franklin Delano Roosevelt, to design and construct an atomic bomb before Nazi Germany could do so, and did. He has been dubbed with the title, "Father of the Atomic Bomb."

from high school, his parents took him for a return vacation to Germany. He soon went off alone into the mountains on a minerology excursion, which unfortunately resulted in his acquisition of an extremely bad case of dysentery which made him so ill that he suffered from bowel and digestive problems the rest of his life.[79]

Consequently, after returning from their family vacation in Germany, his parents decided Oppenheimer was too ill to go to Harvard that year. This meant he had to remain home alone for the most part, and even after his recovery, he remained in an angry and agitated state for months, isolating himself in his room and generally taking a passive-aggressive attitude towards his mother and everyone else. His father wisely paid his English teacher, Herbert Smith, a seasoned woodsman, horseman, and one of his son's favorite high school instructors, to take Robert to the mountains of Colorado and New Mexico.[80] These two traveled on horseback, camping sometimes out in the open trail beneath the stars, and other times at guest (tourist/dude) ranches. Here, Oppenheimer fell in love with living out on the trail in the New Mexico mountains. This area proved to be the area he'd visit repeatedly throughout his life for vacations and that would ultimately play a major role in his professional life as an atomic (nuclear) physicist. He also found beauty and added excitement on this trip with Herbert Smith by falling into a puppy-love infatuation with the female manager (Miss Katherine Page) at the Los Pino's Guest Ranch located north of Santa Fe, New Mexico. However, his emotional immaturity prevented the development of any serious relationship. After these adventures he returned to New York, soon entering Harvard University at age 18 and graduated in 3 years with a Summa Cum Laude degree in Chemistry. From there he attended Cambridge in England where he studied Atomic Structure, Physics Theory, and Mathematics. He next transferred from there to Germany's University of Gottingen which at the time was a scholastic apex of Theoretical Physics in Europe. There he completed his PhD "with distinction" in 1927.[81] Ending the final phase of his educational development, Oppenheimer began his professional career as a PhD in 1929 teaching Physics at the University of California, Berkeley and the California Institute of Technology until 1943.[82]

Going just a step back to 1942, the United States was at war, and Army Major General Leslie R. Groves was put in overall charge of the U.S. Government's beyond top secret Manhattan Project. General Groves was in immediate need for an Atomic Sciences Director to supervise and organize teams of Atomic and other Scientists to design and create a Super (Atomic) Bomb before Nazi Germany did given the Nazis already had a head start. His recruitment efforts led him to the University of California Berkeley's Radiation Laboratory. There, he met with atomic scientist and Nobel Laureate physicist,

---

[79] Ibid.
[80] Ibid.
[81] Ibid.
[82] Ibid.

Ernest Lawrence, who demonstrated for the General the "Calutron Machine" he had made to separate uranium atoms—the heavier from the lighter ones.[83] Lawrence was also a best friend of J. Robert Oppenheimer, who together had vacationed to Oppenheimer's favorite areas in the mountains and woods of New Mexico. Shortly after this consultation, General Groves selected J. Robert Oppenheimer, PhD as the Manhattan Project's Atomic Sciences Director— known today as the atomic scientist in charge of designing the atomic bomb. Tall and formidable, General Groves in terms of temperament was an aggressive and no-nonsense extrovert, whereas Oppenheimer was more the low-key gentleman and calming introvert in manner, yet they worked very well together.

Oppenheimer soon recommended that for reasons of security, plus ensuring the control and job focus of allied atomic scientists, many of whom spoke different languages, that the project site be moved from New York to Los Alamos. The General agreed, and the world's first atomic bomb was developed over nearly a three-year period and successfully test-detonated on the 16th of July 1945.[84]

As Atomic Sciences Director of the Manhattan Project, Oppenheimer was charged with the responsibility for designing and creating the atomic bomb. Hence, he coordinated the research and development of multiple Manhattan Project atomic science teams, individual atomic physicists, and atomic theory researchers. As Director, he interviewed, hired, and had overall responsibility over the atomic scientists, technicians, and workers assigned to the Los Alamos Radiation Laboratory. This latter responsibility extended also to his younger brother Frank Oppenheimer, who had also gotten a job as an atomic scientist on the Manhattan Project. More about his younger brother Frank's story will also follow shortly.

Robert Oppenheimer also consulted with genius and theoretical physicist Albert Einstein at Princeton University who contributed information and research regarding atomic theory and the nuclear fission process. Oppenheimer's many responsibilities, along with constant pressure from General Groves for timely progress and situation reports, was nothing short of Herculean. On July 16th, 1945, at 5:30 AM an 18 by 24-mile site on the U.S. Army Air Corps' Alamogordo New Mexico Bombing Range (dubbed "Trinity" by Oppenheimer) changed from night to day four seconds after the first nuclear bomb in the world's history exploded. After a few seconds the terrific blast of the atomic detonation was heard in a deep bunker 20 miles away, followed on by a thunderous roaring like that of a distant electrical storm. This bunker was where Oppenheimer and other scientists were safely stationed to monitor the test. The following quote from Oppenheimer was taken shortly following the 20-kiloton explosion: "A few people laughed, a few people cried, most people were silent. There flowed through my mind a line from the Bhagavad-Gita in

---

[83] Ibid.
[84] Ibid.

which Krishna is trying to persuade a prince that he should do his duty: 'I am become Death, the Destroyer of Worlds.'" [85] Oppenheimer, incidentally, had taught himself Sanskrit so he could read the Bhagavad-Gita's original text. Unlike many of his scientific peers, Oppenheimer had throughout his life an appreciation for the classics, fine literature, and music. Additionally, he could speak multiple languages and earlier in life had some poetry published.

After the two atomic bombs were dropped on Japan, Oppenheimer's initial feelings of joy and success were rapidly curbed over the next six months. The impact of his success began transforming to horror, especially after the mass death reports came over the radio and American movie theaters' newsreels describing in gruesome detail the atomic bombs' destruction in Japan. Newspapers with the pictures of Japanese children and adult civilians terribly burned, the utter decimation of the cities of Hiroshima and Nagasaki into wastelands, and the slower deaths from radioactive fallout with neutron and gamma radiation exposure could not have been more of a hell on earth. This included ghastly images of peoples' shadows burned into the sides of ruined building walls, sidewalks, and bridge overpasses. [86] These were the sole remnants of a macabre import where people had stood or were walking along at 8:14 a.m. during the city of Hiroshima's morning rush-hour prior to their bodies totally disintegrating in a split-second flash of atomic heat from the atomic bomb dropped on their city. This instantaneous annihilation happened before the shock wave from the atomic bomb's detonation would have even hit them—when the ambient temperature around them changed from normal temperature to that equivalent to the surface of the sun. That, by the way, in terms of Fahrenheit Temperature, is 9,941 degrees. [87] The dropping of the two atomic bombs ended the Second World War and forced the Japanese Empire to formerly surrender to Supreme Allied Commander, U.S. Army General Douglas MacArthur, aboard the U.S. Navy Battleship USS Missouri in Tokyo Bay on the 2nd of September 1945. In the months following, international newspaper photographs of the two atomic bombs' destructive aftermaths were daily displayed, highlighting the blinding, radiation burns, horrible disfigurement, and maiming of civilian Japanese of all ages. Newspapers also featured news stories with casualty statistics about the bombs' increasing "slow-kill" death rates. Pictures of dying Japanese, some with yellow and green spots covering their entire bodies, acute hair loss, and unknown (plus never-before-seen) bizarre illnesses, were all featured in the major newspapers and newsreels of movie theaters worldwide.

In 1946, Congress set up the Atomic Energy Commission (AEC), that provided for civilian rather than military oversight of the nation's atomic energy and weapons

<hr>

[85] Ibid.
[86] Serena, Website: https://allthatisinteresting.com/hiroshima-shadows
[87] Wikipedia: https://en.wikipedia.org/wiki/Sun

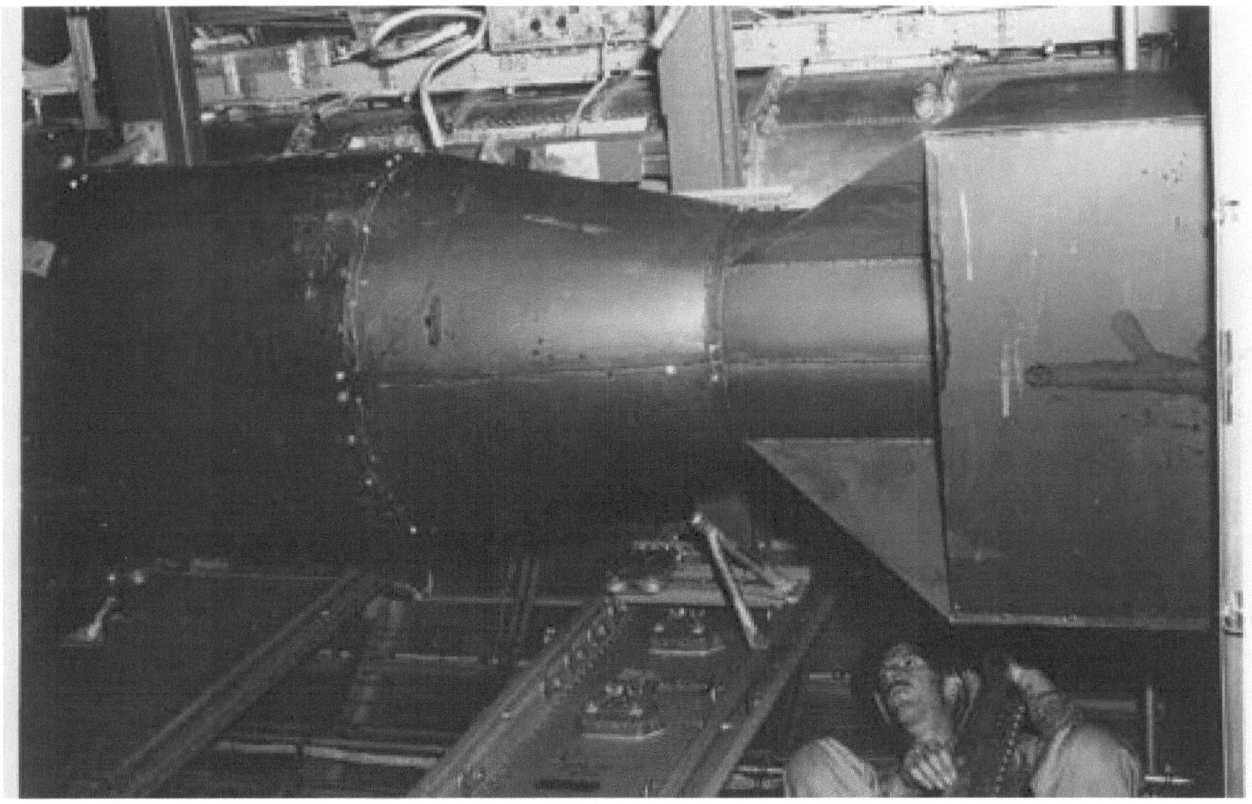

This photo of the first atomic WWII bomb named "Little Boy," which the United States dropped on the Japanese city of Hiroshima on the 6th of August, 1945. It immediately killed over 200,000 Japanese military and civilians according to Japanese estimates.

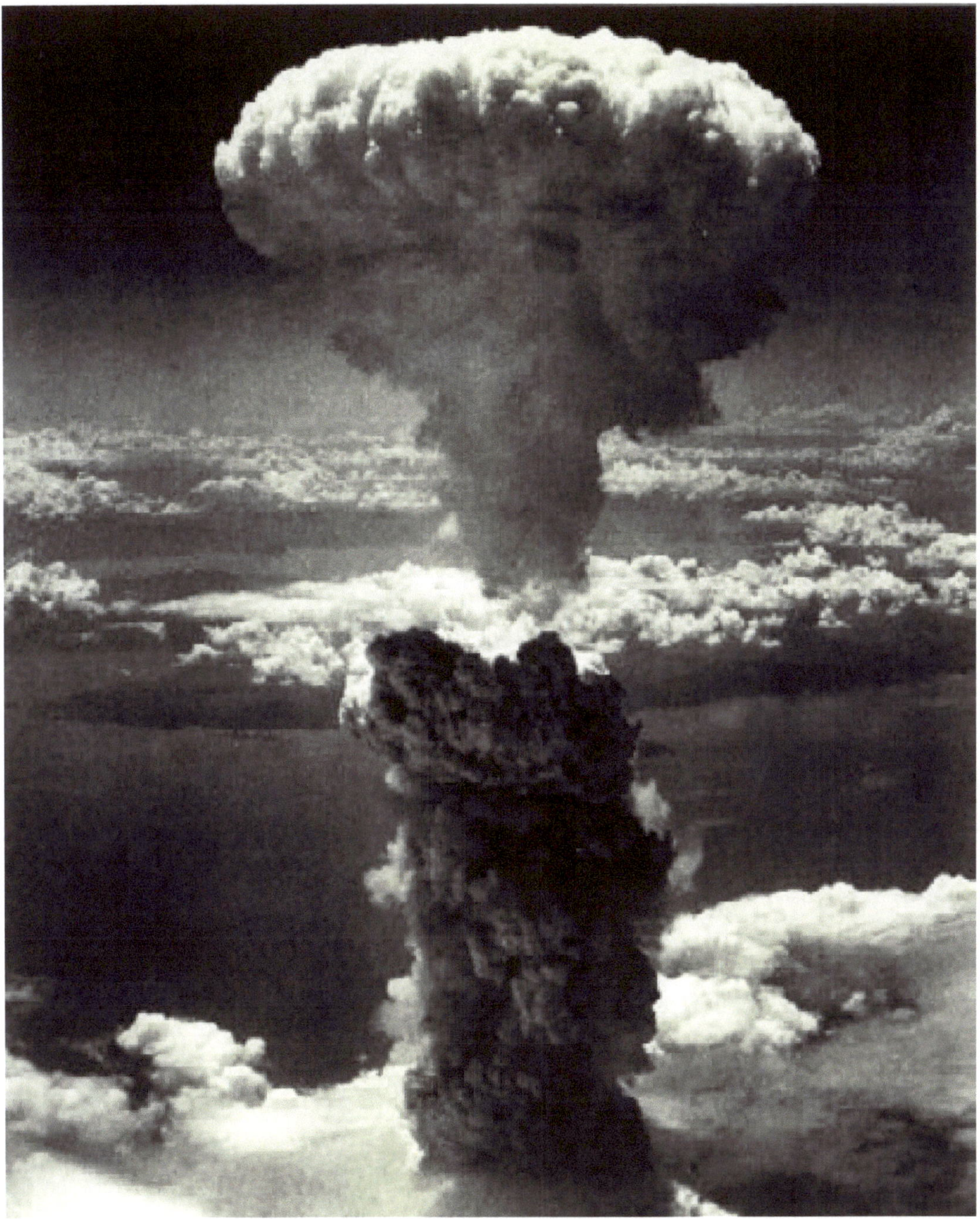

This is a picture of the detonation cloud of the first atomic bomb "Little Boy" taken by an American aircraft over Hiroshima, Japan on the 6th of August, 1945. It was 13 kilotons, or exploded with the force of 13 thousand tons of TNT.

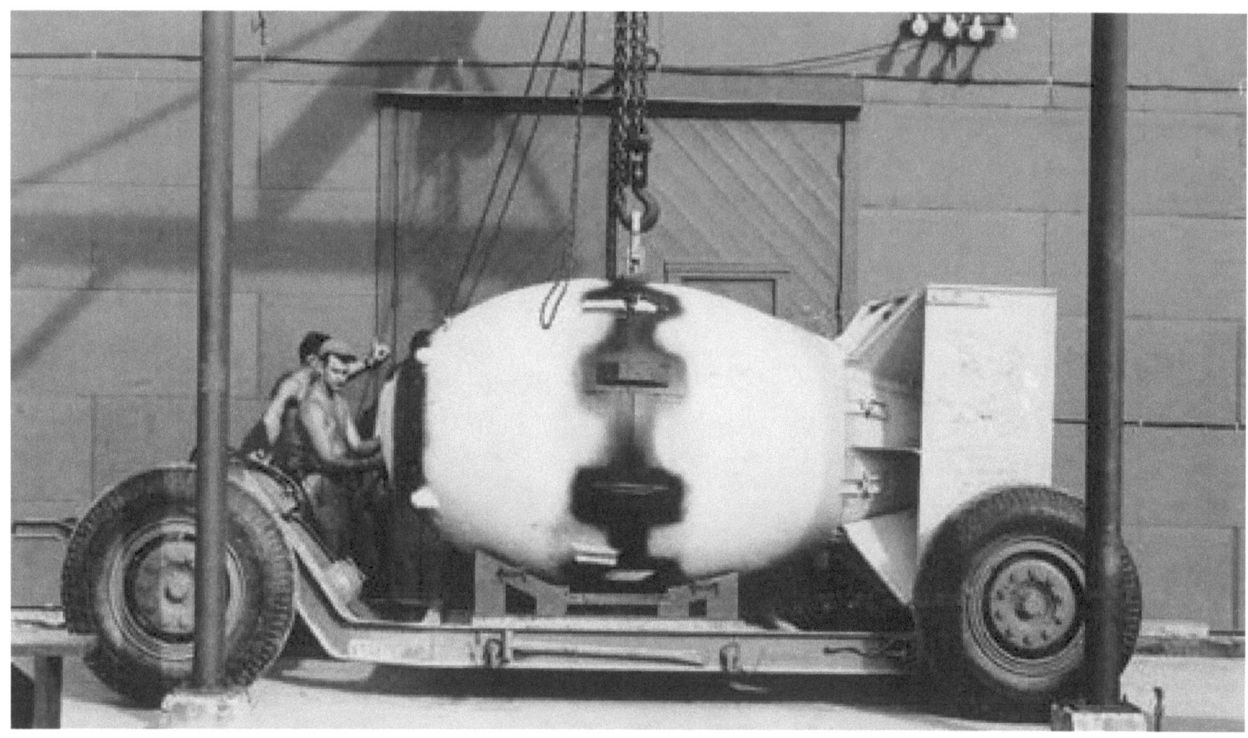

This is a picture of the 2nd WWII atomic bomb which the United States dropped on the Japanese city of Nagasaki on the 9th of August, 1945. It was named "Fat Man" and immediately killed over 100,000 Japanese military and civilians upon its detonation. It also effectively ended the Second World War.

programs.[88] This allowed scientists more freedom for their research under civilian control rather than that under military auspices. Oppenheimer, in view of his notoriety, scientific reputation, and accomplishment, had significant influence in this Commission's membership appointments. First was Chairman of the AEC, David Lilienthal, who was also the Chairman of the Advisory Committee to the United Nations Atomic Energy Commission. It was in this latter Advisory Committee that Lilienthal met Oppenheimer for the first time, as Oppenheimer was a member. Lilienthal was very impressed by Oppenheimer from the start, and since Oppenheimer was the expert when it came to atomic issues, Lilienthal came to rely heavily on Oppenheimer's knowledge and briefing of both himself and other Committee members to help them more effectively perform their duties. These two genuinely liked each other, much to the annoyance of Oppenheimer's Manhattan Project's boss, General Groves, who was a member of a Special Committee to formulate American nuclear weapons policies. Groves felt Oppenheimer had far too much influence on the Chairman of the AEC, as in private conversations he inferred Lilienthal was no more than a rubber stamp for Oppenheimer's opinions and perspectives. Second, General Grove's attitude was further reinforced by the appointment (through Oppenheimer's influence on Lilienthal) to the AEC of one of Oppenheimer's former scientific colleagues at Los Alamos, Robert Bacher, of the five men appointed as Commissioners.

Oppenheimer in his turn was also selected to the nine-member General Advisory Committee (GAC), formed to advise Lilienthal and the Atomic Energy Commission (AEC) about technical, or scientific issues. His Fellow GAC members, prior to Oppenheimer's arrival to attend the GAC's very first meeting, had in the few minutes of Oppenheimer's absence immediately voted Oppenheimer as their first Chairman. Simultaneously, Oppenheimer was also appointed Director of the world-class Institute of Advanced Study at Princeton, New Jersey. Despite these signature laurels of success, especially now being in the ideal position to significantly influence the policies and decisions of the Atomic Energy Commission (AEC), Oppenheimer was never free of his demons and guilt for creating the worst weapon of mass destruction in human history. Within six months of these appointments, he played a key role in establishing the United Nations Atomic Energy Commission, thereby planting a seed that he hoped would someday grow to provide for international control of atomic weapons and energy. Yet even this latest accomplishment failed to alleviate his feelings of guilt.

This guilt was clear in March of 1946 when Oppenheimer lost his composure while in a meeting with President Harry Truman and an Oppenheimer-supportive Dean Acheson, Undersecretary of State. Oppenheimer was describing his reservations to the President about an executive level member's appointment to the United Nations Atomic Energy Commission that he disapproved of when he grew nervous and lost his train of thought. In

---

[88] Wikipedia: https://en.wikipedia.org/wiki/Atomic_Energy_Act_of_1946

hindsight, it appears Oppenheimer's unconscious mind filled in the lost thoughts instead, as his voice shifted to a high pitch while inappropriately accusing and judging himself, confessing; "Mr. President, I have blood on my hands!" Again, Oppenheimer's purpose for the meeting had been to convince the President to remove an adverse (in Oppenheimer's view) political appointment President Truman's administration had just made. The subject appointee was a 75-year-old conservative politician and financier, Bernard M. Baruch. Baruch was an old-school go-along-to-get-along and risk-avoiding politician, who in Oppenheimer's view would negate any chance of serious nuclear arms negotiations with the Soviets. Oppenheimer felt Baruch would follow any directions or proposals for changes in approach and discussion strategy made by the Truman Administration, or the Congress, to the detriment of successful negotiations.

In any case, President Truman decided to sustain Baruch's appointment. Truman also contacted Under-Secretary Acheson shortly afterwards, saying, "Don't bring that son-of-a-bitch around again… After all, he only made the bomb, I'm the one who fired it off." So, it appears Truman strongly disapproved of Oppenheimer's emotional declaration. Oppenheimer, in time, was proven to be all too correct though in his assessment regarding Baruch. The United Nations Atomic Energy Commission's negotiations with the USSR went nowhere.

In October 1949, Oppenheimer was present when the General Advisory Committee was meeting with their commissioners and expert advisors at the Atomic Energy Commission's Headquarters in Washington D.C. Joint Chief of Staff and WWII Hero, Army General Omar Bradley was taking questions after making a presentation about the Soviet Union's recent and successful completion of their own first atomic bomb test and related military considerations regarding their likely development of an H-Bomb soon. Oppenheimer, (who opposed the H-Bomb's development), asked him privately, "What precisely is the military, or any other target of the H-Bomb, General?" To which Bradley responded, "There is no target… It is a weapon of annihilation…" Oppenheimer then said, "Then why build it? Isn't the atomic bomb bad enough for you?" To which the seasoned old General calmly responded, "Psychological deterrence. If we don't develop it, they [meaning the Soviets] will. So, we must have it."[89]

One statement made by this famous WWII Five-Star General (who was the boss of the equally famous Army WWII 4-Star General, George S. Patton) which needs repeating today to all our world's governments, went as follows: "Ours is a world of nuclear giants and ethical infants. We know more about killing than about peace—than we do about living."

---

[89] Wikipedia: https://en.wikipedia.org/wiki/Omar_Bradley

Now some words about Dr. Edward Teller, PhD, are appropriate. He, like Oppenheimer, was an atomic physicist and scientist of the first rank, born in 1908 in Budapest, Hungary. His father Max Teller was a lawyer who introduced his son at age 12 to his very good friend, Leopold Klug, who was a Professor of Mathematics at the University of Budapest.[90] In short, the young Teller took like a duck to water to Klug, who provided him with the adult role model he appeared to need, including gifts of books on Algebra and Mathematics. His mother Ilona (née Deutsch) was also from a Jewish Hungarian family like his father, and a pianist. Religion was not discussed in the family, although Teller once stated, "My family celebrated one holiday, the Day of Atonement, when we all fasted. The idea of God that I absorbed was that it would be wonderful if He existed; we needed Him desperately but had not seen Him in many thousands of years." His early education included the Fasori Lutheran Gymnasium and then the Lutheran Minta (model) Gymnasium both in Budapest, Hungary, where he spent the first 18 years of his life. It was during this period that he met Nobel Laureate for Physics, Eugene P. Wigner and simultaneously met John Von Neumann, later to become a world class master mathematician. Teller left Hungary because of government anti-Semitism and went to Germany to study mathematics and chemistry at the Karlsruhe Institute of Technology from 1926 to 1928. There he found out that chemistry was in the forefront for the study of physics and was opening new ideas about it. From there, Teller went to the University of Munich, Germany from 1928 to 1929. From Munich, Teller went to the University of Leipzig from 1929 to 1930 where he obtained a PhD in Physical Chemistry. He continued as a Research Associate at the University of Leipzig until 1931, and from there held a similar research position at the University of Gottingen, Germany through 1933, when he left for England upon Nazi Adolph Hitler's rise to Chancellor of Germany.

Teller next studied Theoretical Physics at the University of Copenhagen in Denmark from 1933 to 1934. He then Lectured at the City College of London from 1934 to 1935. In 1935 he came to the United States with his wife Augusta Maria "Mici" Harkanyi. He became a Professor of Physics at George Washington University in Washington D.C. from 1935 to 1946. He and his wife both became naturalized citizens of the United States in 1941 and had a son and daughter. As a physicist, he worked from 1942 to 1946 for the Manhattan Project, doing atomic energy research at various higher educational institutions. This led to his eventual assignment to Los Alamos Science Laboratory, New Mexico, under the Directorship of J. Robert Oppenheimer from April 1943 to 1946.

Edward Teller was initially positively inclined towards Oppenheimer, whom he knew and had worked with as an atomic physicist researcher at the University of California, Berkeley. His feelings soon cooled though, when instead of working on his own (which was his original understanding), and on his main interest and goal, the development of what

---

[90] Wikipedia: https://en.wikipedia.org/wiki/Edward_teller#Early_life_and_work

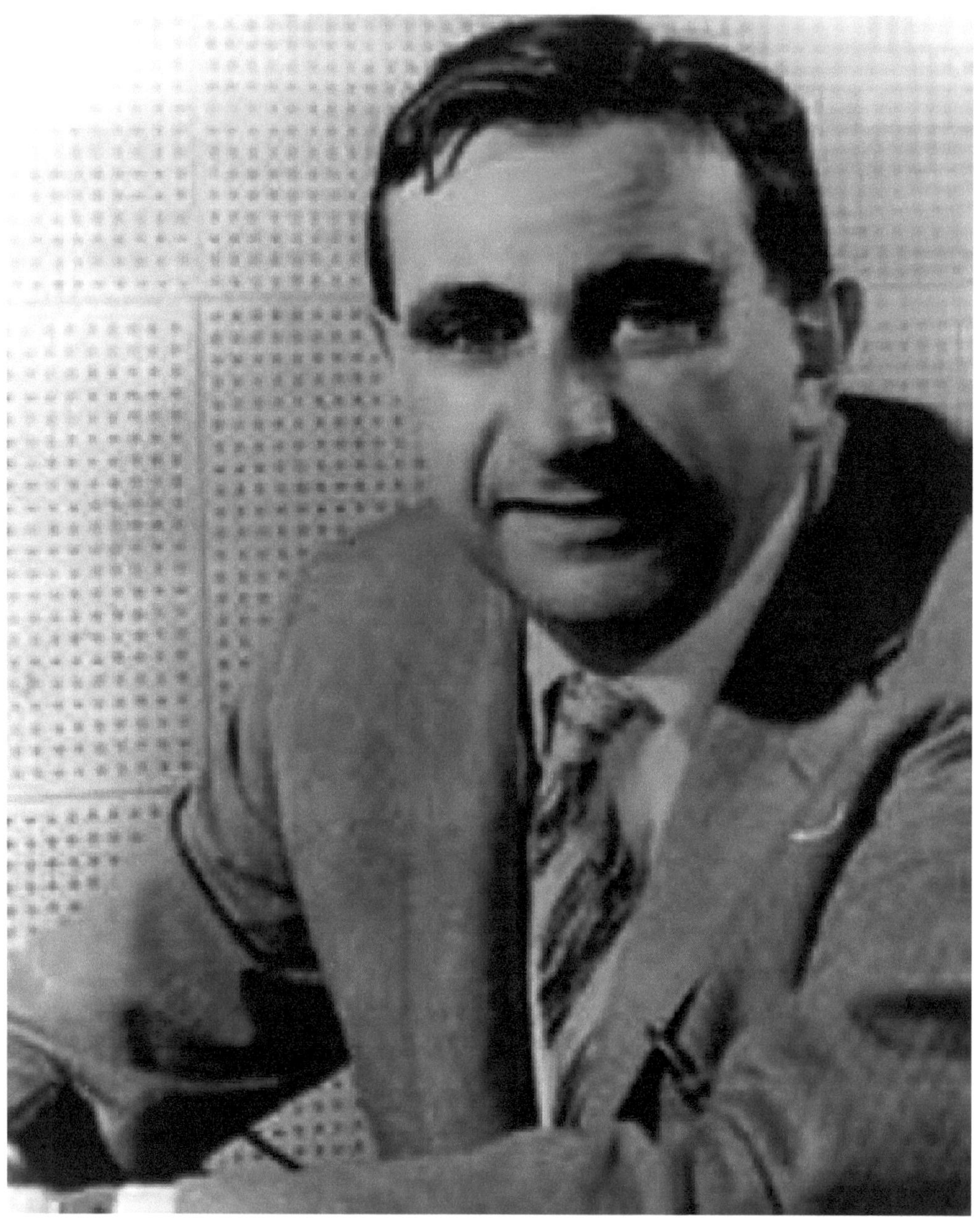

This is a picture of Edward Teller, American nuclear physicist who invented and directed the construction of the world's first hydrogen bomb. The mushroom-like cloud was 8 miles in width and 22 miles high.

he liked to call the "Super" or H-Bomb. Oppenheimer instead made Teller's primary Los Alamos assignment to not only assist but work under the supervision of another physicist in resolving everyday problems with the fission of the atomic bomb, which utterly bored Teller. This planted the first seed of resentment towards Oppenheimer, and it made Teller problematic at best. As time went on, resentment eventually turned adversarial against Oppenheimer.

Teller was somewhat of a loner, and looking at his pattern of migration to different academic institutions and associated jobs every one to two years, this may have been indicative of poor human relations skills. In any event, he soon had a blow-up with his immediate atomic sciences supervisor and fellow physicist, Hans Bethe. Teller refused to work under anyone on a process only he (Teller) originally thought of for producing a critical mass using less of the extremely costly fissionable metal. This made Bethe angry, and he immediately went to Oppenheimer about the matter. Oppenheimer immediately transferred Teller to another area and eventually put him in charge of a small group of his own, working on the "Super" (H-Bomb). It appears Oppenheimer was an able manager, and he perceived Teller could still be useful in problem solving or improving the atomic bomb's fission process. At that time, competent theoreticians in atomic physics were not easy to come by. Some irony seems in play here, as in transferring Teller, Oppenheimer selected Rudolf Peierls from the British Mission to contribute to the Manhattan Project. Peierls in turn brought in his assistant Klaus Fuchs, who was later revealed to be a Soviet spy. In the years following World War II, this decision was to have major consequences for J. Robert Oppenheimer, since as the Manhattan Project's Atomic Sciences Director he was ultimately held responsible for the hiring, management, and security of all the atomic scientists and associated technological personnel working to produce the atomic bomb.

In any case, these two very brilliant men were never fated to reconcile. Teller continued to work with his small nuclear research group at Los Alamos under a different director when Oppenheimer left Los Alamos in Fall of 1945, just after the war. Teller found the new director as cool as Oppenheimer had been when it came devoting more resources and the funding Teller needed to produce a controllable and effective Hydrogen bomb. However, in 1949, after the Soviets had detonated their country's first atomic bomb, Teller had renewed hope of receiving government funding support for atomic scientist recruitment and finally develop it. Teller's fellow atomic scientists who supported Teller's "Super" project met individually with the Atomic Energy Commissioners (AEC). They also lobbied the General Advisory Committee, Department of Defense advisors, and independent atomic scientists and physicists in their respective laboratories and educational institutions. Teller lobbied in-person and was thinking ahead by initiating his own recruiting of atomic physicists for the "Super Project" at Los Alamos.[91]

---

[91] Goodchild, 87-215.

Oppenheimer, however, still had major influence with the AEC Chairman, David Lilienthal, and like Oppenheimer, Lilienthal was aware that the AEC's various laboratories had produced an atomic bomb of 500,000 tons (500 kilotons)—25 times more powerful than the atomic bomb that was dropped on Hiroshima. It could take out any target, so there seemed to be no acute need for a destructive weapon with even more power than that. However, Lilienthal still called for a special meeting of the GAC to get all the members' advice and inputs regarding the hydrogen bomb "Super" Project. Oppenheimer, meanwhile, remained a consultant to David Lilienthal, who now was also Chairman of the Advisory Committee to the United Nations Atomic Energy Commission, including advocating for smaller tactical atomic weapons to keep any nuclear war engagement more in the battlefield environment rather than bombing cities with non-combatant civilians.[92] Oppenheimer had left Los Alamos in October 1945 after accepting a Certificate of Appreciation on behalf of the Los Alamos Laboratory from the Army presented to him by General Groves.[93] Despite returning to academic life, he couldn't shake his international news reputation as the "Father of the Atomic Bomb." Despite teaching and doing research work at Cal Tech in Pasadena, California, he was constantly assailed by phone calls from and trips to Washington D.C. These were for consultations with federal government representatives, the Department of State, Department of Defense, federal government atomic scientists, and senior military officers.

Unfortunately, J. Robert Oppenheimer's personal skeletons shortly started falling out of the proverbial closet on July 12th, 1947, when his brother, Frank Oppenheimer, made the front page of the *Washington Times Herald* newspaper. The headline read, "U.S. ATOM SCIENTIST'S BROTHER EXPOSED AS COMMUNIST WHO WORKED ON A-BOMB."[94] The word spread like wildfire that Frank Oppenheimer, his wife, and many of both Oppenheimer brothers' friends were members of the American Communist Party throughout the 1930s. Although J. Robert Oppenheimer never officially joined the Communist Party, he and his wife Kathryn, who preferred to be called "Kitty" during his early Berkeley career, regularly hosted social gatherings of politically left wing-leaning students and faculty, as well as mutual Communist Party friends. These were considered informal communist group meetings by Federal Investigative sharks, who now began digging for more information, sensing that J. Robert Oppenheimer's blood, as well as his brother's, was now in the water. They soon obtained a report from the Federal Bureau of Investigation (FBI) Director, J. Edgar Hoover, which summarized both Oppenheimer brothers' lives and activities prior to and during the Manhattan Project. In short, it revealed J. Robert Oppenheimer's membership in and financial contributions to American Communist Party front organizations such as Friends of the Chinese People, American

[92] Ibid.
[93] Ibid.
[94] Ibid.

Committee for Democracy, and of the Communist Party membership of his former fiancée and lover while he was working at the Top-Secret Manhattan Project, Jean Tatlock.[95]

It didn't help the Oppenheimer brothers that the Cold War between the USA and former WWII ally, the USSR, continued to accelerate over the next few years. Soon, J. Robert Oppenheimer's brother found himself before the House Un-American Activities Committee on the 14th of June 1949. There, Frank Oppenheimer admitted that he and his wife had both been members of the Communist Party. He went on, though, to say that both had left the Communist Party long before he became involved in nuclear research at Los Alamos. Frank had been teaching physics at the University of Minnesota as an Assistant Professor after leaving Los Alamos in 1947. Unfortunately, following less than an hour after appearing for this hearing, Frank Oppenheimer received word that he was fired from the University.[96] Further, he soon discovered that he had been blacklisted and could never hold a teaching job in the United States again. Consequently, he withdrew to Colorado to raise cattle. Fortunately, the waste of this man's talents and the fact he was living history led government authorities to allow him to teach science in 1957 at the high school level in Colorado. After teaching at that level as a sort of probationary period, the government finally authorized him to teach Physics again at the University of Colorado. Finally in 1969, Frank Friedman Oppenheimer founded the Exploratorium in San Francisco, California and served as its Director until his death in the 1980s.

Perhaps his brother's setbacks at this time, combined with his guilt feelings about the civilian Japanese casualties from the Atomic Bombing of WWII, contributed to J. Robert Oppenheimer's bringing his own situation into his enemies' political view when (contrary to all good judgement) he openly stated to *Time Magazine* during an early June interview the following: "I became a real left winger, joined the teachers' union, had lots of Communist friends. The Thomas House Committee [U.S. House of Representatives' Un-American Activities Committee, with leading U.S. Senator Joseph R. McCarthy] doesn't like this, but I'm not ashamed of it. It was what most people do in college, or late high school."[97] That same month, June of 1949, J. Robert Oppenheimer was like his brother, brought before the committee. He was grilled about various atomic scientists' and former graduate students' political affiliations that he had worked with in the past either while at Berkeley or the Los Alamos Radiation Laboratory. Oppenheimer was protective of his former students and Los Alamos staff, saying nothing that might implicate them in any criminal charges or as potential communist sympathizers. What he didn't know was that investigative work back in 1943 had already revealed that two of the atomic scientists that Oppenheimer had hired to work in the Radiation Lab had been passing on information about the atomic bomb to Soviet operatives.

[95] Ibid.
[96] Ibid.
[97] Ibid.

Further, the Committee was also aware that while married and working at Los Alamos, Oppenheimer had privately visited a former lover and fiancée, Jean Tatlock, who was herself a member of the American Communist Party.[98] Finally, they also had General Grove's Manhattan Project Security Officer's reports by U.S. Army Colonel John Lansdale, who had kept an open investigatory file of his constant surveillance of Oppenheimer since Oppenheimer's arrival to Los Alamos.[99] This included tape-recorded interviews he'd had with Oppenheimer at Los Alamos about his past Communist Party affiliations for security purposes and to prevent Soviet espionage. He had insured that Oppenheimer's comings and goings from the WWII Top Secret Manhattan Project facilities at Los Alamos New Mexico were always under constant FBI or other ongoing military security staff observation.

Again in June of 1949 Oppenheimer appeared before another hearing, in this case the Joint Committee on Atomic Energy, now investigating charges that the Atomic Energy Commission was guilty of vital asset and financial mismanagement.[100] Since the end of World War II in 1946, the Defense budget had shrunk from US$48 billion to US$15 billion, and the separate military services were struggling against each other for a bigger slice of the federal government's declining financial resources.[101] The military services also resented the way in which the Atomic Energy Commission under Oppenheimer's friend, David Lilienthal, exercised civilian control over the testing and deployment of all atomic weapons. The major corporations granted contracts under the auspices of the AEC were thereby firmly controlled, and they in turn highly resented this. These greedy entities preferred the more usually lax "military-industrial complex"[102] management over them by military services, which served to increase their profits considerably. They proceeded to lobby Congress for and got a Congressional Investigation to investigate allegations of major wastages of money, specifically the loss of and unaccountability for large quantities of Uranium 235 and other atomic isotopes, along with an unsatisfactory Security Clearance System.[103]

Oppenheimer soon found himself called on the carpet for his exporting of radioactive isotopes from the Los Alamos Radiation Laboratory to foreign researchers whose interests were not necessarily in accord with the National Security interests of the United States.

---

[98] Ibid.
[99] Ibid.
[100] Ibid.
[101] Ibid.
[102] The reader can see President Eisenhower's final presidential speech in a YouTube search in which he uses this exact phrase and cautions against such interests; while this happened later than the time currently being discussed, the concept had been known and in existence decades earlier.
[103] Ibid.

This steadily led to his eventual conflict with an AEC Commissioner cut from a different cloth than the other AEC Commissioners, Lewis Strauss. AEC Commissioner Lewis Strauss was a former Naval Officer in WWI with a keen intellect and a driving ambition, which was amply noticed by President Herbert Hoover, who made him his personal adjutant and assistant. Consequently, Strauss acquired significant insights about how the Executive Branch of the Federal Government worked. During the period between the World Wars, his shrewdness and drive enabled him to make a fortune on Wall Street. At the beginning of WWII, he again entered the U.S. Navy, rising to the rank of Rear Admiral (two stars), as Chief of the Naval Ordnance Division.[104] Strauss, having been a personal assistant to President Herbert Hoover, had maintained strong executive government contacts. He was known to have an attitude of distrust towards the civilian staff members of the AEC and possessed a "It's my way or the highway" type of attitude. He was very much aware of Oppenheimer's Communist affiliations and had determined that many radioactive isotopes may have been exported by Oppenheimer and his staff to foreign laboratories, overlooking the potential for Communist operatives among their employees working undercover as staff members. This was a major expense and security issue for Strauss, who talked about and had earlier presented a case example, which he considered only one of many, highly indicative of covert Russian activity going on in association with requests from other United States atomic science laboratories and foreign atomic research laboratories for radioactive isotopes from the Los Alamos Radiation Laboratory. This example was a radioactive iron isotope which had been requested by and delivered to the Norwegian Royal Defense research establishment, which Strauss strongly suspected had a Communist operative among their research team scientists.[105]

When Oppenheimer got into the witness chair to testify before the Joint Congressional Committee on Atomic Energy, including to specifically address the Los Alamos Laboratory's exportation of radioactive isotopes to other research laboratories, he knew Strauss was in the hearing room somewhere. Oppenheimer was also aware of—and did not care for—the outlook and attitude Strauss had toward him and his colleagues in this matter. Consequently, Oppenheimer's comments about the radioactive isotopes sent out to other laboratories, in terms of importance for potential military applications, were glib and dismissive. Oppenheimer stated:

> "No one can force me to say you cannot use these isotopes for atomic energy. In fact, you do. You can use a bottle of beer for atomic energy. In fact, you do. But to get some perspective, the fact is that during the war and after the war, these materials have played no significant part, and in my knowledge no part at all."[106]

---

[104] Ibid.

[105] Ibid.

[106] Ibid.

A ripple of muffled laughter echoed against the walls of the hearing room after Oppenheimer's remarks. It was obvious to his listeners that Oppenheimer was making somebody out to be a fool. Yet, to anyone with knowledge of what an important issue the matter was to Strauss would have known Oppenheimer's understatements were intentionally geared to embarrass the Commissioner. By taking this action, Oppenheimer made a powerful enemy that would ensure Oppenheimer paid dearly for ridiculing him— a former Navy Admiral, financial expert, and major government bureaucrat. When Strauss heard about the Soviet atomic bomb detonation in 1949, he generated a Memorandum to Chairman David Lilienthal, advocating that AEC promote an accelerated "Crash Program" to produce the "Super" (H-Bomb) without delay.[107] This caused an eruption of meetings among the AEC and GAC, which resulted in the scientists and key members of both the Atomic Energy Commission and General Advisory Committee deciding (not in small part because of Oppenheimer's opposition) that a Crash Program for constructing a hydrogen bomb would be ethically wrong for the United States. Their recommendation, tempered by the H-Bomb's destructive capacity, was that the proposed project should for now be held in abeyance rather than for the United States taking the initiative in its development at that time.[108]

The military, particularly the U.S. Air Force, was not at all pleased with this outcome. The input of the most senior officers of the Strategic Air Command (SAC), combined with Lewis Strauss approaching his friend, Secretary of Defense Louis Johnson, resulted in Johnson's being persuaded the Soviets were already working on the H-Bomb; further, it was suggested that Oppenheimer by his consistent resistance to making the H-Bomb was selling the country out.[109] Also, when the time came to producing the final draft of the AEC's recommendation letter to the President, there was a shift of commissioners, three for—and two against—supporting a "Crash" H-Bomb production program. One of the two supportive of Oppenheimer's position, Chairman of the AEC David Lilienthal, was resigning from his position shortly, so the recommendation letter to the President was dropped. The decision was also made for each AEC member to individually brief the President. President Truman made the decision not to make a decision, so the policy of the AEC remained in accord with Oppenheimer's to concentrate on the smaller tactical atomic weapons: smaller atomic bombs, atomic tank shells, and atomic artillery shells.

Then on January 27th, 1950, a major broadside event occurred with explosively negative implications for Oppenheimer. Word came from Under Secretary of State Robert Murphy that the British had arrested Klaus Fuchs. Interestingly, Klaus Fuchs was a radiation laboratory atomic scientist Oppenheimer had hired while serving as the

---

[107] Ibid.

[108] Ibid.

[109] Ibid.

Manhattan Project Director specifically to replace Edward Teller.[110] As previously stated, Oppenheimer had found it necessary to transfer Teller to another research area of Los Alamos after Teller had a major blow-out argument with his laboratory supervisor. Oppenheimer placated Teller to some degree by allowing Teller to work on (as Teller called it) his "Super" H-Bomb with his own small research group. The British had caught up with Klaus Fuchs in London, where he confessed to having passed classified information to the Russians while employed in the radiation lab of the Manhattan Project throughout WWII and afterwards.[111] In short, Fuchs had full access to ALL of Los Alamos reports classified as Top Secret, including the technical construction diagrams and scientific documentation about both the atomic and H-Bombs. This meant the Russians already possessed all the information they needed to make both the atomic bomb and the hydrogen bomb. Teller and Oppenheimer were immediately called on the carpet to brief President Truman thoroughly about the information Fuchs knew or had access to. Teller was especially angry and concerned that all his ideas about the Super (H-Bomb), including his most recent Top Secret "Disclosure of Invention" paper, had been passed on to the Russians.[112] So, on 30 January 1950, Teller and Ernest Lawrence made an emergency presentation to the Executive Joint Committee on Atomic Energy. In short, they made it clear to all the Congress members and the Senator chairing it that no other sane choice was possible other than immediately moving forward to create the hydrogen bomb.[113] The Committee agreed with them and took swift action.

That same day, Committee Members contacted President Truman and told him it was vital to overrule the GAC and immediately begin an Accelerated (Crash) "Super" H-Bomb Program, with Edward Teller as Director. The Arms Race against the Russians to produce the world's first Hydrogen Bomb had now at last officially started. The following day, 31 January 1950, President Truman's press secretary read a Presidential statement to the White House Press Corps:

> "It is part of my responsibility as Commander-in-Chief of the Armed Forces to see to it that our Country is able to defend itself against any possible aggressor. Accordingly, I have directed the Atomic Energy Commission to continue its work on all forms of Atomic Weapons, including the so-called Hydrogen H-Bomb, or 'Super-Bomb.'"[114]

Teller now enjoyed the same job status Oppenheimer had held, and now as Director for the creation of the world's first "H" bomb, he returned to work at Los Alamos with high

---

110 Ibid.

111 Ibid.

112 Ibid.

113 Ibid.

114 Ibid.

hopes. In less than six months though, on 25 June 1950, the Korean War broke out. At the same time, Oppenheimer was still Chairman of the General Advisory Committee to the Atomic Energy Commission, and he continued recommending the major use of available funds be reserved for the development of smaller, tactical nuclear weapons.[115] Tactical nuclear weapons development was also more practical for deployment in the battlefield environment of the new war in Korea. Oppenheimer saw this as the most responsible use of major funds rather than the development of the H-bomb, which Oppenheimer perceived as a more long-term project. He also knew Teller's research at Los Alamos had stalled, because the fusion reaction was still too slow to detonate the H-bomb. Teller was all too aware of and highly resented Oppenheimer's influence upon the availability of finances for his project. Worse yet, one of Teller's personal friends (Luis Alvarez) was a member of the panel putting together the final Fiscal Recommendations Report for the AEC; he had agreed with Oppenheimer's view.[116]

In 1949, Teller also believed he had lost an ideal potential atomic physicist recruit for his H-Bomb Project at Los Alamos—a professor who taught physics at Cornell University—due to Oppenheimer's influence. [117] Resentment towards J. Robert Oppenheimer was building up considerable fury within Teller. Never mind, the Cornell Professor Teller had wanted to recruit was his former Los Alamos Supervisor with whom he had the blow-up during the Manhattan Project. Again, Teller's possession of a steadfast sense of personal destiny, combined with a firm resolve to never allow others to receive any credit for his own thoughts and theories, resulted in Director Robert Oppenheimer transferring Teller away from his originally assigned Los Alamos Research Team and former Radiation Laboratory Supervisor whom Teller now wanted to recruit, Hans Bethe.

In the meantime, AEC Commissioner and former Two Star Navy Admiral Lewis Strauss had been reviewing the open security file that Colonel John Lansdale (General Grove's Aide on Security Matters) had passed along among appropriate government channels after Oppenheimer had left Los Alamos. He reviewed a report that had been submitted to General Groves after an investigation on Oppenheimer by the Chief of Counterintelligence for the 9th Army Corps on the West Coast, with jurisdiction over all the West Coast Atomic Energy Facilities, Colonel Boris Pash. (This was while Oppenheimer was Director at the Manhattan Project's Los Alamos Facility). Colonel Pash's recommendation at that time had been that Oppenheimer should be removed from

---

[115] Ibid.

[116] Note: Tactical nuclear weapons are still discussed today as a possibility to accompany conventional arms in modern conflicts; however, given the long-term effects of weapons using depleted uranium (DU) shells and in other small arms/light weapons (SALW), illegal according to international convention though proved to have been used in various conflicts, such tactical nuclear weapons would be even more devastating, potentially triggering further escalation.

[117] Ibid.

the Manhattan Project immediately.[118] Added to this was the political fact that the top Air Force Strategic Air Command Generals and Air Force senior military advisors to the Atomic Energy Commission didn't appreciate Oppenheimer's ongoing technical objections to the H-Bomb Project.

In short, they considered the limits that could be placed upon them by Oppenheimer's insistence on tactical nuclear weapons investment and his "balanced force" concept—counter to the national security of the United States and blockading the full capabilities of Strategic Air Command.[119] At a time when fiscal resources competition between the military services was intense, the U.S. Air Force and its Strategic Air Command wanted to maintain their current status as the primary resource for war time delivery of the new atomic weapons. AEC Commissioner Strauss was aware of this, too, and saw the chance to finally sink Oppenheimer when the Executive Director of the Joint Congressional Committee on Atomic Energy, William Liscum Borden, was investigating the charges of mismanagement at the AEC—and the security clearance procedures that the AEC utilized.[120] In November of 1950, Borden asked the AEC to provide him the files of a dozen of the employees they considered among their most difficult "security cases."[121] Someone made sure that one of the files provided was J. Robert Oppenheimer's.

On the 3rd of August 1951, AEC Commissioner Lewis Strauss and Executive Director of the Joint Congressional Committee on Atomic Energy William Borden met and found they had major security concerns in common about Oppenheimer and questioned his loyalty to the United States.[122] They quickly determined that continuing with surveillance alone would not deliver Oppenheimer's removal, as Oppenheimer was not an idiot and likely had already figured out that his phone was being tapped. They discussed how Oppenheimer's significant influence over members of the AEC, GAC, and his scientific peers needed to be dealt with. This influence and popularity were evident, in that Oppenheimer prior to attending his first meeting as a member of the General Advisory Committee, and before his own personal arrival at what was in fact the GAC's very first meeting, had been immediately elected as GAC Chairman during his absence by the other newly appointed GAC members. Borden had wondered how General Groves, the Officer-in-Charge of the Manhattan Project, seemed not to have duly considered the investigation of the Chief of Counterintelligence, Colonel Boris Patch, and his recommendation for Oppenheimer's complete removal from the Manhattan Project. Rear Admiral Strauss, based upon his own considerable war-time leadership and military experience, likely speculated that General Groves weighed the pros and cons of the matter in Oppenheimer's

---

[118] Ibid.

[119] Ibid.

[120] Ibid.

[121] Ibid.

[122] Ibid.

favor over security concerns mainly because sacking the fluently German speaking Oppenheimer might have fatally disrupted both the morale and efforts of the Manhattan Project's allied atomic scientists. Many of the latter scientists spoke languages other than English, and some were German speakers whom Oppenheimer knew personally from his European educational endeavors while a young man. General Groves was obviously aware of the inherent major security risk, as he had assigned Federal Bureau of Investigation (FBI) agents and military security personnel to monitor Oppenheimer 24/7 for the entire time he was assigned at Los Alamos…and those reports were part of Oppenheimer's personnel file. In any case, Borden had no difficulty with deciding to proceed with the further investigation of Oppenheimer.[123]

About a year later in July of 1952, Borden tasked his new security officer for the Joint Committee on Atomic Energy to carry on the Oppenheimer investigation and passed on to him evidence from British interviews with Klaus Fuchs in London.[124] The British had determined that Fuchs had an accomplice while passing top secret information to the Russians when he worked at Los Alamos. The primary goal of the investigation now was to determine if Oppenheimer was Fuchs' accomplice. Borden then passed on Oppenheimer's security file to his new security officer, Francis Cotter, who'd been an FBI agent prior to the current job. In fact, at one time Cotter had been assigned to Los Alamos as an FBI agent. While J. Robert Oppenheimer's formerly sterling reputation was fading, particularly as he came under ever increasing political attack and ongoing government surveillance and investigation, Edward Teller's fortune and reputation were both now rising. The U.S. Air Force was seriously prepared to give Teller his own laboratory to staff with his colleagues and pursue his dream to finish the development of the H-Bomb. The AEC, however, wasn't about to let the military obtain major control and influence over what they considered to be their bailiwick. So, in July of 1952, they offered Teller the laboratory facilities at Livermore, near San Francisco, for his work—and Teller accepted.[125]

A few months prior to this development, the FBI was performing follow-up interviews on all the people who were known to be critical of Robert Oppenheimer, and Edward Teller was a well well-known and able candidate. During their interviews with Teller, the FBI investigators received a litany of Teller's complaints about Oppenheimer's influence impeding his ability to recruit top atomic scientists to work for him on the "Super" at Los Alamos. He went on to point out to them how Oppenheimer's opposition to the development of the H-Bomb unduly influenced AEC Commissioner Henry Smyth and AEC Chairman David Lilienthal to invest funding in larger atomic bombs or tactical atomic

[123] Ibid.
[124] Ibid.
[125] Ibid.

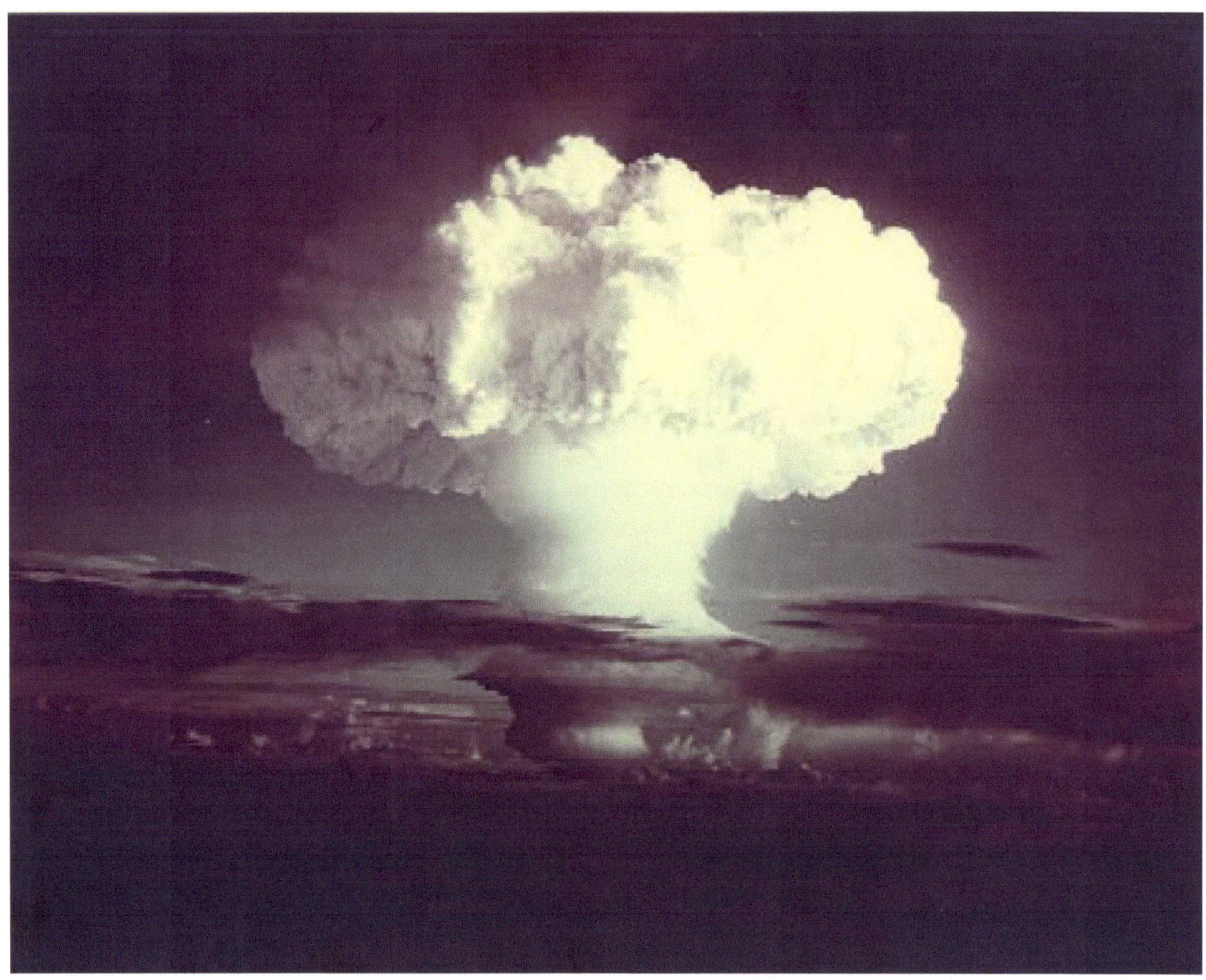

This is a picture of the first hydrogen bomb test explosion, invented by Edward Teller, naturalized American citizen and nuclear physicist. It was detonated on the small Island of Elugelab which was vaporized by this 10 megaton (10 million tons of TNT explosive force) detonation. This occurred on November 1st, 1952.

weapons instead of the H-Bomb.[126] He continued by claiming to them that Oppenheimer had sent atomic scientist Hans Bethe to spy on him at Los Alamos and determine if the creation of an H-Bomb was genuinely even possible. When the interviewing shifted towards describing Oppenheimer's personality and character, Teller was initially complimentary, saying Oppenheimer was "an outstanding man," and throughout his many interactions with Oppenheimer, he'd never seen evidence that Oppenheimer was not loyal to the United States of America. However, he next appears to introduce a preliminary verbal feint, telling the FBI investigators that Oppenheimer was a very "complicated" person. Teller shrewdly set them up for his next negative vocal sword-thrusts by volitionally describing for these investigators not generally known aspects of Oppenheimer's past without having been specifically questioned about it. In short, he told them that a youthful Oppenheimer was oppressed by physical or mental "attacks" which may have had permanent effects upon him. Teller concluded by requesting the FBI investigators not to include his latter remarks in any report for wide distribution, as these could prove "embarrassing, and add fuel to an already smoldering fire."[127]

In any case, Teller finally succeeded in his quest to create the first H-Bomb at 7:15 AM on November 1, 1952. Operation "Ivy Mike" detonated on the small island of Elugelab (one mile in diameter) in the Eniwetok Atoll.[128] From that date forward Teller was given the title of "Father of the H-Bomb" by the international news media. The mushroom cloud was 8 miles in width and 27 miles high. 80 million tons of soil was vaporized, and Elugelab ceased to exist. This was the world's first megaton atomic explosion; the yield was estimated at 10 megatons, or 10 million tons of TNT in detonative force. The explosion was approximately five hundred times greater than the first atomic bomb dropped on Hiroshima, Japan. Edward Teller was not on hand there to witness the product of his labors. Instead, reportedly feeling unwelcomed at the Pacific Proving Grounds, he elected to witness the results on a seismograph in a basement room at the University of California, Berkeley.

Meanwhile, going forward to the 7th of July 1953, former Admiral and AEC Commissioner Lewis Strauss was the newly appointed Chairman of the AEC. On his first working day in this position, Strauss arranged for the immediate removal all classified reports or other secret government documents still in Oppenheimer's possession. In early November 1953, Executive Director of the Joint Congressional Committee on Atomic Energy, William Borden, had reviewed the results of his intensive investigation about Oppenheimer and his Communist Party friends and connections. Borden also had found out that Oppenheimer had ongoing contact with a known Soviet informant since his Berkeley teaching days in 1943. This was a close friend who went to Oppenheimer's

---

[126] Ibid.
[127] Ibid.
[128] Ibid.

cocktail parties, and like Oppenheimer, was a professor at Berkeley, too—but who taught languages instead of sciences—named Haakon Chevalier. On the 7th of November Borden submitted a damning letter and report to FBI Director J. Edgar Hoover and to the Joint Committee on Atomic Energy. This was all occurring while Oppenheimer was lecturing in England and South America as a visiting professor. Hoover passed along the information to the new president, Dwight Eisenhower, who on 3 December 1953 ordered the immediate discontinuation of Oppenheimer's access to any classified, secret, or top-secret information until such time as he was cleared of the allegations and charges.

In short order, Oppenheimer was subjected to a series of Atomic Energy Commission Personnel Security Hearings as opposed to a trial for treason, but over the four weeks of extreme stress to defend himself and give testimonies, Oppenheimer had markedly aged. Oppenheimer never regained his above top secret or other Federal Government security clearances and was also dismissed from his job of being an atomic physicist consultant in Federal Government service. He was not found to be treasonous, disloyal, or guilty of any criminal charges, including passing on secret information to Soviet agents. Of the five opinions rendered by the Atomic Energy Commission Hearing Board, it delivered only one in his favor, but the one in Oppenheimer's favor was profound and clearly revealed a mitigating factor by stating: "The professional review of J. Robert Oppenheimer's actions has been supplemented by enthusiastic amateur help from powerful personal enemies." That Oppenheimer certainly still had many friends and influence among the nuclear science community was soon amply demonstrated by the fact that 158 of the Los Alamos atomic scientists had written a letter of protest to the AEC Hearing Board about the disrespectful way Oppenheimer had been treated.

Lewis Strauss remained personally vindictive towards Oppenheimer and not content with ruining his government and political career; he now did all he could to destroy his academic one. He met with the Chairman of England's Atomic Energy Authority (Frederick Lindemann, 1st Viscount, Cherwell) to ensure no academic post was offered to Oppenheimer in England. Strauss also attempted to get Oppenheimer ousted from his remaining academic position by contacting the Trustees of the Institute for Advanced Study at Princeton, New Jersey. Fortunately, this proved futile, and Oppenheimer lived on the Princeton faculty campus with his family and taught there for the remainder of his days. Julius Robert Oppenheimer died on 18 February 1967, at age 62.

Edward Teller went on to win the honors and rewards he had for so long sought after, but despite all his academic and financial success, he was considered an outcast and *persona non grata* among most of his associates in nuclear sciences, academia, and the nuclear physics community. This was for the key role he played, and the statements he made, as an informant to the FBI and other federal government investigators to the detriment of his old boss at Los Alamos. Worst of all, during Oppenheimer's AEC Security

Board hearing, he gave a damning testimony that Oppenheimer was a security risk and based upon his behavior since 1945, should not have his government clearances restored.

After that event, nuclear science colleagues he knew and had worked with would get up from the table when he'd try to join them for lunch—or otherwise avoid his company. This evading or avoiding extended from months into years, as nuclear science peers and colleagues refused to engage with him or his wife in conversation at professional, educational social parties, or gatherings. The rejection by so many colleagues had a profound effect on both Edward Teller and even the health of his wife, Mici, as they were both considered pariahs at professional social events the rest of their lives.

Some concluding points are appropriate here, that even today are not generally known by citizens of the United States. There was another Manhattan Project atomic physicist, who like Edward Teller was a native Hungarian who became a naturalized citizen of the United States. His name was Leo Szilard, a true humanitarian activist who before and after the first atomic Bomb test at Trinity in New Mexico (July 16th, 1945) submitted a petition to all the Atomic Scientists working at the Manhattan Project for their review, and if in agreement, their signatures. In short, the petition was addressed to President Truman, advocating a test atomic bomb detonation be initiated, demonstrating the destructive capacity of the new weapon to the Japanese people, along with the United States and its allies' terms for Japanese surrender (followed by the Japanese people refusing to surrender) before using any atomic weapons on the people of Japan. Although 70 of the Manhattan Project's atomic scientists signed it, it never made it up the chain of command to the President. Instead, it was intercepted by the United States Secretary of War Stinson's Interim Committee, who recommended the immediate use of the atomic bomb on the people and cities of Japan. Szilard then tried to get the petition to the President through the United States Secretary of State, but that failed too. In any case, the President never saw the petition until after the atomic bombs were dropped, and the petition was then classified and not released to the public until 1961.[129] Edward Teller in later years wrote in his memoirs the following:

> "First, Szilard was right. As scientists who worked on producing the bomb, we bore a special responsibility. Second, Oppenheimer was right. We did not know enough about the political situation to have a valid opinion. Third, what we should have done but failed to do was to work out the technical changes required for demonstrating the bomb [very high] over Tokyo and submit that information to President Truman."[130]

---

[129] Wikipedia: https://en.wikipedia.org/wiki/Leo_Szilard
[130]

What Teller was alluding to here obviously was an Electromagnetic Pulse (EMP)—also known as a Transient Electromagnetic Disturbance (TED)—which would have knocked out the electric power grid of the entire country of Japan, instead of the immediate burn and blast effects and the associated hundreds of thousands of deaths that surface or near-surface atomic detonations would cause.

J. Robert Oppenheimer's nemesis, former Navy Admiral and Chairman of the Atomic Energy Commission Lewis Strauss perhaps had a karmic consequence for his extraordinary persecution of Oppenheimer. In 1959, he ran into difficulty as the United States Senate was considering his nomination for the Presidential Cabinet Secretary of Commerce. In normal cases, nominations at this level routinely went through with little to no challenge. However, in Strauss' case, two former Los Alamos scientists spoke out against him for using his authority at the Atomic Energy Commission to abuse people, revisiting the Oppenheimer case and some others wherein Strauss inappropriately used his power to use the AEC Security Program as a tool for punishing subordinate personnel who disagreed with his point of view. The normally brief hearing in his case went on for a month during which he was voted down by a full Senate Vote—49 to 46—against his selection. He never became a cabinet secretary or held any public office for the remainder of his life. Rumor has it that no less a personage then Senator John F. Kennedy (Former WWII Navy Lieutenant and Hero of PT-109 fame, and later the 35th President of the United States), played the key role in blackballing Strauss.

Chapter Four

Believe Big Brother—Not Your Own Eyes!

It was 2019, the Summer before the COVID-19 pandemic arrived in the United States. My wife and I here in the White Mountains of New Hampshire had jumped into our blue Nissan truck and left the mountainside where we live, towing our 1960s vintage aluminum fishing boat with motor, electric troller, and tackle outward bound. Our goal that day was to go to our favorite lake and do some freshwater pan-fishing. It was one of those beautiful northern New Hampshire bright, early mornings greeting us with a warm glowing sun and clear, cobalt-blue skies. We had left our town going down Highway 16 easterly towards the little town of Errol, New Hampshire, the road free of traffic, as we proceeded unhampered through the Great North Woods' towering evergreens—trees of birch, ash, cedar, and pine, with the Androscoggin River on our right, and shallow ponds interspaced between wooded glens to the left. The river's waters rushed westward, gleaming and crystal clear, its deep bone-chilling coldness spoke of its birth amidst pure springs in the highlands of the surrounding mountains. Its rapids soon transformed into massive liquid fists, pulverizing themselves in turn against steadfast bedrock and granite boulders causing geysers of white foaming water to explode in all directions in an eternal quest to reach the distant ocean. We then spotted two fly fishermen in waders knee deep in the river with tall fishing poles and circular steel reels. These gracefully cast their lines forward, causing their fly lures to land for an instant upon the river's surface, and then in a quick second movement, snap their poles backwards, sending their fly lures soaring into the air in circular graceful arcs, bringing their lures forward again upon the surface of the river for another few seconds, hoping for a fish to strike. If not, then the fishermen's circular maneuvers backwards and forward continued, every few seconds their lures striking different portions of the river's surface waiting a second or two for a fish to strike and get hooked. Fly-fishing is a true art that sadly no longer is seen much anymore, as in older times, like when I was a boy growing up in the late 1950s and early 1960s,

After arriving at Errol, New Hampshire, we turned left to Highway 26 northward-bound heading up to Dixville Notch and beyond. We proceeded through a typical New England small-town area with old homes ranging from single to three story houses, mostly old farmhouses, salt boxes, and 19th Century Victorians. Next, we entered an area of farmlands with extensive green fields and dairy, hay cropping, and lumber yard operations. We couldn't help but to notice numerous giant white and grey U.S. Air Force tanker jets flying over our heads, dumping out from all their engines what I initially thought were smoky white contrails. I pulled over to the side of the road for a few minutes with my binoculars to take a closer look at these jets. So far, we had counted 14 of them flying from the direction of Maine—in an east to west heading—since we left the town of Errol. I could

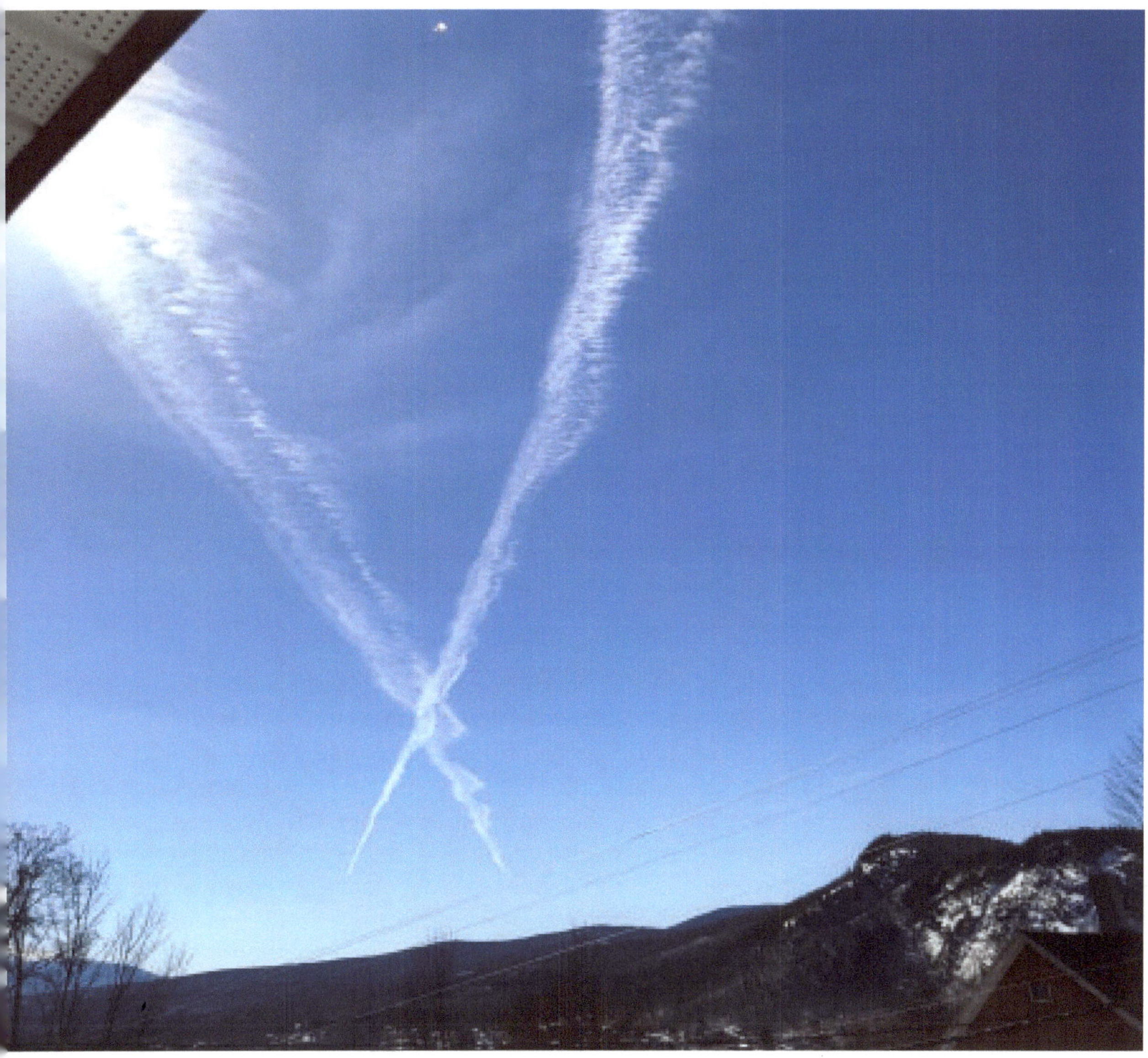

Picture taken from the author's house, top floor balcony (roof of house partially pictured). It shows the aerosol trails of two unmarked U.S. Air Force tanker jets flying in the direction of Mount Washington. This was the first picture taken by the author and his wife about 5 to 10 minutes after they passed over our home on March 10th, 2020. An onlooker can already see the dense white aerosol trails these covert (Global Dimming) geo-engineering jets left behind them, expanding horizontally. Their smog-like effect is herein starting to destroy what was previously a cobalt-blue and clear sky. Three white UFOs are observable, which at this distance look like jets, especially the largest of the three, which has a chevron type of shape.

not see any of the usual military markings on them, although I recognized their jet platforms from my aircraft carrier days in the Navy and when I was stationed in Okinawa, Japan as a Medical Logistics Officer and occasionally had business at the U.S. Air Force Base at Kadina. These jets were all flying at a stratospheric altitude of about 30,000 or more feet, sometimes three to four of them in an informal parallel pattern but all in the same direction, separated at approximately three-mile intervals.

The strange thing was that these jets were all simultaneously dumping white aerosol trails from all their wing and/or tail engines, their cloudy trails extending 10 or more miles behind them. I also observed that these trails being streamed from all these jets were not dissipating. Rather, they were all exiting from their engines in thick and white straight cumulus-cloud-like lines. After about four minutes upon exit from the respective jet engines, I noted that these trailing lines of clouds began losing their thickness, expanding horizontally slowly outward into what looked like cirrocumulus clouds. In any case, I'd wasted enough time looking at clouds, so we proceeded towards our destination, Diamond Lake.

Upon arrival at the lake, we launched the boat from its trailer and commenced our voyage to the far northerly shore of the lake where groves of green reeds (or "tulles") grow in abundance. The deep shade and coves the reeds provide make that area of the lake a favorite spot for bass and other pan-fish to hang out. We had caught one small-mouth bass, about a two to three pounder, when we heard another jet passing over our heads. It was yet again one of those grey U.S. Air Force tanker jets, but it had already passed over the lake before its sound caught up to our ears. I took out my binoculars once more and saw that there were no airline or military identification signs on either the jet's fuselage (body) or wings. It was like the other jets we spotted earlier all without identification markings, cruising at 30,000 feet or more. Four streams of thick white aerosol were exiting from all four of its wing engines, extending for miles behind it, over my head and as far back easterly from the direction it had come as far as I could see. It was a repeat of the same phenomenon seen earlier, wherein the jet aerosol trails initially appeared like lines of white cumulus cloud within a few minutes after their release from the jet's engines, then these white cloudy trails all slowly expanded horizontally looking like cirrocumulus clouds. Then we noticed two more tanker jets about two to three miles distant on both sides of the original jet that had just passed over our heads, both with similar cumulus cloud-like trails extending for miles behind them. I noted the time on my wristwatch, which was about 1pm, and we continued fishing.

Later, it was getting near to 3:30pm, and we stopped fishing for a snack when we both noticed that our previously cloudless cobalt-blue sky, indeed the entire western horizon where the jets had gone, was changed into a smoky white to greyish smog. This was the kind of sky common to what we'd seen in California prior to retirement in either Los

Angeles, Sacramento, or San Jose, before moving to New Hampshire. The sun itself was no longer bright because of the thickening smog, and now we could even look at it directly and make out its now bright white and circular shape to the west of our boat's position. My wife, Sydney, asked me if this was normal, and all I could say then was that to me it certainly didn't appear so…that normal jet contrails didn't linger, or have such long-lasting effects, let alone completely smog out previously clear skies like we were observing within a few hours.

The following day, I got on to the internet via our PC and entered "extended or extensively long jet contrails" into my browser. One of the results that came up was a documentary about geo-engineering titled, "What in the World are they Spraying?"[131] I knew from my Navy experience that the military had been pushing to achieve partial weather control since the late 1970s. I also knew that normally jet contrails didn't persist for the length of time or have the kind of environmental impact like what my wife and I saw from our boat. I next began looking into the history of the United States Military's covert epidemiological biological warfare studies on the PC, and readily found that the military had secretly experimented with flu virus and bacteria on civilian big city populations in the United States many times in the past. It further appeared to me that these jet trails acted far more like they were aerosols being purposefully sprayed by these jets into stratospheric altitudes instead of just normal jet contrails. A classic example of a sprayed aerosol which many older readers may have heard of was the toxic chemical Agent Orange, which was a defoliant aerosol the military used during the Vietnam War. Its purpose was to reduce and/or destroy the plant-life of the jungle canopy, ideally for better ground targeting by jet bombers, fighter jets, and combat helicopters. The only problem was that it poisoned and eventually killed a lot of American military personnel (and no doubt countless Vietnamese) with cancers years later after their service in Vietnam. These unknowingly inhaled it into their lungs. The casualties included Communist North Vietnamese Army soldiers, Republic of Vietnam Army Soldiers, Communist Viet-Cong guerilla soldiers, Vietnamese civilians, and American military in the field—all five Military Services: (U.S. Army, U.S. Navy, U.S. Marine Corps, U.S. Air Force, and the U. S. Coast Guard).

From there, I discovered other internet sites that spoke about jet engine aerosol discharges, like Aircrap.com and eventually GeoengineeringWatch.org. At the latter, I found further documentaries and reports from ecologists, forest biologists, civilian airline jet pilots, PhD chemists, hydrologists, soil scientists and others, all presenting damning testimony and information that not only our government, but governments internationally have been using these jets to control the weather.

---

[131] Whittenberger (2010).

I followed up with more research to refresh my memory over the next few weeks, and sure enough, the military had been performing epidemiological studies and germ-warfare experiments with aerosolized flu virus and other biological agents since the 1950s on American cities. One example that I had heard about occurred off San Francisco, California's coast, in September of 1950. It was both covert and secret, and called "Operation Sea-Spray," wherein a Navy mine-sweeping ship had released an aerosol of pathogenic bacteria called "Serratia Marcescens" into the fog banks as they drifted into the city of San Francisco from the ocean over a 6-day period.[132] The Navy and federal government researchers were experimenting to determine the answer to a "What if" situation, specifically to realistically test the likely spread and distribution of an aerosol biological agent among the population were a city the size of San Francisco ever hit with a germ warfare attack. So, the mission here was to answer the following question: "What would the epidemiological spread of a biological warfare agent throughout a large American city's population look like?" Operation Sea-Spray experiment was considered a success, as many San Franciscans had come down with the signature urinary infections and pneumonia-like symptoms specific to the Serratia Marcescens infection. Not only had the aerosol-delivered pathogen spread throughout the city, but it also spread throughout the bordering cities, towns, and country areas as well. As only one civilian had died from this experiment, the government researchers considered the experiment highly successful with minimal collateral damage[133]. Similar experiments were performed upon the crews on Navy ships too—without their knowledge.

The U.S. Army did epidemiological/biological warfare research in New York City in 1966, when light bulbs containing massive amounts of a bacteria known as "Bacillus Subtilis Variant Niger" were broken open by federal government researchers on the tracks of the subway system in mid-town Manhattan. Although it was at that time considered harmless, in more recent times this bacterium has been known to cause food poisoning. Between 1949 and 1969 the military performed 239 open-air tests with pathogenic agents. Beyond that, these were all violations of the Nuremberg Code, which was law constructed for all the nations of the world after the trials of Nazi German criminals for their crimes against humanity after World War II. The Nuremberg Code requires that all people must be advised of, and their permission obtained, prior to their being a human subject or subject of any involvement in any kind of human experimentation program.[134] Other branches of

---

[132] Wikipedia: https://en.wikipedia.org/wiki/Operation_Sea-Spray

[133] In 1981 the family of the sole civilian casualty of Operation Sea-Spray, Edward J. Nevin, took the U.S. Government all the way to the United States Supreme Court for his wife's loss and some sense of justice. The Supreme Court Justices ruled the same as the lower courts that refused restitution because it couldn't be proved that the Serratia Marcescens Bacteria had specifically caused her husband's death.

[134] The Declaration of Helsinki (1964) by the World Medical Association further adopted set ethical tenets regarding medical research on human subjects. While not legally binding, it is considered the standard by which all medical research on human beings must be measured to be considered legitimate.

the service performed similar experiments in other American cities, and it wasn't until 1969 that President Richard Nixon withdrew the military's authorization to continue such devious and secret human experimentation.[135]

I suppose we can all trust the government not to do such things anymore, but when my wife and I see these giant white or grey jets about every two weeks, going back and forth spraying out these jet aerosols over our heads, we can't help but to wonder why.

Through further reading and internet research, I found out about a worldwide United States and NATO Stratospheric Aerosol Geoengineering (S.A.G.) or "Global Dimming Program."[136] In short, this has been and continues to be a covert program run in this country by federal government contractors and other operatives using commercial and military unmarked jets to spray aerosols containing barium, strontium, and aluminum nano-particulates. Private and commercial airline pilots have reported seeing these unmarked, big white or grey colored (usually) jets spraying out aerosols from all their engines to Federal Aviation Administration (FAA) and other government authorities at both federal and state levels. Yet, all that's received in responses are dismissive declarations such as, "No such thing is going on that we are aware of." Also, "All of that is nothing but conspiracy theory." And finally, "Those are simply jet contrails."

What was interesting about it all though, was that the public narrative had changed and/or shifted from the initially presented purpose of the jet trails being a tool for controlling the weather, to that of the major purpose being to block the sun's ultraviolet (UV) light and heat radiations from causing damage to life on the planet's surface. By September of 2019, I had received letters of response from two U.S. senators from New Hampshire, the current one belonged to the Democrat Party and the other senator (the previous incumbent), had been Republican. Both provided the same answer verbatim to my concerns about what these unmarked jets were doing: "Mr. Sullivan, all you are seeing are jet contrails. There may be a lot of them, but that's all they are. We have had our experts look into the matter, and if you hear anything different, it's just conspiracy theory." This all sounded just too much like a typical bullshit-government "party line" for me to believe, never mind an insult to my intelligence, as I used to be a Navy Division Officer on an Aircraft Carrier.

So, came later September 2019, and we were getting the usual cool and gusty north winds from Quebec, with flurries of rain from time to time. The tree leaves of the Great North Woods were turning from their spring and summer green to their brilliant fall colors of gold, orange, and scarlet. The night-time temperatures were also dipping into the lower

---

[135] Wikipedia: https://en.wikipedia.org/wiki/United_States_biological_Weapons_program
[136] Whitman, Website: http://aircrap.org/stratospheric-aerosol-geoengineering-aka-chemtrails-facts/33450/

40s. My wife and I were in our back yard garden, harvesting our potato, pumpkin, and squash plants during a sunny and rain-free day. Suddenly, we heard a low roar and looking up saw an unmarked, grey-colored U.S. Air Force (geoengineering) tanker jet fly right over our house, on a northeast to southwest heading, towards Mount Washington. It was lower in altitude than usual, at perhaps 10,000 to 15,000 feet, apparently coming from Maine bearing in mind the jet's trajectory. Then we heard yet another low roar in the sky and looked up to see another unmarked big tanker jet fly over nearby although white in color and about two miles to the left flank of the previous jet.It was also proceeding southwesterly in its heading, and again like the previous jet, towards Mount Washington. They were both lower than the usual 20,000 or more feet in altitude, spraying out aerosol from all their engines, forming straight lines of white cloud-like discharges following for 10 or more miles behind them. Within a few minutes after exiting the jet engines, these cloud-like trails in turn began expanding horizontally, slowly but steadily fanning out into a greyish white smokey haze, changing a previously turquoise-blue and clear sky into a smoggy mess.

Sydney told me per the weather reports that it was slated to rain the following day, so I got a glass laboratory flask that I kept with my hard apple cider producing equipment. We placed it outside to collect a rain sample so we could test it and see for ourselves if any aluminum was in the water. Aluminum I could at least test for of the three components (strontium, barium, and aluminum particulates) these covert geoengineering jets were supposedly aerosol-spraying into the stratosphere. It rained beginning that night and into the next day, so I got a great water sample. I'd placed the flask in an open area of the back yard, away from the cars, garage, and house to alleviate any outside source from contaminating or otherwise compromising the water sample. Here my nursing and science education helped, as I took a medical laboratory reagent test strip (I had previously ordered these Med Lab Diagnostics 16 in 1 Reagent Test Strips for water testing) and carefully placed it into the water contained in the flask for two seconds. I next removed the reagent strip from the water and then shook it off, holding it horizontally for just over 60 seconds before comparing the color the reagent strip had turned into against a color chart, for the presence of aluminum in the water. It read 25 ppm (or 25.0 parts per million).

Such ppm scores are way over the top for the presence of aluminum in such amounts, especially in rainwater. The Environmental Protection Agency (EPA) lists the maximum contamination of aluminum in drinking water should not exceed 0.2 ppm. There are no aluminum mines in my area or factories processing aluminum ore (Bauxite). Consequently, there should be no traces of aluminum at all in the local atmosphere—or from the rainwater I took for my water sample.

The following month (October of 2019), another group of these jets flew over and near our house, which is halfway up a small mountain, at around 1,350 feet above sea level.

Again, my wife and I watched from our top floor balcony, as the formerly blue and clear skies outside turned to a smoky off-colored white, progressing to a greyish-white smoggy mess over about a two-and-a-half-hour period. Within three hours, our sky and the southwest and western horizon looked as bad as Los Angeles or San Jose California in terms of air pollution and appearance. It rained a few days later and this time the water sample tested out at 10.0 ppm, not as bad as before, but still an over-the-top score for our local atmosphere. I concluded from these findings that some of what environmentalists and activists are saying about the purpose (or mission) of these jets we see on any given day, crisscrossing in the stratosphere above us may in fact be a government program to deter, or hold in abeyance, the planet's global warming for as long as possible. Hence, the goal of the aluminum particulates and other chemicals these geoengineering jets are spraying are to promote cloud-cover, or a global dimming.

These geoengineering jets' aerosol spraying activities, particularly on such a massive and international scale, appear to be our species' technological response to climate change. In short, it is a covert federal government and international program to create and maintain a synthetic ozone layer that will to some degree address the planet's ozone layer's Arctic and Antarctic holes and its overall thinning, all of which has been directly caused from human activities. In any event, in 1991 a U.S. Patent was issued (#5,003,186) to Hughes Aircraft Company and "The Stratospheric Weisbach Seeding for Reduction of Global Warming Patent."[137] With it was a proposal to inject into the upper atmosphere a white powder containing barium, strontium, and aluminum oxides for the purpose of reducing global warming. A research paper presented to the U.S. Air Force in 1996 by an Air War College Study Group consisting of several senior military officers is also significantly revealing, pointing out the strategic advantage of using technologically simulated weather to achieve goals and victory on foreign or domestic modern battlefields by making the results of deliberate offensive actions appear to enemies as the consequences of natural weather events.

So, it appears that putting an aerosol of metals and chemicals into the atmosphere has multiple purposes, being weather control, reduction of global warming, and battle or wartime objectives. Since aluminum conducts electricity, it may serve to enhance the intensity of electrical storms to cause more atmospheric contact with lightning, which enhances the creation of more ozone in the lower atmosphere, which eventually migrates up into the stratosphere. The bottom line appears to be that these covert programs have all been running not only without the informed consent of the American public—but in potential violation of the Nuremberg Code, as such experimentation has not been the product of informed consent by those affected. Incidentally, aluminum particulates, if they

137

are put out into the air we breathe, have been implicated as a potential etiological (causation) factor for the onset of Alzheimer's Disease in adults and autism in children.[138]

I can't help but to think of the potential for class action lawsuits if this is true. No wonder then that the government may want this stratospheric aerosol geoengineering program to remain covert. It's all too much in keeping with the old military proverb: "That it's easier to ask for forgiveness than permission…" a proverb Navy Chief Petty Officers and Naval Officers traditionally adopt to justify taking the initiative to do the right thing and get the job needed done, despite military protocols, policies, or regulations to the contrary.

The reason this is important is in getting back to some history in our story where science, experimentation, covert operations, and public information (or profound lack thereof) once again find a significant nexus. This, of course, builds up to the ultimate point of this book: in both US and world history there are power players who rely upon secrecy to conduct operations for myriad reasons—not the least of which is profit or individual/group interest that have little or nothing to do with public interest. Were the public to know of such machinations, there would hopefully be a severe accounting among those responsible. There is too much we often don't know—to our detriment—that later we find out was happening all along.

So, let's go back to where we left off: once again—the "Father of the H-Bomb," Doctor Edward Teller. In 1952 Teller left Los Alamos to become Chief Atomic Physicist in charge of the Lawrence-Livermore National Laboratory, in Livermore, California. The reader I trust will recall that we left him entering the later 1950s, when Teller was at his zenith of celebrity and wealth outwardly. But unfortunately for his interests, as you might remember, he was privately considered a pariah among his scientific community and associated academia for his past statements to the FBI, and legal testimony at a federal government hearing of the Atomic Energy Commission (AEC) against his former boss, fellow atomic scientist and atomic (in current parlance, "nuclear") physicist, Julius Robert Oppenheimer. Oppenheimer thereby lost his federal government atomic scientist consultant's job and related federal confidential, secret, top secret, and beyond top secret clearances, in large part because of Teller's testimony at the hearing.

I believe that by the late 1950s, the federal government and other nuclear-armed countries' governments, nuclear scientists, and militaries discovered that their respective atomic bomb and thermo-nuclear (H-Bomb) test detonations between 1946 and 1963 had not only collectively seriously damaged the Earth's ozone layer, but they had thinned out what remained. Edward Teller, and many other top federal government atomic scientists

---

[138] Weather as a Force Multiplier: Owning the Weather in 2025 (1996).

and science consultants were contacted to see what, if anything, could be done—and Teller demonstrating anew his brilliance, was the first to experiment and come up with the theory that if millions of tons of heavy metal particulates, sulfates, and chemical oxides were aerosol-sprayed into the stratosphere that the planet would eventually cool. In hindsight, it certainly appears Teller's theory may have been covertly implemented, late in the decade of the 1970s, initially by U.S. and followed by NATO (National Atlantic Treaty Organization) countries. Aluminum oxide, titanium, barium oxide, and sulfur hexafluorides were apparently aerosol-sprayed by the tons into the stratosphere. By the way, sulfur and related oxides attach or mix with rainwater in the atmosphere, thereby making the rainwater falling to the earth acidic. This "acid rain" destroyed the bark and outer protective exterior of trees, eventually killing them. So, this may well be the original cause of the "acid rain" we older folks may recall that was happening early to mid-1970s. The bark of trees today, especially dying ones, are being found to contain aluminum, barium, strontium, and titanium through certified laboratory testing, which make them vulnerable to fungus and insect pests.[139]

Acid rain also removes essential metals from plants like calcium, magnesium, and potassium from the soil, reduces crop yields, and kills aquatic life in rivers, streams, and lakes. It additionally speeds up the corrosion of buildings and structures made of limestone or reactive metals like steel. Consequently, by the late 1960s and early 1970s, American biologists and environmentalists began noting and complaining about acid rain and its impact on forest trees, plant life, and aquatic wildlife. But by the late 1960s, volcanic activity, industrial pollutants, and automobile exhaust were all implicated as contributors to global warming (now climate change). In my own lifetime, underarm deodorant sprays, cow poop, automobile exhausts and my own and readers' individual "carbon footprints" have all been developed and added to the federal government's list, leaving out our government's primary role and responsibility for causing global warming in the first place.

The foundation for the loss of clarity as to the original and most significant cause of global warming in my estimate was presented by no less a speaker then Doctor Edward Teller. The year was 1959, and Teller's celebrity and status as a giant in the scientific community brought him many invitations to make public, private, and academic presentations, and speeches. By 1959, Teller knew the major cause of global climate dangers were the combined atomic and nuclear weapons tests previously done, and at that time were still being performed by the United States and the other countries that possessed nuclear weapons. So, I found it significant that in 1959 Teller was a guest speaker at the "Energy and Man" Symposium organized by the American Petroleum Institute and Columbia Graduate School of Business. In attendance were directors, CEOs, owners, academic professors and major shareholders of national and international oil and gas

---

[139] Website: https://www.geoengineeringwatch.org/category/tree-die-off

corporations. Without any mention of the role of nuclear weapons and testing, Teller proceeded to put the primary blame for global warming upon the oil and gas industries.

Teller presented the following:

1. That burning fossil fuels in increasing amounts, as time moves forward, releases more carbon dioxide into the planet's atmosphere, causing atmospheric contamination.

2. That this carbon dioxide in turn absorbs infrared radiation emitted from the Earth.

3. This process in turn causes a "Greenhouse (Gas) Effect" wherein the carbon dioxide captures and absorbs the heat, which in turn warms the planet.

4. The Arctic and Greenland by themselves have icecaps over 15,000 meters thick.

5. It has been "calculated" that a temperature rise combined with a 10% increase in carbon dioxide would melt the icecaps enough for the ocean to submerge New York City. In fact, all U.S. coastal cities would be submerged by ocean level increases, and since most people in the United States live along the coasts, the ongoing increasing use of fossil fuels (oil) is much more of a serious problem than people realize.

6. Teller outlined the danger from increased atmospheric levels of carbon dioxide. In 1959 he calculated the carbon dioxide level in our air as about 2%, by 1970 it would be 4%, by 1980 it would be 8%, and by 1990 it would be 16%.

I googled the difference in ppm of carbon dioxide in our air from about the time Teller did his 1959 calculations, specifically 1960, as 300ppm. By 2020 this had increased to just over 400ppm, so that roughly is a 33% increase of carbon dioxide worldwide over that period of 60 years.

In any case, Teller's conclusion was that if the US and the world kept on with an exponential rise in the usage of conventional fuels (gas, oil, coal etc.), that it would result in a serious impediment for radiation (heat) leaving the planet. Hence, the overall temperature of the planet would rise and melt the icecaps of the planet, which in their own turn cause the oceans to rise worldwide. This is certainly happening, as we can see by the cracking open and melting of the glaciers in Greenland, the South Pole (Antarctica), and certainly the North Pole, where the massive melting of the permafrost is destroying homes and buildings in Alaska and affecting the natural habitats of countless wildlife.[140]

Now, the drumroll: Teller's relevance continues, as we now get into his involvement with certain phenomena that was, after WWII, also addressed among scientific, political, and military contingents, which as we shall see also has relevance to both humanity's nuclear adolescence and its reaction to climate impacts.

Teller, in addition to his work as a physicist on the H-Bomb and impacts of subsequent nuclear and chemical contamination of the atmosphere, was officially mustered into the federal government's above top-secret MJ-12 group between 1979 and 1980, though I suspect he had already been recruited many years prior. MJ-12 (or Majestic 12) was a secret government group originally made up of the 12 people President Harry Truman selected for dealing with covert matters surrounding EBEs and their technology shortly after the two crashes of 1947 in Roswell New Mexico. The only reason it's known is because of the interception of a Top-Secret Assignment Memorandum signed by President Truman designating this group of people as "Operation Majestic 12."[141] This was sent to the Secretary of the Navy James W. Forrestal on 24 September 1947. Should this group continue to exist, and evidence suggests it does, this group today is likely larger but made up of the "alphabet soup" of agencies' top directors (FBI, CIA, NSA, etc.), Presidential cabinet members like the Secretary of Defense, political and legal advisers (as Henry Kissinger was in the past), the top U.S. military generals, and naturally the top engineers and allied scientists of the country.

Again, UFO phenomena and the nuclear threat converge. In February of 1949, Edward Teller attended a secret conference at Los Alamos, New Mexico to address the green "fireball" UFOs being reported in the nuclear testing area and near the Los Alamos Radiation Laboratory.[142] Military officers, federal government and contractual scientists were in attendance too. One of these was a PhD astronomer from the University of New Mexico, Dr. Lincoln LaPaz. His expertise was called upon often during this conference, and he was certain that these green fireballs were neither conventional fireballs nor meteorites. He went on to share he'd observed one in December of 1948, saying:

---

[140] Incidentally, also possible from the melting of the permafrost is the exposure of bacteria, viruses, and other biological threats that have not been present among humans for some time—if ever. As is seen when rainforests are clear-cut, similar phenomena have been released—or combined—among both human and animal populations without the necessary immunities to such obscure or previously unknown pathogens.
[141] Wired (2007): http://wired.com/2007/09/dayintech-0924/
[142] Good, 265-7.

"This fireball appeared in full intensity instantly…there was no increase in light… Its color, estimated to be somewhere around wavelength 5200 angstroms, was a green hue, such as I have never observed in meteor falls before."[143]

(Author's note: the angstrom in this case refers to the wavelengths (units) of visible light in solar physics, usually ranging between 4000 to 7000 angstroms).

Dr. LaPaz continued, saying, "The path was as nearly horizontal as one could determine by physical observation, and just before the end the green fireball broke into fragments; still bright green."[144] Dr. LaPaz went on to rule out conventional but infrequent and unusual types of meteors and fireball-like phenomenon he'd experienced but left all attending no doubt that the green fireballs were a phenomenon up until then unknown. By the late 1950s, the governments of the USA, Canada, England, and the USSR were all becoming increasingly alarmed at the attention UFOs were giving to their respective nuclear weapons military bases, military ICBM silos, command and control centers, and nuclear weapons depots and storage facilities.

As described earlier in this narrative, UFOs had buzzed our jets and eventually our space capsules and destroyed some of our military jets when these were ordered to actively engage them in battle and jammed military communications, and as mentioned earlier interfered with United States and Russian ICBM missile test launches, actually turning them on and off. Further, there were unexplained instances of something having killed, dissected, and removed all the blood from livestock like cattle and horses, and worst of all have been continued reports of abductions of tens of thousands (or more) people. Further, unless they have done so covertly, there is no public information about them making any direct attempt to openly communicate or otherwise peacefully engage with either the United States or the USSR (now the Russian Federation) despite attempts being made to do so by both major powers. In fact, UFOs appear to evade and avoid direct contact, and their covert activities and monitoring of the United States, UK, and Canada's most secret military bases and nuclear facilities certainly are not indicative of any peaceful intent on their part.

UFOs looking like gigantic "green fireballs" of energy were again first observed hovering and moving around desert areas where atomic bomb test detonations had occurred, especially near Los Alamos, New Mexico. As far back as 1947, leading WWII General of the U.S. Army and Chief of Staff George C. Marshall and WWII Hero and 5-Star Army General Douglas MacArthur created a secret group of Army Intelligence called

---

[143] Ibid.
[144] Ibid.

the Interplanetary Phenomenon Unit or IPU.[145] In 1955, General MacArthur stated to the New York Times the following:

> "The Nations of the World will have to unite, for the next War will be an Interplanetary War. The Nations of the Earth must someday make a common front against attack by people from other planets."[146]

[145] Ibid.
[146] Ibid.

Chapter Five

Local Case Study:
The Abduction of Betty and Barney Hill in the
White Mountains Of New Hampshire

Although most people of my "Boomer" generation and older folks have heard about the Betty and Barney Hill alien abduction incident, I still suspect many younger people today have not (unless watching the History Channel about alien and UFO phenomena), and since it occurred here in the White Mountains near Lincoln, New Hampshire on the 19th and 20th of September 1961, their significant story needs retelling. This story is also significant, as it was also the first major published news report of an extra-terrestrial alien abduction in the United States.[147]

Betty and Barney Hill were an interracial married couple during a period when such relationships were uncommon in the United States; Barney was Black and worked in Portsmouth, New Hampshire as a postman. He was also an U.S. Army veteran and was a member of the local board of the United States Commission on Civil Rights. His wife, Betty, was white and was a social worker. They were actively involved with their Unitarian Church and were both members of the NAACP and considered leaders in their community.[148]

Betty and Barney Hill's UFO experience began on September 19th, 1961, at approximately 10:30 PM as they were driving home from vacationing in Montreal, Canada and Niagara Falls in New York State. Barney was driving down New Hampshire's Highway 3, at that time designated U.S. Route 3, and Betty while looking out the window thought she saw a falling star (meteorite) in the sky. There was only one problem with it, and that was that it was moving upward. Betty thought that was more than a little strange, but now she noticed that the meteorite was moving straight in their car's direction, and it was growing larger and brighter as it approached their 1957 Chevrolet Bel Air. Betty alerted Barney about these developments and requested for him to stop the car both to get a closer look and let out their black and tan Dachshund dog named Delsey so that she could relieve herself. Barney then pulled over their car at a picnic area south of the Twin Mountain area and let Delsey out to do her business. Betty now got out of the car to look at the "star" through Barney's binoculars and saw an "odd shaped" airplane, or "odd

---

[147] Wikipedia: https://en.wikipedia.org/w/index.php?title=Barney_and_Betty_Hill&oldid=1072665388
[148] Their story is also told in the 1966 book titled *The Interrupted Journey* by John G. Fuller and later in 1975 in a TV film called *The UFO Incident* starring a wonderful young James Earl Jones as Barney.

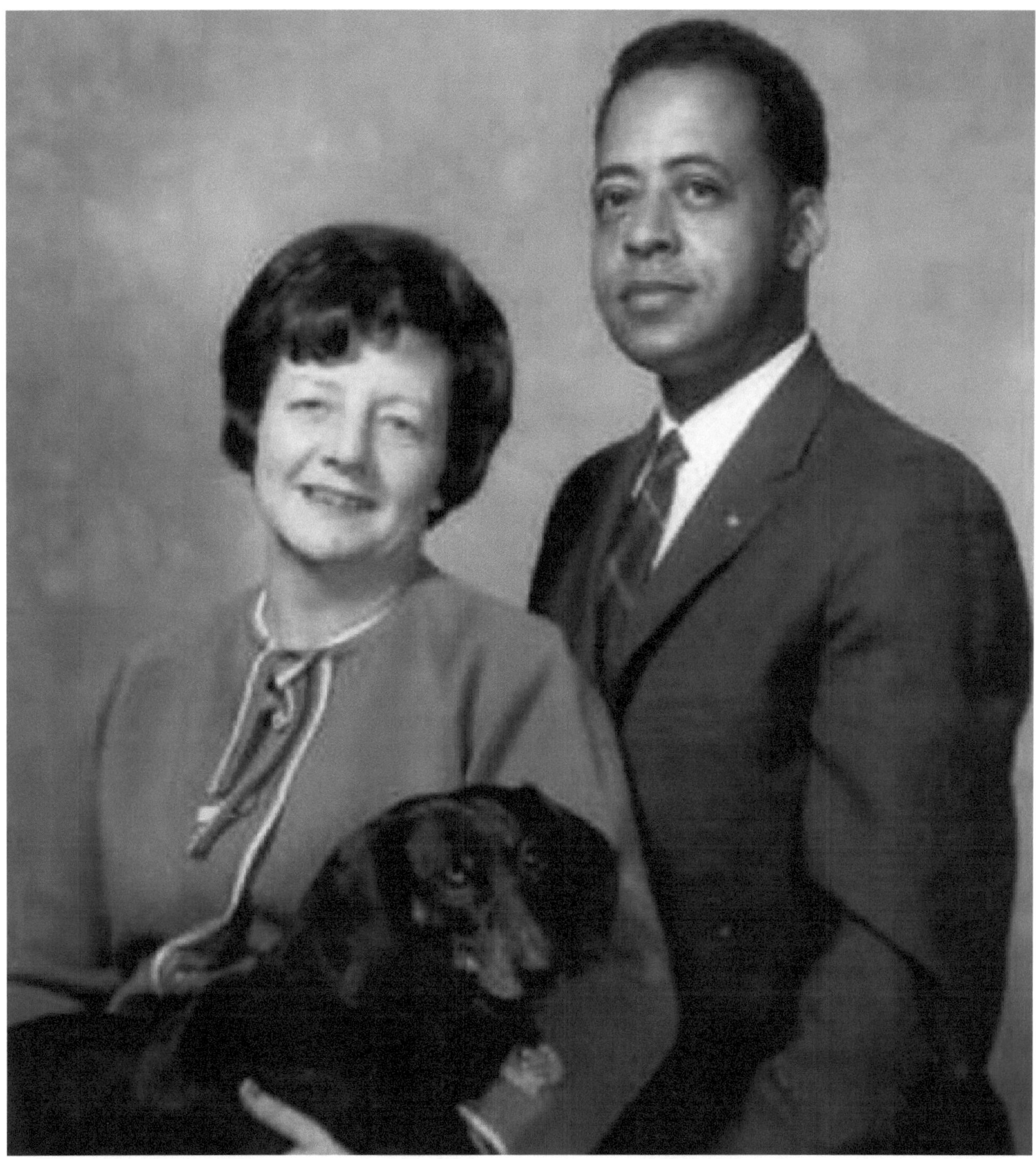

This picture is of married couple Betty and Barney Hill and their female dachshund named "Delsey." They were both abducted by combined Grey Alien and human hybrid "beings" in the White Mountains near Lincoln, New Hampshire on the 19th and 20th of September, 1961. Their story was the first major published news report of an extra-terrestrial alien abduction in the United States.

shaped" aircraft" flashing green, red, and blue lights near the moon. She recalled how her sister had several years ago claimed to have seen a flying saucer. Betty thought at the time, "Could this be a UFO?" and "What am I seeing?"

Barney, having returned Delsey to the car, took the binoculars himself to have a look and observed what he believed was a commercial airliner traveling westerly towards Vermont, perhaps on its way to Montreal. But as he looked again, he changed his mind and became alarmed, because without looking as if it had turned, it was now not only rapidly descending in altitude, but it was indeed coming toward their car rather speedily. This development made Barney think, "This object that was a plane is NOT a plane!" The Hills quickly got back in their car and drove perhaps a bit rapidly towards the Franconia Notch, as towering yet majestic granite mountains carved ages ago by prehistoric glaciers closed in on them on both sides of a narrowing—and at that time isolated—highway on a cool moonlit night.

The object continued to follow behind them to their right, passing over a closed restaurant and a signal tower on the top of Cannon Mountain. The UFO next veered to their left coming close to the famous New Hampshire landmark, "Old Man of the Mountain."

Betty later stated that this UFO was at least one and a half times the length of the "Old Man's" granite Native American profile. So, it must have been hundreds of feet long. The illuminated and now oval craft continued to follow them, and when they were about one mile south of "Indian Head" (yet another granite naturally carved monolithic head, which itself appears as the epitome of the face of a Native American warrior) when the UFO descended so close to their car that it caused Barney to stop in the middle of the highway. This huge and silent craft hovered about 80 feet above the Hill's car and filled the entire view looking out from their car's front window. Barney later stated that it reminded him of a huge pancake. With his pistol in his pocket, Barney then exited the car and bravely moved closer to the UFO.

Using his binoculars, Barney saw between eight and eleven humanoids who were themselves peering at Barney from their own craft's windows. Then, all of them except one moved to what appeared to be a large hatch or doorway, like an elevator on the rear wall of the canopy of the UFO. The remaining humanoid stood motionless but was looking directly at Barney, who suddenly heard a voice in his mind saying, "Stay where you are and keep looking." Barney, upon telling what happened sometime later to a therapist, had a partial recall of these humanoids wearing shining black uniforms and black caps on their heads. He also recalled red lights on bat-wing shaped fins, which slowly extended out and downwards to the ground from both sides of the UFO. Lastly, a long structure was lowered from the bottom of the craft. Barney dropped the binoculars from his eyes and ran back to the car. In a state of panic, he yelled at Betty, "They're going to capture us!" He then looked up to see that the UFO had moved its location to directly above the Hill's car. Barney jumped into the car and immediately drove away at high speed. He ordered Betty to keep her eye peeled for the proximity of the UFO. She recalled rolling down the passenger side window and looking up. At that instant, they both remembered hearing a cacophony of rhythmic beeping and buzzing sounds, which they both recalled seemed to impact and bounce off the trunk of their car. Their car then began vibrating and a tingling sensation like some sort of electric energy passed through their bodies. The Hills in telling their story said that the next thing they recalled was the onset of an altered state of consciousness which left their minds feeling dulled. They then recalled hearing a second series of beeping and buzzing sounds that returned them to full consciousness in their car, which was parked along the highway.

They determined that they had traveled 35 miles south but had only clouded and unclear memories of arriving at this section of the highway. They also both remembered making a sudden and sharp turn off the highway on to a side road, encountering a roadblock, and seeing a fiery looking orb in the road. On arriving home in Portsmouth about dawn, they both had some strange impulses to do things that they could not logically explain. Betty insisted that their travel luggage be kept by the back door instead of the normal closet located in the main part of their home. They discovered neither of their watches were working, and as it turned out, they never in fact did again. Barney noted that the leather strap on his binoculars had been torn, but he couldn't remember the cause of it. The toes of his best shoes were also terribly scraped, and he was compelled behaviorally to examine his own genitals privately in the bathroom, though he didn't know why he was doing it, and that he found nothing unusual. They both took long showers to remove possible contamination, and each of them drew a picture of what they had seen.

The following day, truly perplexed and anxious, the Hills did their best to together reconstruct the events in correct order pertaining to the UFO and their drive home. But when they came to the part where they had initially heard the beeping and buzzing sounds, their memories were vague and foggy. Betty placed the shoes and clothes she had worn during the drive home into her closet and noticed that her dress had been torn at its hem, zipper, and lining. They also noted shiny concentric circles on their car's trunk that had not been there the previous day. They experimented with a compass, noting that when they moved it close to the spots, the needle began whirling rapidly. But when they moved the compass away from these shiny spots the compass needle dropped back to its normal position.

On the 21st of September 1961 Betty Hill decided to telephone the Pease U.S. Air Force Base to report their UFO encounter, though for concerns about being labeled insane, she refrained from revealing all the details. Shortly after, a Major Paul W. Henderson contacted the Hills requesting a more detailed interview. Henderson's report, dated September 26, 1961, was in keeping with the long-standing military policy to deny the reality of UFOs, determining "that the Hills had probably misidentified the planet Jupiter." This was later amended to include meaningless technical jargon like "optical condition," "inversion," and "insufficient data" to discourage any serious follow-up investigation.[149]

Shortly after this, Betty Hill then began having a series of nightmares that were very vivid, almost tactile, and very disturbing. In November 1961, Betty began journaling the details of her dreams immediately after she had them if she woke up, or otherwise detailed what she could remember upon arising first thing in the morning. In one dream she and Barney were at a roadblock, and a group of small men had surrounded their car. She then recalled two of these men forcing her to walk through a forest at night, also seeing Barney walking behind her. She called out to him, but he appeared to be in a trance or sleepwalking. These men were short and wore matching blue uniforms and had black hair, dark eyes, prominent noses, and bluish lips. Their skin was a grey color. She next recalled she, Barney, and these little men walking up a ramp into a metallic, disc-shaped craft. Upon their entry, Betty and Barney were separated. She began to resist and was told by one of these men she referred to as "the Leader" that it would take much longer for them to "conduct the exams" if she and Barney were examined as a couple. They were then escorted into separate rooms. Her dream continued with a new man like the others entering the room to conduct her "examination" with the "Leader." She referred to this new man, who had a calming voice and manner, as "the Examiner." The "Examiner" told Betty that he was going to perform a few tests to determine the differences between humans and the UFOs occupants. She was placed in a chair where a bright light flared down on her. The "Examiner" proceeded to cut off a lock of Betty's hair and went on to examine her eyes, ears, mouth, teeth, throat, and hands. He also cut the rims of her fingernails and saved the trimmings.

He then examined her legs and feet, and inserted what she perceived as a dull instrument, like a letter opener, and scraped some of her skin on to some material which looked like cellophane tape. Her examination took an untoward turn when the "Examiner" claimed to be testing her nervous system and thrust a needle into her navel, which caused Betty excruciating pain. The "Leader" immediately waved his hand in front of her eyes, and the pain disappeared. After Betty and the "Leader" left the room, he advised her that "the other men" did not want her to remember this encounter. Betty told him she'd eventually remember no matter what they did. She and Barney were then taken to their car, and the "Leader" suggested they wait to watch the starship's departure. They did so and resumed their drive home.

---

[149] .This is *Report 100-1-61*, Air Intelligence Information Record, forwarded to Project Blue Book, the U.S. Airforce's UFO research project, to be duly filed and forgotten about.

As time went on, Betty and Barney decided to be interviewed by UFO researchers from the National Investigations Committee on Aerial Phenomena (NICAP). These brought to the Hill's attention that they had taken much longer to arrive to their home in Portsmouth from Colebrook, New Hampshire than should have been the case. The Hills' 178-mile drive was normally a 4-hour drive, versus the 7 hours the Hills had taken. The Hills could not recall hardly anything about the 35 miles of U.S. Route 3 between the towns of Lincoln, Indian Head, and Ashland New Hampshire.

The Hills next remembered the image of a fiery orb sitting on the ground, but in hindsight they figured it was probably the moon, but the researchers advised them that the moon had set earlier in the evening. The UFO researchers discussed the Hill's traveling time discrepancy, for which the couple had not come up with a logical explanation. The researchers explained to them that such a phenomenon Ufologists call "Missing Time." They also discussed and suggested professional hypnosis to restore previously unrecallable memories. Barney thought it might be of benefit to Betty to clear up "the nonsense" referring to her dreams.

During the next year, the Hills made frequent weekend trips to the White Mountains, the purpose being to hopefully find the road areas where they had encountered the UFO, retrace their route, and revisit where the UFO had landed, and find the area they were captured. They thought that such revisitations might trigger by association their recalling more specifics about their abduction, as well as what happened during the "Missing Time" the NICAP UFO researchers had educated them both about.

In November of 1962, close to the Thanksgiving holiday, the Hills were attending a meeting sponsored by their Unitarian Church which rather coincidentally featured a guest speaker who just happened to be a Captain in the U.S. Air Force, and rather coincidentally made a presentation about hypnosis. The Captain's name was Ben H. Swett. The Hills were drawn to him like flies to sugar, approaching him privately and sharing the story of their "Close Encounter" experience. The captain is alleged to have been especially interested in the "Missing Time" component of their experience. The Hills went on to ask him if he would consider hypnotizing them, but he declined, claiming he was only an amateur hypnotist and that they should seek out a professional one.

In early March of 1963, the Hills made their first public disclosure about their UFO encounter with a large group of people at their church. About eight months later, Captain Swett once again returned to the Hill's Unitarian Church to give another presentation about hypnosis to their study group. The Hills once more took the "opportunity" to approach Captain Swett privately again, and Barney shared that he was planning to see a male psychiatrist that he personally knew and trusted. The captain (whom I suspect was CIA-affiliated), responded that Barney should tell the doctor about the abduction, and then ask the doctor if he would recommend the services of a professional hypnotist in view of what he and his wife had experienced. Barney did precisely that, and the psychiatrist referred Barney to a Benjamin Simon who lived in Boston, Massachusetts.

In any case, the Hills grew confident and comfortable enough in November of 1963 to make a presentation about their alien abduction experience to an amateur UFO study group called the "Two State UFO Study Group" located in Quincy Center, Massachusetts. The following month in early December of 1963, the Hills met up with this Benjamin Simon hypnotherapist character whose mind had already been made up prior to his interviews with them by already concluding that their extraterrestrial hypothesis was quite impossible prior to hearing a word from them. Simon also made it very clear after his hypnotic interviews with them that the Hills genuinely "thought" they had witnessed a UFO with human-like occupants. Unfortunately for the Hills, they both submitted themselves to the influence of a man whose mind was already made up at best, or at worst was less than objective. Simon may have genuinely sought to discredit their account of the matter, particularly if he was covertly cooperating with federal government authorities' UFO denial policy, which was standard operational procedure at that time. In fact, instead of Barney alone being hypnotized, (as he was the person referred to Simon originally in the first place) the sessions with Mr. Simon were now going to be extended to Betty, wherein Simon allegedly "hoped" to uncover more about their combined experience through hypnosis. Further of interest, and indicative of his apparent government-supported agenda, he "reinstated" the Hills' "amnesia" at the conclusion of each session that he individually had on a 1:1 basis with his subjects. Betty Hill, during her sessions with Simon, maintained her account of her abduction in accord with her dreams and consistent with Barney Hill's account of the abduction while he was under hypnosis.

While under Simon's hypnosis, Barney Hill said that his binocular strap had broken, when he anxiously ran from the UFO back to his car. He also remembered an overwhelming compulsion to veer suddenly off the highway and go onto a side road into the woods. He recalled seeing six men standing on this road instead of his non-hypnotic previous testimony in which he encountered the cement "roadblock" and saw "a fiery orb" in the road. Barney Hill (while under hypnosis) recalled three of the six men approach his car and tell Barney that he didn't need to fear them. He remembered one who seemed to be a leader tell him to close his eyes. Barney then said, "I felt like his eyes had pushed into my eyes." He described these men as Betty had in her dreams, short statured with greyish skin, black eyes, black hair, and bluish lips. Barney stated that these men had a terrible mesmerizing impact, saying, "Oh… those eyes… they are there in my brain!" He went on to say that he and Betty were escorted into the aliens' disc-shaped craft, where they were then separated. Three of the men guided Barney into a room and told to lie down on a rectangular examination table, like one would see in a doctor's office. He kept his eyes closed during most of the exam because he was so frightened. A cup of some kind was placed over his genitals, and although saying he didn't experience an orgasm, he believed that a sperm sample had been taken from him. Then one of the men scraped his skin and examined his eyes and mouth. A thin tube was inserted into his anus, and then quickly removed. He also felt a hand feeling up his spine and Barney thought they were counting his vertebrae. Finally, he heard the men speak in a language he couldn't understand, but during the few times the men spoke to him directly it was in English. Barney also said they weren't speaking directly, but rather communicating with him by (as Barney described the phenomenon) "Thought Transference," being unfamiliar at that time with the term of "Mental Telepathy." The Hills while under Simon's hypnotism both said that the aliens' mouths never moved when they chose to communicate with them. Barney recalled the men escorting Betty and him back to their car and staying parked to watch their ship leave. Betty while under hypnosis started to cry profusely when describing the "Examiner" alien examining her.

Simon examined the Hills several times each. He also claims that Betty had severe mental distress while describing her examination by the alien "Examiner" while under hypnosis. (Simon also stated that he had to close one of his sessions with Betty early, as tears were "flowing down her cheeks" while describing her examination by the alien.) Simon additionally "suggested" during one of his sessions with Betty that she could sketch a copy of the "Star Map" that one of the aliens told her was where they came from. This was the source of both public controversy and ridicule over the map's accuracy as time went on, causing many to reject the Hills' story. Unfortunately, we lack potentially additional details, as Barney Hill died young at age 46 in 1969.

Simon's conclusion after his sessions with the Hills was "possibly" that Barney's memory about this UFO encounter was a fantasy brought about by Betty's dreams. Psychiatrists later suggested that the "supposed" abduction was a hallucination given the stressors of being an interracial couple in the early 1960s United States. In a 1980 episode of the TV Program "Cosmos," the celebrity astronomer Carl Sagan demonstrated that without the "lines drawn" in the Betty Hill map, it bore no resemblance to the "real life" map which scientists could then produce of the double star system of Zeta Reticuli. Looking at the records available, I think that the celebrity the couple obtained, Betty's early loss of Barney (Betty never remarried), and Betty's psychiatric problems in her later years contributed to many people rejecting the entirety of the Hills' original story. This was certainly in keeping with the government's agenda at the time, to keep the general public believing UFOs were not real—and any people believing otherwise were nuts.

I must give the thumbs up to Betty's map. Though Betty Hill was no astronomer, I must ask what are the odds of Betty being correct after all? Particularly since modern 21st Century science has determined there are in fact planets in the Zeta Reticuli system that are inhabitable. Further, she was an educated person (graduated from the University of New

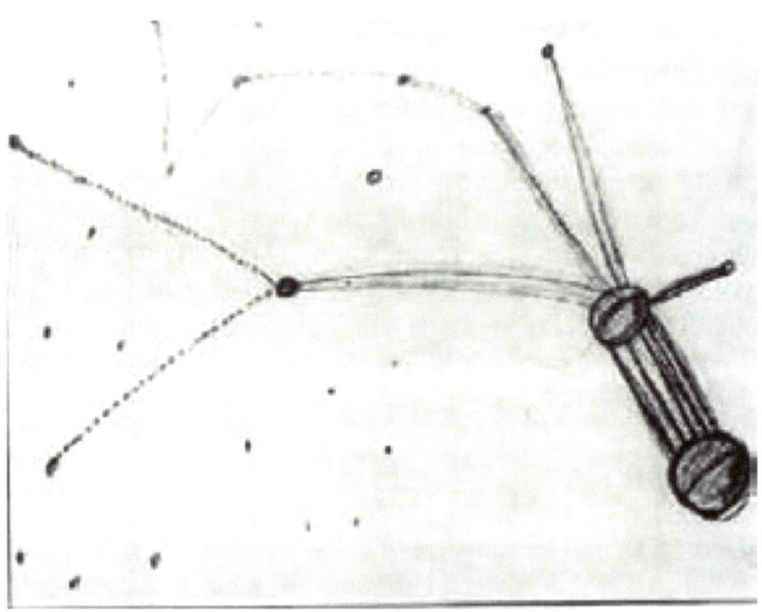

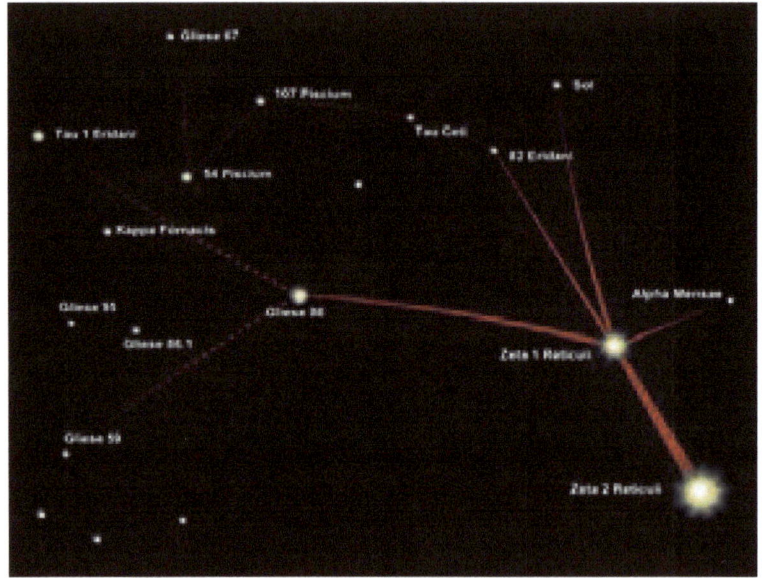

The top black and white picture is what Betty Hill drew from her memory, of a star map she saw while being abducted by combined Alien Grey and human hybrids (EBEs). One of the EBE hybrids (which in this case were not a natural species, but the scientific genetic combining of Grey Alien and human species to form a hybrid (human and Grey Alien species) told Betty that the map actually showed where they (the EBEs) had come from. The star system represented is the double star galaxy of Zeta Reticuli, which had not yet been discovered when Betty Hill created her Map. The colored chart below Betty's is a modern day star chart of the star system "Zeta Reticuli."

Hampshire), was feisty, and obviously had guts (especially to argue and directly challenge the aliens abducting her and her husband). When alien-abducted at the age of 58, she was at the top of her game as a social worker and civil rights advocate, and certainly ahead of her time to have found happiness in an inter-racial marriage in an area and time (1961 and earlier) in the United States, whereby the social norms were (how can I say this delicately?) more often less than accepting of such relationships and marriages. To sum it all up, when it comes to Betty Hill, I can only objectively conclude she was one highly intelligent, assertive, and gutsy Lady. I salute her.

Chapter Six

The Final Chapter for Humanity?

I'm an old man as I write these lines in October of 2021, and I sometimes wonder if it's an exercise in futility for me to continue writing. I believe the United States is upon the brink of civil and world war. The United States population has never during my lifetime ever been as divided as it appears to me to be today, even during the Vietnam era of my early adulthood. It rather is reminiscent of our earlier Civil War, except this time in an information and technological age that we are approaching like toddlers. The days of journalists of the caliber of Walter Cronkite or Mike Wallace, in providing genuine world news, clearly seem over. Instead, all we receive on the major news networks for the most part is through the lens of corporate conglomerates more interested in ad revenue and making news more like a game show than as a purveyor of facts. We no longer have war correspondents regularly on the ground to genuinely find out what's going on in often unknown, meat-grinding and limited "undeclared" wars, usually in multi-national/global corporate interests, which kill and maim our citizens in the military in what the brass hats and higher ups in the federal government call, "Low Intensity Conflicts (LIC)."

In my parents' time, such wars were called "police actions," which I suppose is a backhanded way of discrediting their importance or significance, especially because despite our supposedly being a Superpower, we never win in such wars. The propagandists assure us of the enemy's inferiority, or that they are a third world (now called "developing") country, yet they consistently still win against any major power…and this despite the billions of dollars spent and the countless lives lost.

Perhaps these consistent failures in such wars, which have been of no benefit to the majority of people of this country, combined with the U.S. Government's continued corruption, are a major contributor to the unrest and a spirit of rebellion against the *United States Constitution*, and our traditional rights and freedoms. The spirit of rebellion is not significant solely to our country alone, either. The same type of Marxist or Nazi-style rebellion is occurring within the other traditionally democratic nations like Australia, New Zealand, Canada, England, and throughout most of Europe—and all of it simultaneously. I'm no political scientist, yet I can't see how this was not thoroughly planned out by some well-funded entity, that has international connections and makes billions—if not trillions of dollars—from destruction, surveillance, and lives lost.

Chernobyl is leaking again—the Soviet disaster that Ukraine inherited, once again taken over by Russian forces. The Russian Federation also recently had an incident with an underwater UFO off the coast of Siberia, in which a Russian military research submarine that encountered it had its power shut down, and it was initially reported (before the story itself was shut down), that they had barely avoided another major world-impacting nuclear disaster. And on August 5th, 2019, the Russians had a major fire at one of their army's nuclear weapons storage depots near the city of Achinsk, located in the Krasnoyarsk region of Eastern Siberia. Thousands of stored nuclear tank and artillery shells, along with other conventional high explosives, detonated over a two to three-day period. There was nothing anyone could do, as these exploded unimpeded into the planet's atmosphere. Putin showed up with military personnel to tell civilians that they had to evacuate because of the radioactive fallout. He himself couldn't stay there too long either because of the fallout.

In our own country, too many of us, by not paying enough attention to what government has been doing, have unknowingly been contributing to the building and maintenance of the surveillance police state we are now suffering under. A tyrannical government can now easily identify, locate, and detain us anywhere and lock us down. We also need term limits for all Senate and Representative positions at the Federal Government level to help deter corruption and the negative influences of big corporate lobbyists.

It has been the Federal Government's actions that have led to this deterioration of our freedom and liberty, like environmental freedoms to use parks, access to healthy and non-genetically altered or chemically-affected food, medicine without evoking fear, the degrading of our freedom to travel, and the government's backdoor dealing with covert parties.

This is where we now get into the issue of what the government knows about EBEs and their potential agenda. Through research into the government's past actions and policies associated with UFOs, and the documents I've reviewed, it appears the US Government has made at least two treaties, or agreements, with what some consider "the Greys," which is purported to be the alien species which crash-landed in Roswell, New Mexico in 1947. There are also reports that certain EBEs (suggested: Greys) worked with the Nazis during WWII, and helped them to develop superior weaponry, and encouraged their inhumane and monstrous medical eugenics research on people they considered sub-human or deplorable, specifically all Jews, homosexuals, the insane, the physically and mentally disabled, opposing political activists, prisoners of war, Roma (once called "Gypsies"), political prisoners (like politically outspoken Catholic priests, and university intellectuals) and opposing political party members, and others of non-"Arian" heritage… These comprised the people which the German National Socialist Party (Nazis) of WWII sent to the work-camps, which turned into death-camps, as the Nazis pursued their "Final Solution" wherein millions of Jews and countless thousands of "undesirable" people (including children and babies) were stripped naked, separated from their families and herded into the gas chambers for "Showers" of Cyclon B (a Cyanide-based poison insecticide). Afterward, their bodies were collected and cremated in gigantic ovens, either while barely still alive or dead, and their remains were used as road filling as the Nazis paved the camps' roads, for example, at the Auschwitz Birkenau Concentration Camp in then Nazi-Occupied Poland.

These "Greys," it appears logical, based upon my review of the available information, would have still maintained contact with the Nazi scientists who entered the United States for fresh starts at life, under the U.S. Government's "Operation Paperclip." This happened just before the end of, and just after, World War II. It also is clear that the Greys had underground bases in the southwestern United States for 100 or more years. As previously discussed, President Truman established a top-secret Group of 12, known as the MJ-12, to be responsible for contact with such beings, retrieval of any of their crashed vehicles to harvest technology, to overview and control the reverse engineering of crashed UFOs, and to continue updating all top secret and above top-secret information/documentation. This group comprises, in my judgement, an important portion of the secret back-door government of the United States, which conducts Black Operations and makes vital decisions behind the scenes which our presidents are privately (but not always) advised about. While the books, movies, and television shows dedicated various conspiracies (never mind YouTube and other social media) have their culprits (valid or not), it does bear mentioning that conspiracy is sometimes based on a grain of truth that has run amok according to the predispositions of others' interests. One potential grain of truth is found via a source I would tend to trust, suggesting The Bilderberg Group and other combined political/multinational corporate entities have also been implicated and identified in former Canadian Minister of Defense, Paul T. Hellyer's book, *THE MONEY MAFIA: A World in Crisis,* which carries my strongest recommendation that Americans read, to understand the nature of some of the evils we are facing.

Because my own book has been about the history of UFOs in conjunction with both human contact and subsequent government cover-ups (including their potential reason for being here), it appears major contact with the Greys was formerly made on or about February of 1954, when former 5-Star WWII Army General and then President, Dwight D. Eisenhower met with representatives at Muroc Air Base, which today is called Edwards Air Force Base in California.[150] These offered their assistance to help the United States develop incredible new technologies, and according to certain sources, this was in exchange for giving up all of our nuclear weapons. The President and the MJ-12 Group soon determined, (based upon information received, apparently, from other advanced civilizations), that some of the aliens that had reached our planet were hostile. Added to that was the fact that the U.S. Military could take no effective offensive action (at that time) against the Greys' superior technology. Consequently, the President responded with a "No

---

[150] Hellyer, 199 -200.

Thanks." However, as the story goes, some agreement WAS made it appears for some advanced technology to construct military bases and cities far underground. Hence for this and other advanced technological information, the Greys were given permission to abduct a limited amount (thousands) of U.S. Citizens, and animal livestock (like sheep and cattle) to conduct their experiments. The Greys were to provide the government with an identification manifest (or list) of the people abducted, the location of the houses, ranches, and farms where these lived, plus a list of any animals they selected for their experimentation. This was to ensure the people involved would remain unharmed, healthy, and the government could then monitor them for potential medical and/or mental health treatment as, or if needed (and, I might note, ensure National Security interests = public ignorance, or the general perception by the Public that UFOs and Aliens were nonsense, practical jokes and hoaxes, or mistaken identification of normally encountered weather, atmospheric, or space "phenomena").

Prior to the 1980s, all the United States Government could do at that time (early 1950s), was take a defensive stance and bide their time. This time was needed for research and development of weaponry that would enable the U.S. Military to take offensive action against these visitors if needed. There was no way they could stop these aliens from coming and going to our planet, and quite frankly doing anything they wanted to do, from the 1950s up through the 1980s. This purportedly serves as another reason WHY the government denied the reality of UFOs for so long. They did not want the added pressure the public in those days could wield, for them to do something prematurely about the UFOs, before having the technological means to successfully do so.

Finally, the "arrangements' with the Greys was thought to have fallen through for two major reasons. First, the Greys went FAR beyond the parameters of the original agreement to abduct thousands of people. Instead, the military had determined the aliens were abducting tens of thousands of Americans and more.

This is where the reports of abductees and others suggest programs of Grey-human hybridizations and abductions (which for example, the Betty and Barney Hill abduction is suggested to be a classic textbook case of Grey-human hybrids' abduction of other humans) has been going on now for more than 60 years. These Grey and (reportedly) allied other alien races have consistent physical examination procedures and uniform environmental arrangements for human abductees which never vary, once the abductees are taken aboard a UFO. Their agenda is always about genetics and reproduction including, specifically, the creation and curation of Hybrid Grey and human "beings" that can pass for and/or look just like a human being, and most importantly of all, for the hybrid being to be able to reproduce like a human being normally can.

Another truly frightening thing is that these Greys and the Grey-human hybrids not only communicate with us through mental telepathy, but they can read our minds and are prone to take advantage of human susceptibility to suggestion. In short, their minds possess the power to make us dream while we are awake. They also use these telepathic abilities to make humans forget they were ever abducted at all, and what procedures or experimentations were performed upon them. For those interested, I suggest reading David M. Jacobs, PhD's book, *The Threat* wherein he addresses the "Mind Scan" power of these beings which can force us to do things against our will, and that this ability is genetically passed on to hybrid beings. He is a retired former college professor and professional hypnotist who has investigated thoroughly the alien abduction of humans' phenomenon for decades. One major point of Dr. Jacob's work is to disabuse us that these aliens are merely "studying" or "learning about" our species.

The 2nd reason the "agreements" with the Greys purportedly fell though was because of a genuine pitched battle in 1977 between the Greys and a United States Delta Combat Force with yet another alien species' military assistance at the Dulce underground military base, near the city of Dulce, New Mexico.[151] This was at that time a location where the Greys were sharing their cloning, crossbreeding, and genetic manipulatory procedures (like the outrageous experimentations and scientific "testing" the Nazi German scientists and medical doctors were doing in the 1930s, to create "beings" they could potentially use for military applications.) The situation got out of hand when some human Black Ops military guards found totally sane people, some on the U.S. "missing persons list," that had been placed in "holding cages" that were only "supposed to be used" for the "mentally deficient people" scheduled for experimentation. The end-run was a top-secret investigation reportedly by President James Carter, which revealed large numbers of abductees being held in the base's underground jail cells against their will, including female hostages. Beyond that, huge containers of "fluids" were discovered prior to or during this battle, containing human and alien fluids and body parts.

Mr. Phil Schneider (now deceased) was a federal government geologist and structural engineer possessing above top-secret clearance who was purportedly present and wounded critically at this Dulce, New Mexico underground U.S. military base during a battle between the human military Delta Force (with the assistance of another technologically advanced alien race) against the Greys. This led to his retirement, during which he used to give public seminars about Federal Government Black Ops personnel having 129 bases like Dulce, with three-to-five-mile underground cities which he helped build with alien technology. Specifically, this included laser drilling machines capable of making tunnels seven miles long in one day. He also claimed these cities were made to accommodate "New

---

[151] Schneider (August 1995).

World Order," or "Globalist" people and their families, and had he known that fact he claimed he would have never done the job.

Schneider also claimed that the Black Ops budget during the 1970s consumed $1.25 trillion dollars every two years. In any event, the "New World Order" doesn't apparently appreciate "whistleblowers," and Schneider claimed Federal Government Black Ops personnel had made multiple attempts to kill him for presenting seminars to the general public about what was really going on between the extra-terrestrials, and the U.S. Government. Mr. Schneider was found eventually in his apartment, strangled to death with one of his own foley catheters, although the "official" cause of his death was suicide.

Add to this that we have now arrived at a time in history where humanity (or our species) is truly at a fork in the road of our development. We will either destroy the planet and ourselves, or we will make the adjustments required to become a benevolent species on our planet and perhaps beyond it. It is a scary but at the same time exciting time to be alive.

One of the most important things I've learned from my research, and a major talking point of former Defense Minister of Canada Paul T. Hellyer's 2014 Book, *The Money Mafia, A World in Crisis*, originally comes from long-time abductee Jim Spark's 2006 book *THE KEEPERS: An Alien Message for the Human Race*. This message from a group of a dozen advanced aliens, is addressed to us, the "Species of the Planet Earth" (if we want to survive). Jim Spark's Book Publisher, Mr. Brian L. Crissey of Wild Flower Press, in Columbus, North Carolina, gave his generous permission to me, as Mr. Sparks himself did to Mr. Hellyer, to quote verbatim what the group of alien beings asked Mr. Jim Sparks to pass on to all our human species to hear. And I quote:

> *There are some things you need to understand. Yes, it is true that we have been in contact with your government and heads of power.*
>
> *It is also true that agreements have been made and kept secret from your people. It is also true that in the past some of your people have lost their lives or have been badly hurt to protect this secret.*
>
> *Our hands had no part in this.*
>
> *We contacted your leaders because your planet is in grave trouble. Your leaders said the vast majority of your population wasn't ready for anything like us yet, so we made time agreements with your leaders as to when your people would be made aware of our presence. This part of the agreement has not at all been kept.*

It was also agreed that in the meantime steps would be taken to correct the environmental condition of your planet with our advice and technology. We say "advice" because it is your planet, not ours. They also broke that agreement.

Your air, your water, are contaminated.

Your forests, jungles, trees, and plant life are dying.

There are several breaks in your food chain.

You have an overwhelming amount of nuclear and biological weapons, which include nuclear and biological contamination.

Your planet is overpopulated.

Warning: It is almost to the point of being too late unless your people act.

There are better ways of deriving energy and food needs without causing your planet any damage.

Those in power are aware of this and have the capability of putting these methods into worldwide use.

Mr. Sparks at this interval asks them, "Why are they (leaders) not doing this now, since they have the technical means?" The Aliens in unison telepathically continued:

Amnesty… Complete amnesty to those in power, governments and leaders who have been suppressing the truth, they can't be held liable for any past wrong deeds. It is the only way these leaders can come forward with the truth. It is necessary that you do this in order to work together and survive.

Do we have the capacity to forgive and not hold those who have been dishonest with the world accountable, if only to know what they have concealed—what may be necessary for us to save ourselves, if all of this is true? We already know—even without the presence of UFOs and EBEs—that we have consistently chosen poorly as a species when it comes to greed over cooperation, violence over peace, destruction over creation, and lies for the sake of certain interests over the facts necessary for humanity to make necessary decisions. We have proved that we often cannot be trusted with power; those with it wield it most often with dark, self-serving intent rather than the common good.

We have a choice that we need to make about how we intend to walk forward, and it sometimes takes brutal reminders for us to realize that darkness is no answer when all living beings strive toward the light for a reason. It is who we are. Now we just need to remember it.

Truly,

John A. Sullivan

Former LCDR, USNR and Senior Psychiatric Technician, California Dept. of Corrections, (Retired)

Appendix: Exploring the White Mountains and Documenting UFOs

The White Mountains: Environment

This story begins in the White Mountains, which stretch approximately 88 Miles across North and Central New Hampshire with a small portion extending into western Maine. These comprise the tallest elevations in the northeastern United States. The highest mountains range from 5000 to over 6000 feet, occurring in a line of well-defined summits named for Presidents of the United States. These higher mountains have consequently been dubbed the Presidential Range. The highest of them all is named for our first president, the Six Star General in charge of the Continental Army during the American Revolutionary War and Founding Father of our country, George Washington. Mount Washington is 6,288 Feet, or 1,916.6 meters high, reached by a narrow road to the summit for a fee, just off New Hampshire's Highway 16. This road was originally a horse carriage path for sight-seeing dating back to 1861. The Mount Washington Auto Road Company, which runs the ticket booth, also offers a van service to drive visitors up and back down from the summit. (Note: I recommend anyone fearful of driving at high elevations, on a narrow road, and where cars may have to maneuver carefully by one another, to consider using the van service. I also suggest that those driving down the mountain do so slowly and are confident their vehicle's brakes are in excellent condition.)

Mount Washington has a treacherous history in that it has an Arctic—or polar—weather capacity. Its winds have been clocked up to 231 miles per hour at the summit, and its temperatures during the winter months can often exceed 30 degrees below zero Fahrenheit.[152] Mount Washington, plus the White Mountain Range's hiking trails and ski paths, are all subject to rapid weather changes within a few hours. Spring days extending into the month of May, may begin sunny and warm, but can change suddenly to thick blankets of dense, frost-forming fog. Further, such adverse weather is often accompanied by high winds containing sleet, freezing rain, or snow. This unpredictable weather annually results in hikers getting lost and sometimes becoming hypothermic from extended exposure to frigid weather. Even seasoned hikers, if unprepared for such conditions, can have accidents resulting in serious injuries and sometimes death. Although Mount Washington isn't high in terms of global mountain ranges, there are days especially during winter when its dangerous weather rivals the extremes associated with Arctic lands or mountains 20,000 or more feet high. Realize too that times have unfortunately changed, especially now when you must pay for emergency medical and Conservation Officer Rescue Services. Consequently, I recommend that all visitors hiking, cross country skiing, paddling, and/or

---

[152] Camerino (October 2020).

otherwise recreating in the White Mountains get a "Hike Safe Card." These are available online from the State of New Hampshire for, as of 2021, either Individuals ($25) or Families ($35). Possessing this card can alleviate the holder's financial vulnerability to potentially major search and rescue, emergency air medical transport, or other emergency medical expenses.

The Mount Washington Valley and the White Mountains of New Hampshire were carved out many millions of years ago by the action of glaciers. These glaciers were prehistoric mountainous rivers of ice, which scraped and carved their way through solid rock, leaving behind the current steadfast granite mountains that themselves were formed at the foundation of time. These glaciers also carried and left behind them huge boulders, signposts of their passage throughout the White Mountains. Madison Rock near Conway, New Hampshire, and Jockey Cap in nearby Fryeburg, Maine, are monolithic gigantic boulders cut away from their once mountainous vastness and carried far distances by these ancient oceanic giant rivers of ice. The streams and rivers of the White Mountains abound with rocks and boulders, containing fossils of fish, squid, plants, insects, and other fossils. These date as far back as the Devonian Period of Earth's Prehistoric Era; between 360 to 408 million years ago.[153]

Our Discovery of UFOs

Well, now I need to explain what led up to my wife's and my own first "up pretty darn close" UFO experience. October 2019 went by, and by mid-November the leaves had all fallen from the trees, and we received the normal lower temperatures and increasingly icy cold rains of late fall. By the first week of December our town and the surrounding White Mountains were hit by the strong easterly winds blowing in from the west, combined with the icy north wind from Quebec, along with the usual blizzards and snow falls, which in the upper Mount Washington Valley are always measured in feet rather than inches. The snow stayed on through the 2nd week of March, and the winter had been rather bland for us, as many of the various book shops, antique stores, folk music concerts, karate studios, gyms, and eateries were closed by governmental authority, due to the onset and march of COVID-19.

Sydney and I did our usual three mile walk with our black and tan dachshund dog (named Angus) to stay in shape. We'd bundle up with layers of clothing, waterproof jackets, snow boots with cleats, warm Canadian fur hats, and ski-masks with Angus in his sweater for these often up-hill hikes. In any case, that day we finally had our first major snow melt, meaning that major portions of the snowdrifts the town's snowplows had piled

---

[153] New Columbia Encyclopedia, 971.

up over the last 3+ months were melted off. This development signaled that we could again walk freely along previously snow-covered sidewalks and streets. It was a cool and crisp late morning, and we had a strong easterly wind, and a bright but not overly hot sun at about our 11 o'clock position overhead. The skies were cobalt-blue, clear, and without a cloud in sight so the three of us took our first extended outside walk of the year, since the first blizzard hit back in December. The temperature was around 56 degrees Fahrenheit, (truly a warm day, by New England standards), and we wouldn't have to worry about Angus sinking in the snow or getting too cold. We had been following the progress of COVID-19 since it had entered the country on both coasts. There had up to this time only been a few cases of COVID-19 in the entire state of New Hampshire, and most of them were in the southern portion of the state. There were not a whole lot of people traveling this winter thanks to the lockdowns, and we felt relatively safe up here close to the border of Quebec.

Anyway, we three had completed our stroll, and were all just walking into our driveway, when one of those big gray geoengineering jets went over our house yet again, billowing out the white aerosols from its engines in a northeast to southwesterly flight path towards Mount Washington. We had just gotten to the stairwell to get inside our home when I heard the report of another jet, and sure enough another one of this same kind of white but unmarked U.S. Air Force tanker jet was going over head about a mile or so to the left flank of its partner, spilling out the usual initially cloudy white aerosol trails from all its engines. Keeping in mind just how clear and cobalt blue the sky was that day, I told Syd to grab her phone camera as I opened the door to let Angus in and get to the 3rd deck upstairs balcony of our home. I told her, "Now is our chance to get some really great photographs of what these jets do to the sky; we couldn't ask for more perfect conditions to demonstrate the 'before' and 'after' effects of these geoengineering jets!" We thought at the time that we could send such photographs in to Geoengineeringwatch.com or Aircrap.com, for potential inclusion in their community outreach seminars, and/or publications.

Our home is about halfway up Mount Jasper, so named for a secret Native American cave where for hundreds of years Indians used to mine green and white jasper to make their spear points, arrowheads, and tools. We are at about 1,360 feet above sea-level and live in a three-story Eastern salt box house. This gives us a great frontal view of Mount Forest, called "Elephant Mountain" by the locals, and a left side view of Mount Washington, Mount Madison, and Mount Jefferson. Sydney began to take pictures of the white aerosol trails of both jets as they sped southerly in the direction of Mount Washington.

I then took the camera and took pictures of the western horizon and Mount Forest, going on to take a few more pictures of the north to northeast skylines in the direction of Maine, the direction from which both jets had flown. All the skies were still a clear cobalt-blue and free of clouds, but after about 10 minutes that steadily began to change. We took a series of pictures of where the jets had passed over our house from our third deck balcony, and from in front of our house overhead, following their flightpath's direction. We also took more pictures as the once cloudless, cobalt-blue and clear skies slowly transformed into a smoggy, smokey and haze-filled one, at intervals over a two-and-a-half-hour period. With these pictures we hoped to secure vividly clear "before and "after" skyborne effects of these geoengineering jets and send them in to Geoengineering.org and Aircrap.com to assist them in their publications and/or educational community-outreach goals.

A few days passed, and we finally got around to checking the pictures to see the results, particularly the "before" and "after" photographs, and they certainly told a story! The smoky, smoggy sky was so bad it had blocked the sun itself, which at the time we could look directly at it without blindness, shining brightly as a white circle against the smoggy haze which after an hour and a half had extended to all four horizons. The cobalt-blue and clear skies in the "before" pictures also told a story. In short, they provided ample evidence that these cloud-like jet aerosols were certainly not behaving like jet contrails. It was then that we both noticed what we initially thought was ice-melt dropping off our roof was in fact what looked like a couple of fleets of UFOs…some coming down close to our house, apparently to check us out! Not only that, but the pictures had captured different types and configurations of UFOs; some had flattened white metallic shells, three had what looked like jet wing tips, but these were all located too far to the back of the UFOs' fuselages, in such positions that any lift capacity from them would be questionable at best. At a far distance, these could possibly be mistaken for jets. These three jet-like white metallic UFOs were very proximal to the geoengineering jet aerosol trails that were actively expanding towards them in the pictures. We had not heard any jet sounds other than the two geo-engineering jets that had initially passed over our heads that day. We certainly did not spot these, or the two formations of circular bright silver metallic orbs approximately 200 feet in diameter, two of which along with a small neon-green energy probe or UFO came down next to us on the balcony as we took photographs. Neither did we hear any of these UFO crafts make any kind of sound… Nor could we see them at the time we were taking the photographs! The fact that we couldn't see them convinced us that these UFOs all possessed cloaking technology that were it not for the Japanese camera's zoom functions (and color-filter lens), we would have never suspected the UFO activity that was at that time occurring all around us!

Looking at the 2 formations of smaller metallic orbs, they were constructed of a silvery metal that brightly mirrored the sun's rays. I would judge them to have been about 150 to 200 feet in diameter, circular, each with a dark filtered black glass-looking colored canopy—or cockpit—on top. The two that came down closest were near houses, power poles, and trees that I used as benchmarks to estimate their size. There appeared to be two bright exhausts of light energy from two specific areas on the hulls of these silvery metallic orbs, yet despite two of them in relatively close proximity we heard no report indicative of their propulsion while taking the photographs. When we enlarged some of the orb's photographs, we couldn't see any humanoid or other figures in the dark and black colored tops, or shaded canopies of these UFOs. There were also two huge—I'd estimate a thousand feet or more in diameter—respectively neon-green and white colored circular balls of light energy. These came down to treetop level past us and above the southerly portions of Berlin just above the houses and trees. Further pictures revealed these UFOs were all headed in the direction of Mount Washington and the Presidential Range of the White Mountains. The white and green balls of energy seemed too large to be probes but may have simply been UFOs for transport—the same as the jet-like white metallic UFOs and silver metallic orb-shaped UFOs appeared to be. None of them were detectable to either our eyes or ears… Our experience does appear to prove that "cloaking technology" such as that portrayed on popular TV science-fiction series certainly could exist.

We found it (their near proximity without our ability to see or hear them) certainly concerning… We also had inadvertently taken pictures of the front of our house during our "before" and "after" photographing of the geo-engineering jets' aerosol trails passage, and under an eave of our roof we had captured the image of a small green ball of light—of pulsating neon-green energy—with an electrical field all around it. It had been hovering to the immediate left of the balcony and apparently nearly right next to us while we were taking pictures. Of further interest was that it had located itself on the other side of the house wall, proximal to our home's computer. The field of electrical energy surrounding the small orb (it was not more than two feet in diameter), made it resemble the planet Saturn. I had taken some comfort in my sister Elizabeth's comment (she used to do professional-level photography) that the green orb-shaped reflections on pictures were often caused by a camera lens reflecting the light of the sun. That is until the following day when I took another picture from my driveway and saw this same small ball of neon-green energy following me. In the days immediately following these events, I found many UFOs were now passing by or hovering over our house, seemingly to not only check us out, but presumably to allow us to film their vehicles.

One interesting thing I've observed about both small and large UFOs is that most of them tend not to have the stereo type of circular classic flying saucer or orb shapes and are in fact diverse and highly variable. The same is the case with large UFOs. On the other hand, the smaller crafts I've photographed close-up tend to have dark portals, windows, canopies, or cockpits that are shaded or black, and usually I have not been able to see any life forms, humanoid or otherwise. The UFOs, both larger and smaller sized, appear to use both cloud cover and cloaking technology, or combinations thereof, to remain unseen and covert in their travels. I've observed after taking hundreds of photographs since, that these individual orbs and other smaller shaped UFOs can combine their platforms, or merge their smaller craft with others, irrespective of individual UFO size or initially pictured physical configurations to form conglomerates of larger and even gigantic mother ships or starships. In short, they appear to be able to routinely combine their individual craft's hulls, fuselage, bulkheads, or walls into the very substance of other UFOs to either reduce or increase their size and/or perhaps capabilities.

I've photographed UFOs in size ranging from about two feet in diameter like the green plasmid-energy "probe" or "will-o-the-wisp," to starships the size of U.S. Navy nuclear aircraft carriers and beyond. The most remarkable UFOs I've photographed so far were two UFOs shaped like giant squids, except that they were miles in length and width! Yet, even more amazing than these alone were the follow-on series of photographs that captured literally thousands of smaller UFOs the size of big city skyscrapers, mostly in the shape of squares, rectangles and other block-type shapes were all entering giant cavities centralized within these two gargantuan squid-shaped UFOs! These "smaller UFOs" were penetrating the hulls of both these monolithic squid-shaped, and apparently Intergalactic Transport Starships through white and brilliant energy fields serving as doorways… I've especially included these photographs within this work, as they in my estimation certainly prove that our planet, its species, and the White Mountains of New Hampshire in particular are a popular destination for interplanetary scientists, tourists, and mining operations. (Granted, this is in my opinion.)

We have taken many more pictures of these geo-engineering jets since March of 2020, sometimes silver colored ones, but always without markings, and not necessarily the big white or grey U.S. Air Force tankers.

To our amazement, upon looking at the photographs we have taken of what we believed were jets, our camera's lens often revealed instead a UFO pouring out the aerosols from behind their craft! How, we wondered can these one or more UFO craft or their operators be affecting us from such distances? Are these UFOs which appear to be from advanced civilization(s) actively assisting the federal government in the International Global Dimming Program? Or are these spraying something else? How can a smaller UFO craft as compared to a U.S. Air Force jet tanker, hold such massive amounts of aerosol? And it appears they may even be capable of controlling what we see and hear, since we saw NONE of, or heard nothing from the UFOs, in terms of fuel exhaust reports while taking pictures to memorialize the cause and effects of the geoengineering jets that passed over our home.

My wife and I since March 10th, 2020, have taken dozens of pictures of these geo-engineering, or Strategic Aerosol Geoengineering (S.A.G.) jets whose activities have been documented now for years as a covert operation going on world-wide throughout the United States and NATO Countries. I recommend in strongest terms that readers get hold of a book I mentioned before: former Canadian Secretary of Defense, Paul T. Hellyer's Book, *The Money Mafia, A World in Crisis*, which reveals his experience with the U.S.

Military and U.S. Government's disinformation about UFOs and advanced civilizations. In fact, I think it is the most important book to have been written in the 21st Century.

Mr. Hellyer's Book further reveals that the United States federal government has already been given a technology the size of a box capable of running all the energy needs of a modern household without pollutant oil, gas, coal, or nuclear power. It could liberate people from having to pay ongoing utility bills. Yet not a word of this has ever been passed along to the people of the United States. American citizens and residents are the ones footing the bill (via taxation) for all the federal government's research projects (including covert ones) and now to the taxpayers comes the added expenses for the newest military branch, the United States Space Force. In view of these developments, we all now have a genuine stake and "Need to Know" (using military, FBI, CIA, and federal black ops "spook" security parlance) about the identities of these documented advanced civilizations and what "deals" (treaties or agreements) the U.S. Government has made with them in exchange for advanced technologies.

To continue then, I can, after taking hundreds of pictures of UFOs, answer one of my own questions raised earlier, which is how can a small UFO, in no manner as large as a U.S. Air Force tanker jet, spray the same or more amounts of aerosol into the Earth's stratosphere? Well, this is because there is more to be seen than IS seen.

That is, because of UFO cloaking technology, pilots, and other observers of UFOs only see a portion of what is really flying—or actually there. The fact is you may see ONE UFO, from either a plane or from the ground, but any first-rate camera lens can usually penetrate their cloaking technology enough to reveal that what appears to be a single UFO is composed of many smaller UFOs or robotic drones, all working together in whatever configuration or platform which the piloting intelligence or EBEs want to make.

The same is true of mother or gigantic starships, many of which are as large as U.S. Navy aircraft carriers or a mountain, in the latter case miles long. Those of us who are veterans like to sometimes make the quip that "military intelligence" is a contradiction in terms. The military for example has publicly speculated the aliens are hiding either in the deepest canyons and depths at the bottom of the oceans or underground in Antarctica's vast wastelands. What is true is that single or groups of UFOs have been observed and followed by nuclear submarines under the ocean as well as by jets when they fly over land near or upon military bases and nuclear installations. It could very well be that many of them are in cities constructed deep underground, or within the inside of, or under mountains.

But, if the White Mountains are any example, then they obviously like living in the sky…and in plain view! This could well be an explanation for our species' stories and legends about Biblical entities such as "The Watchers" and the "Anunnaki," the latter going back to the ancient Sumerian civilization. They were considered sky-dwelling deities whose name comes from the Elder Old God of the Sky named "ANU." These were the same beings who were said to have impregnated mortal women (as described by the Bible in the Old Testament's Book of Genesis) and created giants.

Taking Photos of UFOs: A Primer

Last, but certainly not the least, the White Mountains National Forest of New Hampshire Provides a marvelous studio for photographing all types of UFOs. Its hiking trails, lakes, and wondrous mountain vistas provide superb photographic opportunities, without the risks of arrests, fines, or detention associated with entry into or near government military bases and other restricted areas. What you will need in terms of equipment include the following:

a. A good set of binoculars, or a telescope
b. A cell phone with an upper grade photographic capacity.
c. A basic knowledge of normal cloud formations, specific types of clouds and their characteristics.
d. A field guide (book) I recommend, as it's been most valuable in differentiation between normal and unusual clouds. It is titled, *The Cloud Spotter's Guide: The Science, History, and Culture of Clouds* by Gavin Pretor-Pinney.
e. A Personal Computer
f. A Software "Photos" program, or the equivalent.
g. A Printer capable of printing on photo-paper.
h. A cell phone capable of transferring the photographs you take to your computer.
i. The possession of—and ability to use—a compass.

Once you have downloaded your photos of UFOs individually into your photo software, you select which picture you want to work on to see what's there.[154] You must be observant of unusual-looking clouds during your UFO hunting. When you see markedly strange clouds, outside the norms illustrated in your field cloud spotting guide, take a picture of it or a group of out-of-the-ordinary looking clouds. Also look for black spots amidst clouds, which may be circular, square, or horizontal in shape in front of, besides, or within clouds and photograph them. Similarly, look for brilliant white areas, often cubic, circular, rod, and pillar (or column)-appearing shapes. These shapes are frequently luminescent, shining

---

[154] Note: The best to work with is Adobe Bridge and Lightroom; this does not allow fundamental changes to the photo taken except to work with the original to scan in, clarify, work with gradients, etc. Photo manipulation except to better see what is within the photo will not lend credibility to your images. Photos taken in digital formats these days includes original information; software will further reflect changes made to the original image.

like a light bulb against and within the darker regions of large clouds. Photograph these when you see them.

Bear in mind that individual UFO shuttle vehicles will be small in comparison to large mother ships, or starships, which can vary in size from a Naval Aircraft Carrier to the size of a mountain. Look additionally for straight lines within a cloud, which are more brilliant than the rest of a given cloud's body. That often indicates a mother ship or other type of gargantuan UFO. Now I'm really going to let the cat out of the bag, UFOs usually always use concealment which clouds offer, along with their cloaking technologies that most often render them invisible to our eyesight—yet not so to our camera lens. Another remarkable characteristic is that they don't make noise like modern planes and jets do. The photographs I've taken often reveal light energy being discharged, apparently as a propulsion exhaust from many UFOs. This silence is also a common trait of UFOs, as reported by many people who have observed, been close to, or been abducted by these vehicles.

In any case, after you download your UFO pictures from your phone to your computer, tablet, etc., do the following steps (delineated here for users who are not familiar with the steps):

a. Download each photograph into your respective photo program and save it with identifying information, including date and location (though if using Adobe Bridge and Lightroom, this will be in the photo information automatically).

b. Perform the following steps for each individual picture.

c. Click the Download Image Icon on the top right of your computer screen

d. Click (or select) the photo of the picture image that will appear on your computer/tablet screen or in your photo downloads folder.

e. Either import the image to your photo software or click the "edit image" icon that will have now automatically appeared above the picture you took. In my case, the "edit image" appears along with a few other control icons on the far left, as one faces the computer screen.

f. Your picture will again appear on the screen. Choose the function that will allow you to "Save a Copy." This will then store an original copy of your picture into your photo's application or program.

g. You will then return to the image of the original to edit the image. On my computer it's (Ctrl + E).

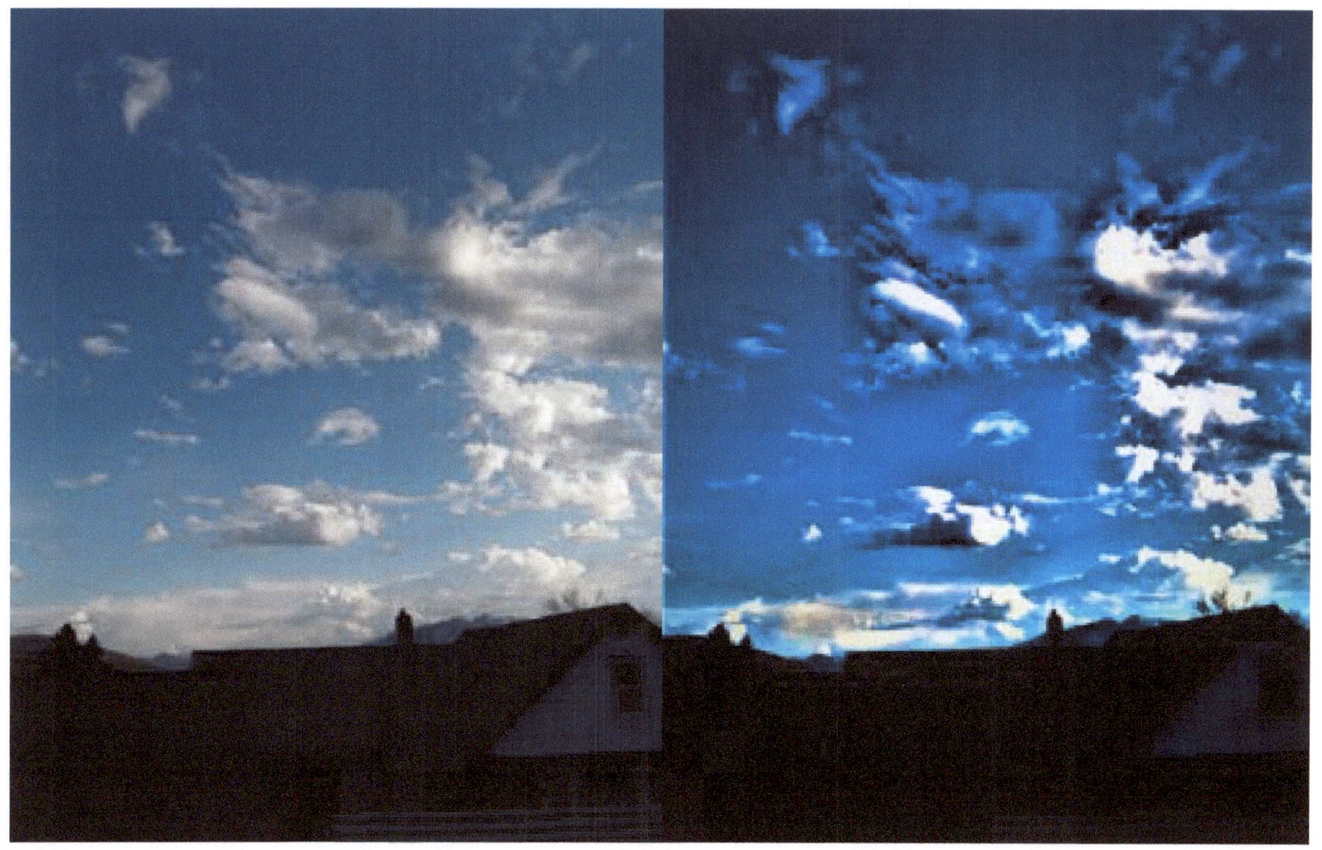

Photo sequence demonstrating my process. The first is the untouched photo as I took it. Look at it yourself...do you see anything herein indicative of UFOs? In the second photo I have highlighted the photograph with different levels of color/lighting from my computer photo program to bring out the UFO images more.

h. In your program, select "Filters."

i. Next, you're going to enhance your photo.

j. Depending upon your photo program, find the adjustment function that will allow you to zoom/move towards the cloud(s) or UFO(s), that if captured in the photograph will start to appear (IF present). This includes moving toward the dark spots or squares spotted by your binoculars, or any other uncommon features of the cloud(s), potentially including UFOs.

k. Once near, or as close as you want to be to an area of interest, use the clarification function to get better clarity on the part(s) of the image you want to see.

l. You might need to adjust the color, warmth, and tint to see different aspects of the image. This is also true of lighting adjustment between the lowest value of zero (0) to focus in UFO(s) and/or areas of interest as best as you can. Don't give up if the Object(s), UFOs, or areas of interest remain out of focus.

m. Proceed by saving a copy of the photo at this stage.

n. Now, if you have an area of interest, a UFO etc. in a portion of the photograph, use the "crop and rotate" or "resize" functions to cut off areas of the picture not significant to your area of interest and then create the size that will be workable for you.

o. You can also use the "filters" function at this point. In my software, I usually use Original, Zeke, Napa, Slate, Neo, and Icarus, singularly or in tandem.

p. Next, select "Adjustments" and try your "clarity" function once again, adjusting it from low to high until you get the best picture possible of your item or area of interest. If not suitable, then return to the original image, make a copy, and make selections. Don't be afraid to try different combinations of things for learning purposes, eventually you will get a knack for the process, and it will be something you look forward to.

Additionally, here are some additional pearls for enhancing your success as a UFO watcher and photographer:

First, location is a key factor in going to places where UFOs are known to have appeared, particularly mountain areas with a history of religious sacredness. Classic

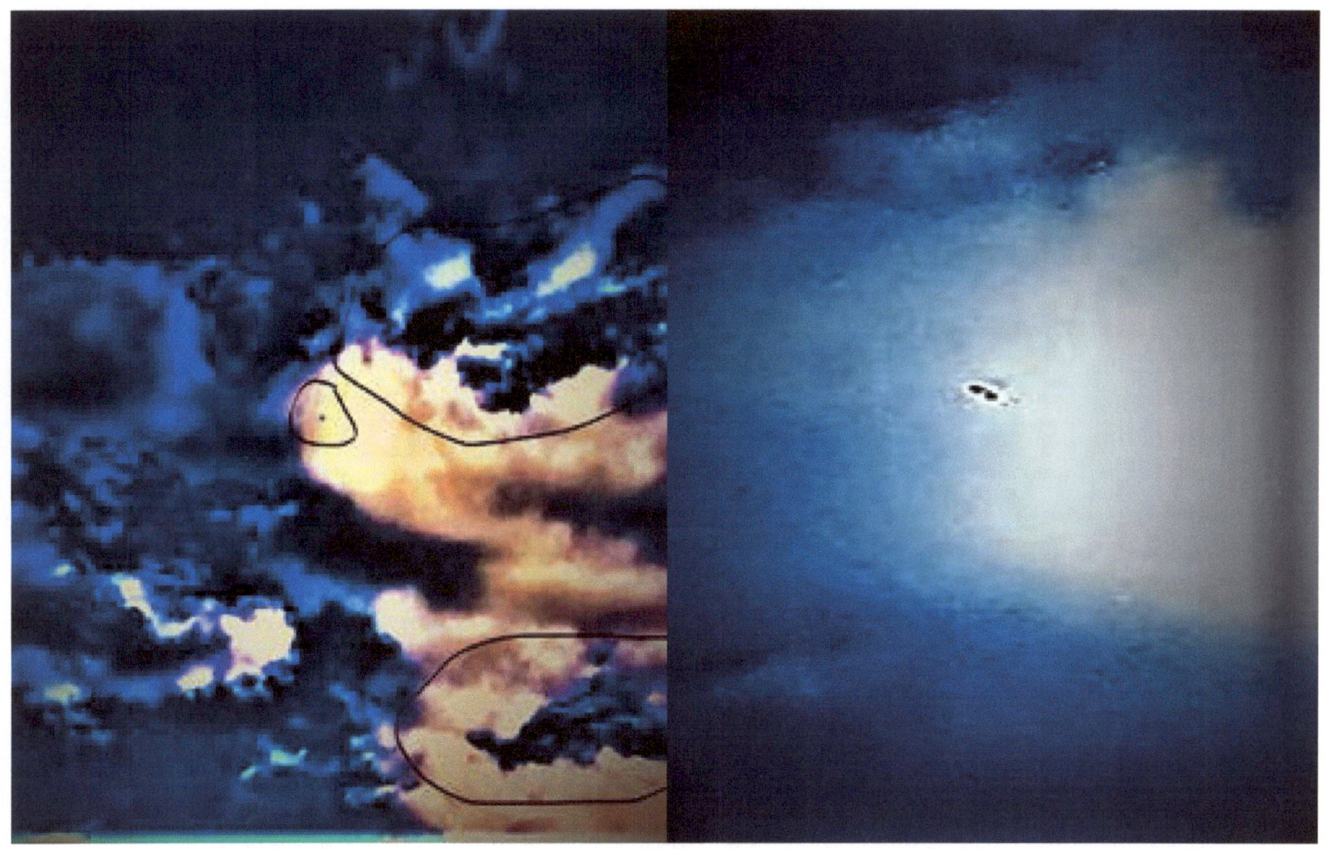

The third and fourth photos of the sequence. The image to the left is a close-up of a portion of the same photograph wherein I am drawing around areas of interest and concentrating my efforts on the largest starships and a small shuttle UFO closest to my location, which is half way up one of the smaller White Mountains. I was particularly interested in the top UFO circled, which resembles a robotic dragon-fly. In front of it is a small UFO that is perhaps a shuttle UFO craft. The shuttlecraft is enlarged here in the image to the right as the final picture of this series.

Importantly, I want to point out a common effect to be anticipated: a phone camera's lens can't focus or effectively penetrate the cloaking device energies of dozens to hundreds of UFOs that can occupy a given area. So the best solution is for the watcher/photographer to concentrate his or her efforts upon a specific area of the photograph that interests them, as I did in this case a few starships of interest and the shuttle UFO. Otherwise, the UFO enthusiast will encounter some considerable frustration perhaps. I have no doubt though, that as professional photographers enter the field, the skies won't be as limited as they are presently. In any case, I've been having a ball!

examples would include Mount Rainier in Washington State, where a female Manitou dwells named "Tacoma" meaning "She Who Gives Us the Waters." Tacoma was also the Native American and original name for this mountain. Further, the first fleet of UFOs flying in formation were first seen in modern times (1947) flying beside Mount Rainier by a civilian pilot flying a private airplane nearby. Two of these UFOs later crashed in Roswell, New Mexico. Hence, Mount Rainier National Park would likely be an ideal observation area for UFO watchers and photographers.

In like manner, Mount Washington, located within the Presidential Range of the White Mountains of New Hampshire, is a place where UFOs have been spotted going back to the 19th century and earlier. As mentioned previously in this book, it was also in the White Mountains, near the town of Lincoln, New Hampshire, that the first and most famous alien abduction in modern times occurred, that being the case of married couple Betty and Barney Hill in 1961. Folks traveling by vehicle in either direction from or towards Lincoln, New Hampshire on Interstate Freeway 93, should exit to the old Highway 3 (the Daniel Webster Highway), and head for the Indian Head Resort. The hotel there offers a first-rate restaurant, with spectacular views of the White Mountains, as well as hotel accommodations.

Most notably to us UFO watchers, the Betty and Barney Hill Historical Marker is posted within walking distance just to the North of the Indian Head Resort, on the right side of Hwy 3. This area is proximal to the location where the Hills were abducted by a group of aliens piloting a UFO. The nearby freeway didn't exist in their time nor anywhere near the infrastructure and urban buildup of our own time. In 1961 there was only a two lane, lonely highway through the towering mountain passes and dark brooding woods. The area where the Hills were abducted by aliens piloting a UFO is proximal to this monument, and along this very highway.

I would be remiss were I not to mention one of the best places of all for getting pictures of UFOs. It's the monolithic "Indian Head Mountain" for which the resort is named. The trailhead for hiking up this monolith isn't marked very well. But head south on Highway 3 towards the city of Lincoln from the Indian Head Resort. You won't travel very far before you see a brown State Government sign which merely says "Parking Area" to your right side. There will be a dirt and gravel road next to this sign, which you can enter and then park your vehicle. The Indian Head Trail is there, the major one leading to the top of the Mountain. The scenery is beautiful, but it is uphill and no cakewalk. When my wife and I first climbed up this hill in our mid-60s, people coming down from the mountain looked at both of us and commented, "Just take it SLOW, you two…" It took us old duffers about an hour to get to the top, which was crowned with a grove of pine trees. Huge flat slabs of granite worn smooth through millions of years of snow and rainfall were remarkable, and it provided great tables for sitting upon and picnicking as well as taking breathtaking photographs.

There are plenty of clouds there to take pictures of, along with a sensational view, where to the left side you can observe the Victorian vintage Mount Washington Hotel and the base for hosting many of the past's major historical and political events like one of the first Globalist Bilderberg Group Meetings in the early 1950s. There are also, by the way, other trails you can take branching off from the main Indian Head trail. Folks can take these alternate trails (get a trail map from the gift shop), which will lead them to the bottom front of the Indian Head, whereby they will marvel at the front of this monolith. The front of this mountain truly and absolutely looks like a grim, yet proud and confident Native American war chief, or warrior. In short, it rocks!

So, to sum it up, the White Mountains' recreational areas, including Mount Washington and all the other mountains of the Presidential Range White Mountains' hiking trails and lakes, have proven to be nothing less than sterling when it comes to obtaining pictures of UFOs.

Mountains where mining operations, both past and present, are other good destinations with the potential for photographing UFOs. Mountains and adjacent valleys rife with "old timers'" stories, folklore, and legends about fairies, elves, and even dragons, are also important factors, potentially indicative of UFO activity. Additionally, my primer for photographing UFOs is only a starting point. Patience combined with practice in trying different adjustments of light, filtering of color, and experimenting with different camera lens are the keys for successfully filming these amazing phenomena. I never thought at this advanced age that I would ever again experience the true awe and wonder of experiencing something so new and exciting, like when I was a young lad in the traditional Boy Scouts during the early 1960s.

Another pearl I'll share is that the closer a UFO watcher or photographer is physically to the clouds, the better the chances for his or her success for beating the odds and obtaining photographs of UFOs. Sometimes the UFOs will come into a near perfect focus immediately without my having to go through an exhaustive methodology. If, for example, there is only one UFO or a small group of them, say between 6 and 12, your photographic results will generally be better. This is because their cloaking technologies are less effective in blocking a modern camera lens. On the other hand, when I've found myself confronted with 50 or more of them in the sky immediately above or nearby me, their combined mass of technological cloaking energies, radiating out from and around all these UFO vehicles, render it nearly impossible to get clear pictures of them. What I mean, based upon my experience, is that some of them will be clearly visible in each photograph, but not many of the other UFOs that at best appear as shadows or silhouettes. Much depends upon how

I adjust the lighting and color tinting at the computer. I've often gotten a group of them that make up the mass of their numbers focused clearly, but when I adjust to attempt getting clear picturing of nearby UFOs, I may get them into clear focus but then lose those clear images that I initially had focused in. One solution that works is to concentrate on focusing clearly one portion of UFOs within a large mass of them at a time. But that gets to be mighty expensive, bearing in mind the costs today for decent printing in order to produce the pictures taken from my cell phone and loaded into my PC.

Again, all their combined cloaking technologies when there are 50 or more of them cause havoc with my cell phone's lens. I look forward to what professional photographers will be able to do soon and will undoubtedly develop lens or other tools for such situations. Besides location, patience is needed too. There are many strange looking clouds in the sky, like cirrostratus undulatus, and although a UFO photographer or watcher may think there are and/or should be UFOs within or near them; there are no guarantees for an associated presence of UFOs simply because of unusual or massive amounts of clouds. Now I frequently take pictures of large masses of clouds, and huge ones like thunderheads, and I am infrequently lucky to capture a photograph of a UFO shuttle craft or even more than a few starship UFOs.

New Hampshire in my opinion has got to be the All-Terrain Vehicle (ATV) capital of the Northeast. And yes, I have one. For those of you not necessarily into hiking, there are hundreds of ATV off road trails throughout Jericho Mountain State Park. The summit of Mount Jericho is also second to none for UFO photography. Also, but for more seasoned hikers, Mount Forest (called "Elephant Mountain" by locals), offers sterling views of the upper Mount Washington Valley and the White Mountain's Presidential range, as well as UFO photographic opportunities. I also want to share the fact that my eyes aren't as good as they used to be. In short, although I can and have spotted UFOs directly with my binoculars when they are amidst the clouds and not cloaked, what I often do is photograph huge and or massive formations of clouds. I then check them out at home after loading them into my PC. It's a lot of fun because you never know what you will find.

To get to Mount Forest's summit, just leave the Berlin, NH downtown area northerly via Highway 110, via Wight Street which turns into Jericho Road. As you proceed down Jericho Road you will see to your right blue metallic buildings which constitute Berlin Mini-Storage. Directly across the road from it on the left you will see a sand and gravel road, so proceed up it. At the first fork in the road you encounter, bear left when you see a small sand and rock quarry. Continue to bear left past a large sand and rock quarry. Continue onwards bearing to the left. When you come to the next fork with a trail to your right leading downwards to lower elevations, pass this by and continue proceeding down the sand and gravel road to its end, where it will then turn into a trail head and bear to your left.

On this main trail you will soon note an acute right turning of the trail in a crescent or half-moon form, which three quarters through it you will find yet another trail fork. The trail to the right is safer and will lead you to a lower portion of the mountain's summit to take pictures of clouds, views, and potentially UFOs.

Now, for the more adventurous, and seasoned hikers, you may decide to opt for the lesser used and fainter trail located on the left side of the previously mentioned fork. As you proceed, the trail will become fainter and will shortly make a right turn into an opened, somewhat cleared area, probably a secondary loading point for logging operations long ago. In any case, bear to the left side of this area, following it straight on till it ends. At that ending point you will see an old trail leaning to the left where it will eventually lead you into a large tree forest which is located on the crown of the summit.

This is important: Immediately upon entering this forested area, mark the trail end with a hiking stick, branches crossed, or an article of clothing wrapped around or in the lower branch of a tree proximal to the trail end. That will make your route easier to find for the return trip down the mountain. Now you or the leader of the group needs to make an oblique (or half turn of their body to the right) and take a compass bearing. Follow that bearing slowly through the forest and cautiously approach the summits top where the tree line abruptly ends…

Although there are outstanding overlooks from which to take photographs, the glacially cut summit crown's cliffs are abrupt, steep, and slippery. If rain or fog are present, or have recently impacted the mountain, the sheer glacially sharpened open granite rock offers no ledges or handholds to break a fall. During such conditions the summits edges are especially dangerous. I don't recommend this area for children weather under wet or dry conditions, even with adult supervision; as it's too dangerous.

For those folks physically incapable or otherwise unable to physically pursue the previously mentioned spots for getting pictures of the clouds and UFOs, I recommend you park your car in the Walmart parking lot in Berlin's sister city of Gorham, New Hampshire. Just take HWY 16 out of Berlin and you will see the Walmart to your right. For some reason the clouds come from all directions over and near this parking lot. I've gotten some choice photos of UFOs hiding in the clouds from here, while my wife was shopping. Additionally, toward the end of autumn, Syd and I went to the Fryeburg Fair in Maine, We took a ride on the largest Ferris wheel there, and while staff were helping other passengers disembark, we found ourselves dangling at the uppermost vantage point possible. I happened to note that the sky above the fair was chock full of white cumulus clouds. So while sitting there I took four pictures in all cardinal directions. Upon our return home, I found I had captured about 25 UFOs watching the people, animals, and festivities going on below.

I also strongly recommend the Town and Country Inn and Resort, located just outside Gorham, New Hampshire if any readers take a holiday in our area. It is on the right side of Highway 2 headed easterly toward Maine. The Inn is a great place to stay at and dine. It also happens to be a great place to take pictures of the clouds and mountains from the front of the Inn. A couple of our friends recently came to visit us during our Fall season from Washington State. My wife Sydney took her counterpart, my friend's wife for lunch at the Inn, and she took a picture from one of the Inn's dining room windows. Her photograph captured the brilliant orange, gold, crimson and green leaved trees and foliage with nearby mountains in the background, themselves covered in a blanket of the same majestic colors of Fall extending up the mountains meeting a cobalt-blue sky.

A few weeks later we received an E-Mail message and a photograph attachment from of the beautiful photo she took, remarking that we should pay special attention to the left upper portion of the sky, located in the left upper portion of the photograph. To our delight and surprise, we saw that she had unknowingly photographed a fleet of cube-shaped UFOs, flying in a circular formation over a mountain in a westward heading towards Mount Washington. She also generously allowed me to include her beautiful photograph in this book.

As I conclude, my hope is that my readers will consider educating themselves more about this fascinating yet alarming subject and become watchers and professional photographers of UFOs. Also, that others will adopt it as a hobby and create true works of art and beauty.

The discoveries I have made have expanded my own outlook about not only extra-terrestrial lifeforms and space travel but have inadvertently introduced me to the fact that many of our visitors are potentially from other dimensions and not just from other galaxies. The technological marvels I have observed have firmly led me to conclude that these advanced civilizations and beings are not hundreds of years—but tens of thousands to millions of years ahead of our own world and species when it comes to technological achievements. Although most of them are benevolent and peaceful, there remain a few that are dangerous and openly hostile to our species. Consequently, I recommend that folks avoid UFO contact (Third Kind) should one ever appear in their vicinity—and from anecdotal evidence and abductee accounts (particularly if they are female and of child-bearing age).

Those who follow my directions for photographing UFOs need to realize that they will see things wonderful, but also frightening, and sometimes very funny. We have a unique

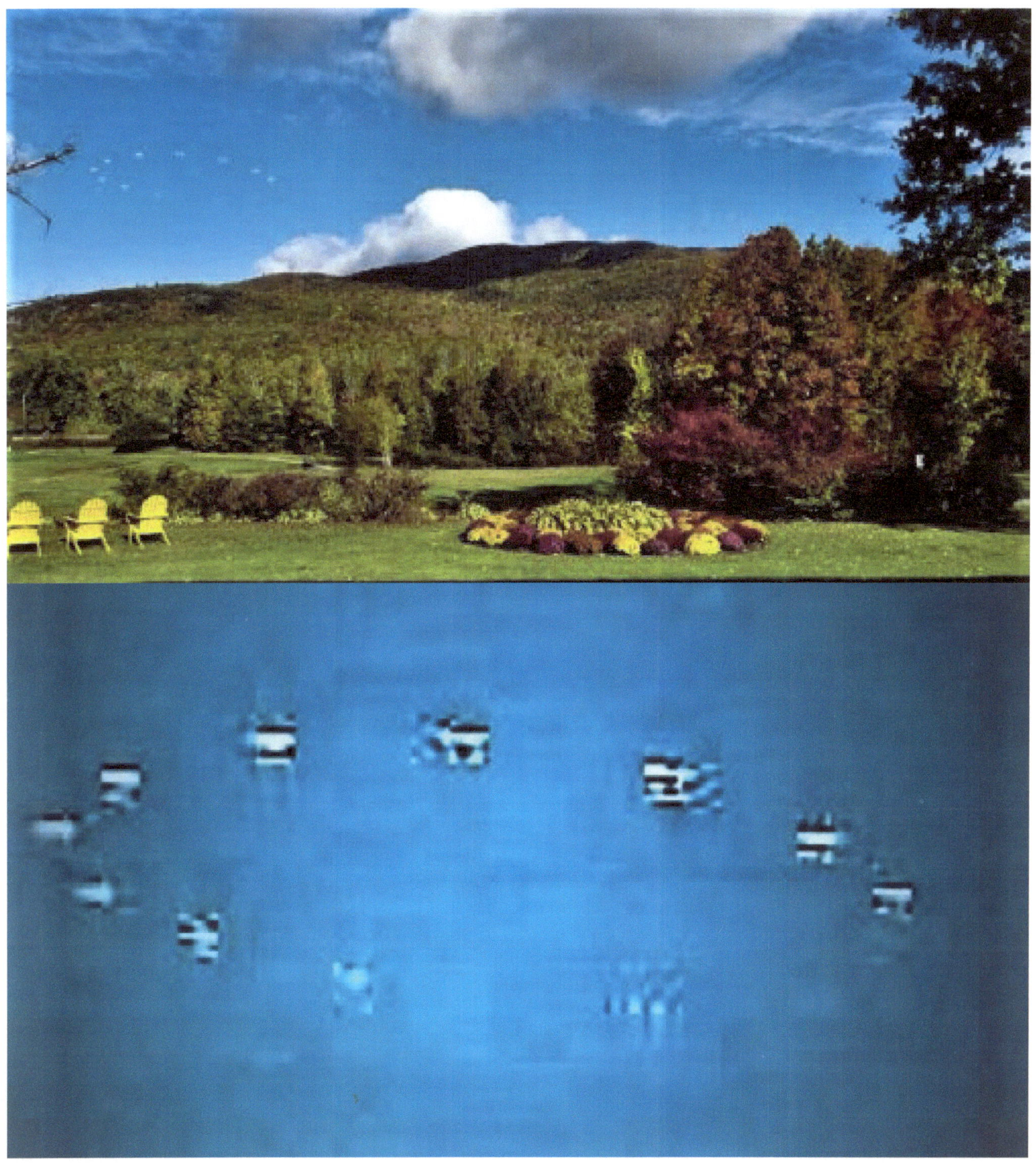

The 1st photo is the original photo by Linda Wilson. The second photo is zooming in on the formation of UFOs seen in the upper left of the original photo.

planet, teeming with life in the oceans and in the air, as well as on our planet's continents. They are concerned that such an intelligent species, living on an extraordinarily beautiful world that has just recently begun to develop a technological civilization that unfortunately seems to be using its most advanced technologies to bring about its own extinction. I have to think that while we have no way most often of seeing EBEs with our eyes, they can go anywhere to observe and watch what is going on and are highly amused by and interested in our species. This brings on an entirely new meaning to the saying, "We are not alone." In fact, we may more often than we think believe ourselves to be alone when we are not…

In any case, when "official" contact is made, I think our species is in for a most humbling experience. But think about it: there were life-forms once on our planet like the dinosaurs, and then and now crustacean life, whales, and even forms we haven't yet discovered in the deep ocean. Many extinct species according to the geological and paleontology records and charts reigned over this earth for hundreds of millions of years… Is it not probable that these species in time developed the physical dexterity and brain power to create an advanced civilization? Our ancestors as a species according to the same records, only came out of the trees about a million years ago…

I think we may soon be in for a surprising, shocking, and humbling awakening regarding our species' place in the Milky Way galaxy.

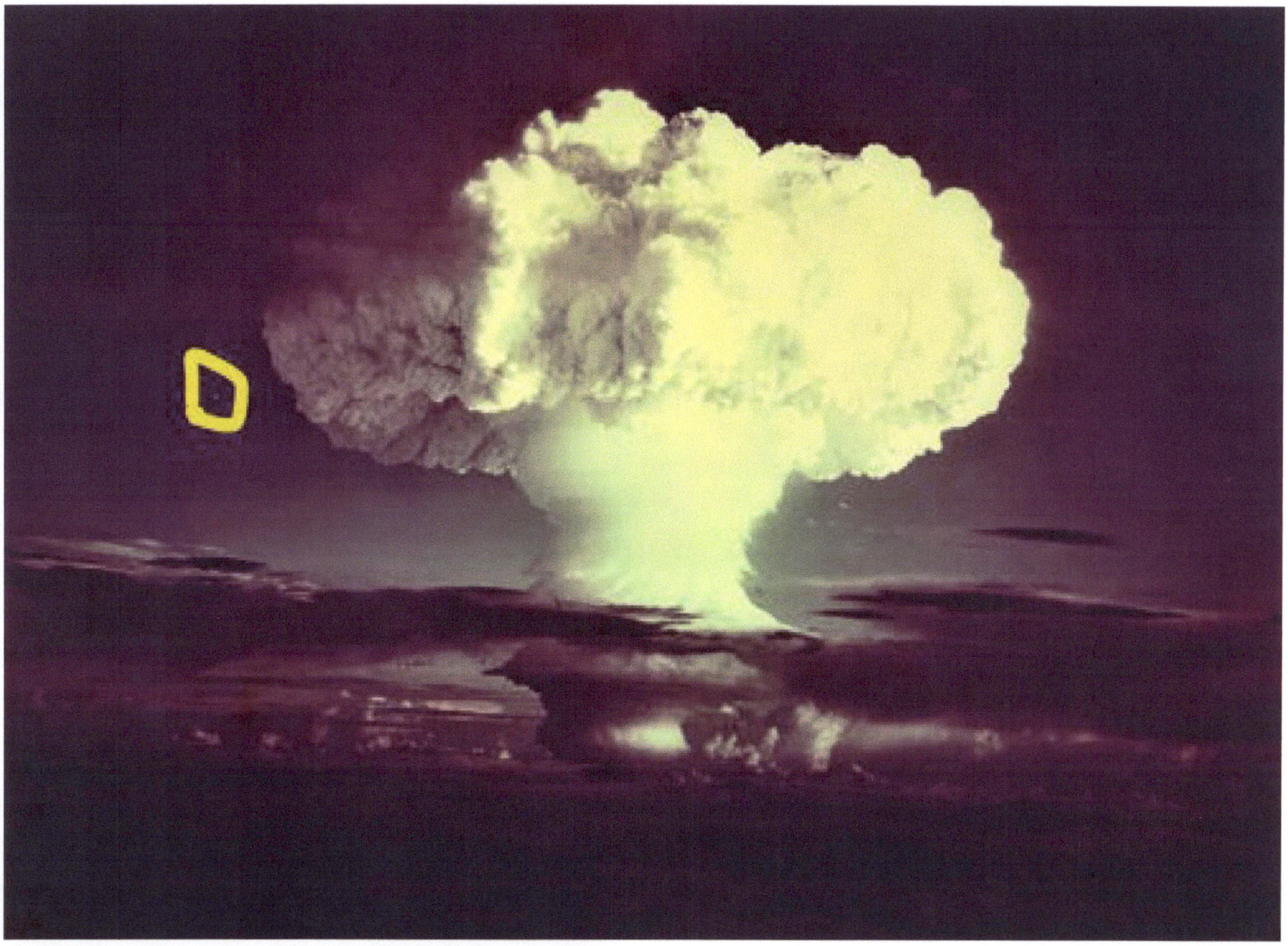

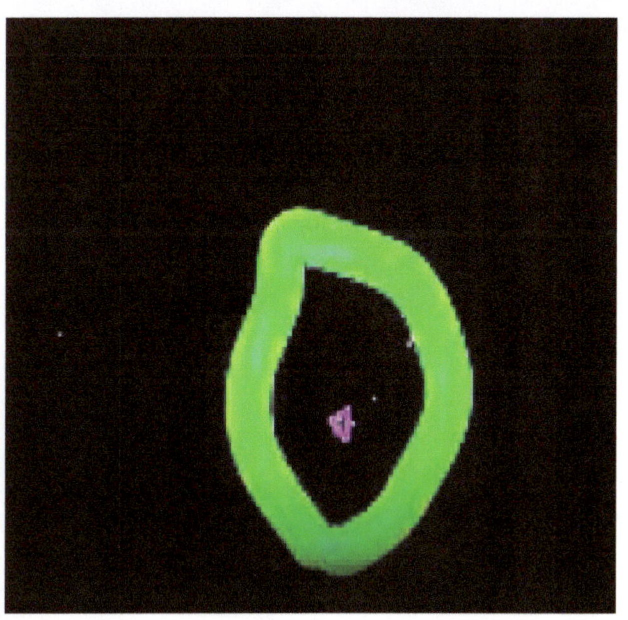

Another look at this same photo: Phil Schneider PhD was a Federal employee and an architect/engineer who told the public during his lectures in the 90s (up until he was allegedly murdered) that the USA had targeted a gray alien base with this new weapon's first test in November of 1952. I enlarged the photo so I could bring what appears to be a mothership into focus.

Two small formations of UFOs flying towards Mount Washington over Berlin, New Hampshire in straggled lines, taken about one hour after the two geo-engineering unmarked U.S. Air Force tanker jets passed over the author's house. Their shapes are that of silver metallic orbs, about 200 feet in diameter with canopies of a dense black (not transparent) glass-like material. A white energy plasma-type UFO is also observable herein, similar to the type that Julius Robert Oppenheimer ("Father" of the Atomic Bomb), and Edward Teller ("Father" of the Hydrogen Bomb) encountered in the Atomic testing areas near Los Alamos, New Mexico. These energic plasma-type UFOs are also neon green and electric orange in coloration. These energic UFOs are all about 2000 feet in diameter, and reportedly capable of splitting apart into smaller energic plasma-type UFOs…

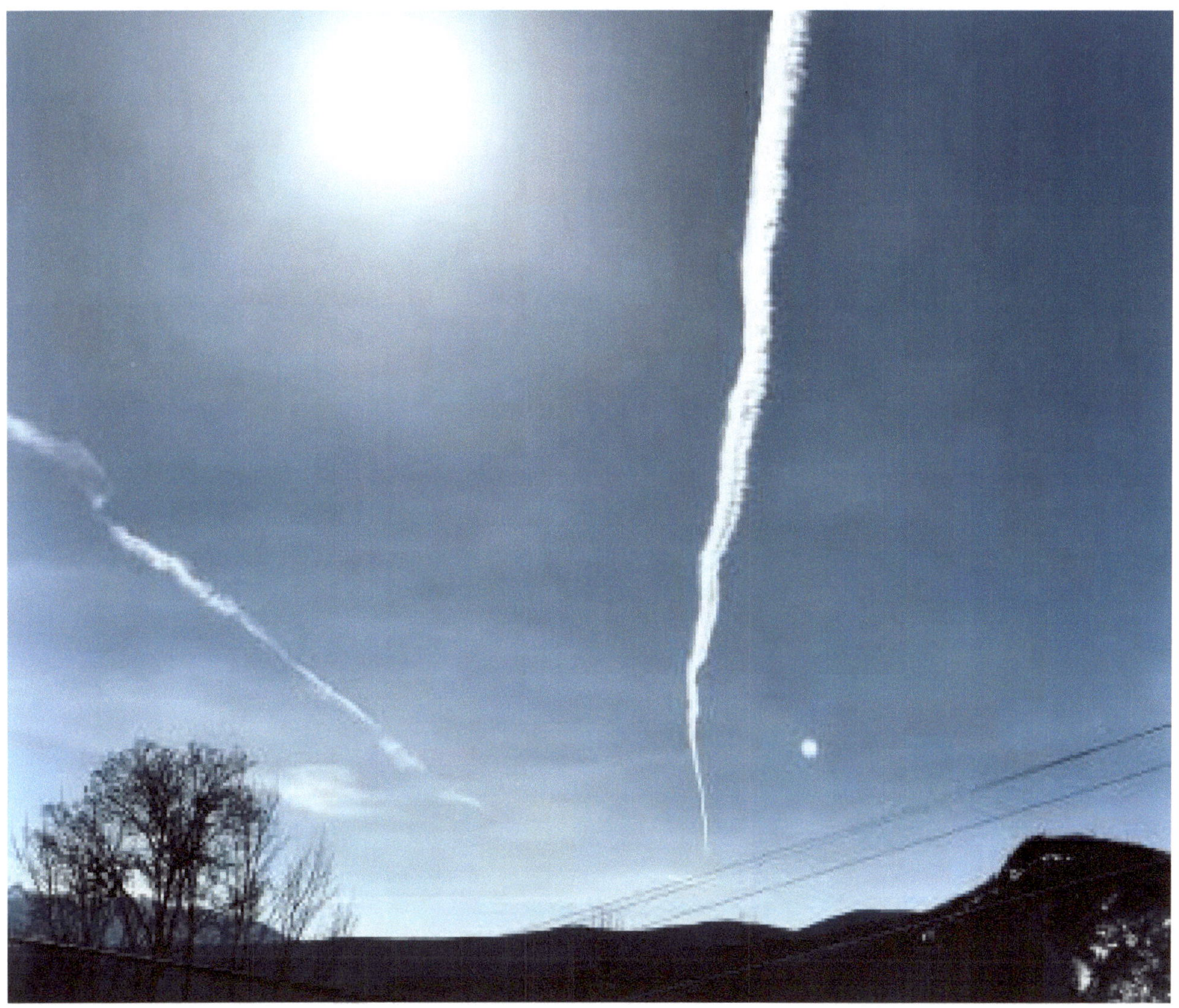

Another Look at a white energic UFO to the left side of Mount Forest in Berlin, New Hampshire. This was taken about one hour after two geo-engineering jets passed over author's house on Mount Jasper. Note the "dimming" impact of the aerosols on the sun. The smog-effect was so intense the author could look head on at the sun and actually see its shape and outline. The previous cobalt-blue and cloudless sky was now only a memory.

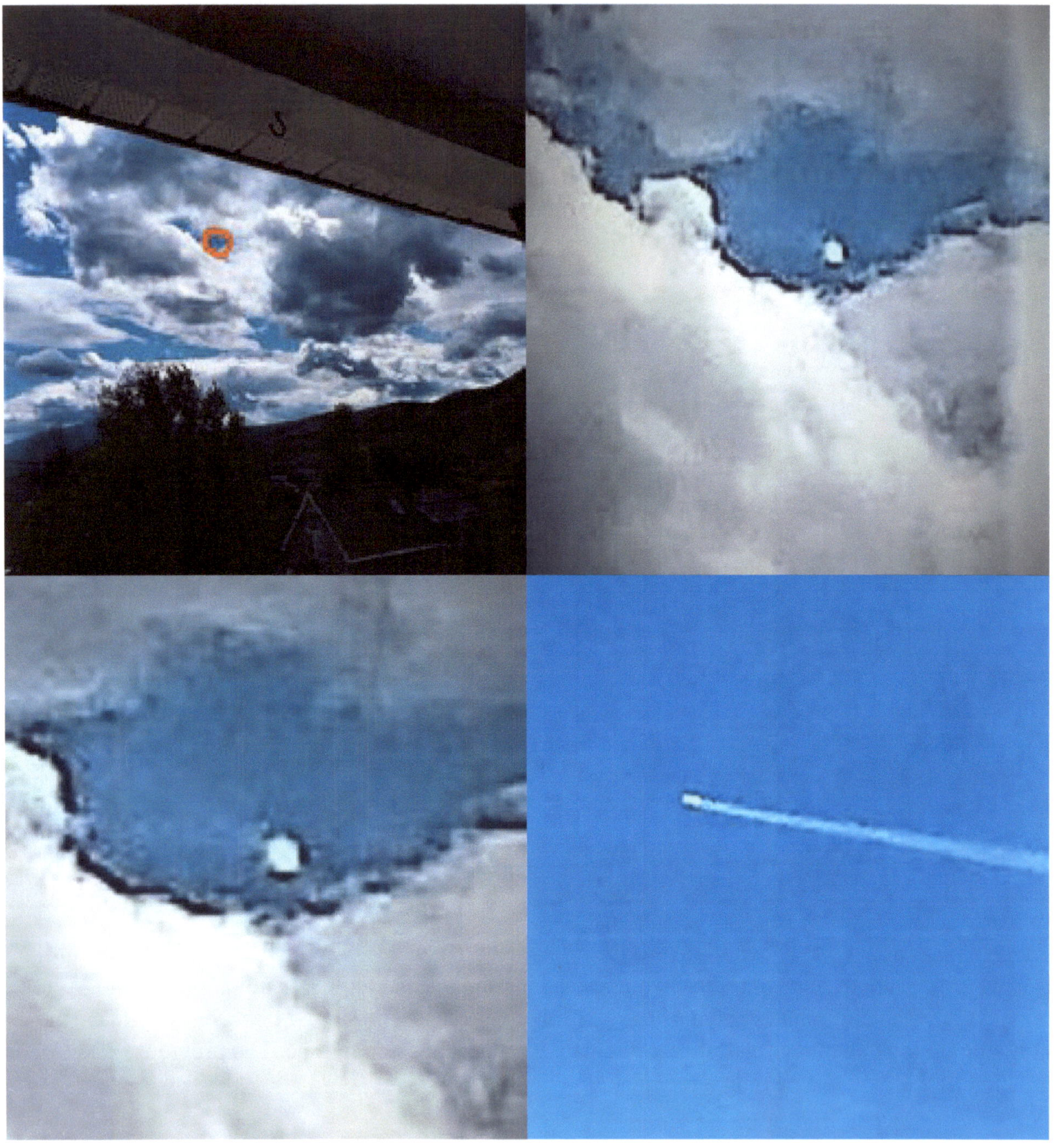

This is a block-shaped UFO I often see outflowing aerosols, same as what the Government's geo-engineering jets do regularly over our own and NATO countries… I am unable to determine if one of the advanced civilizations are assisting the government with its "Global Dimming Program" or doing something else…

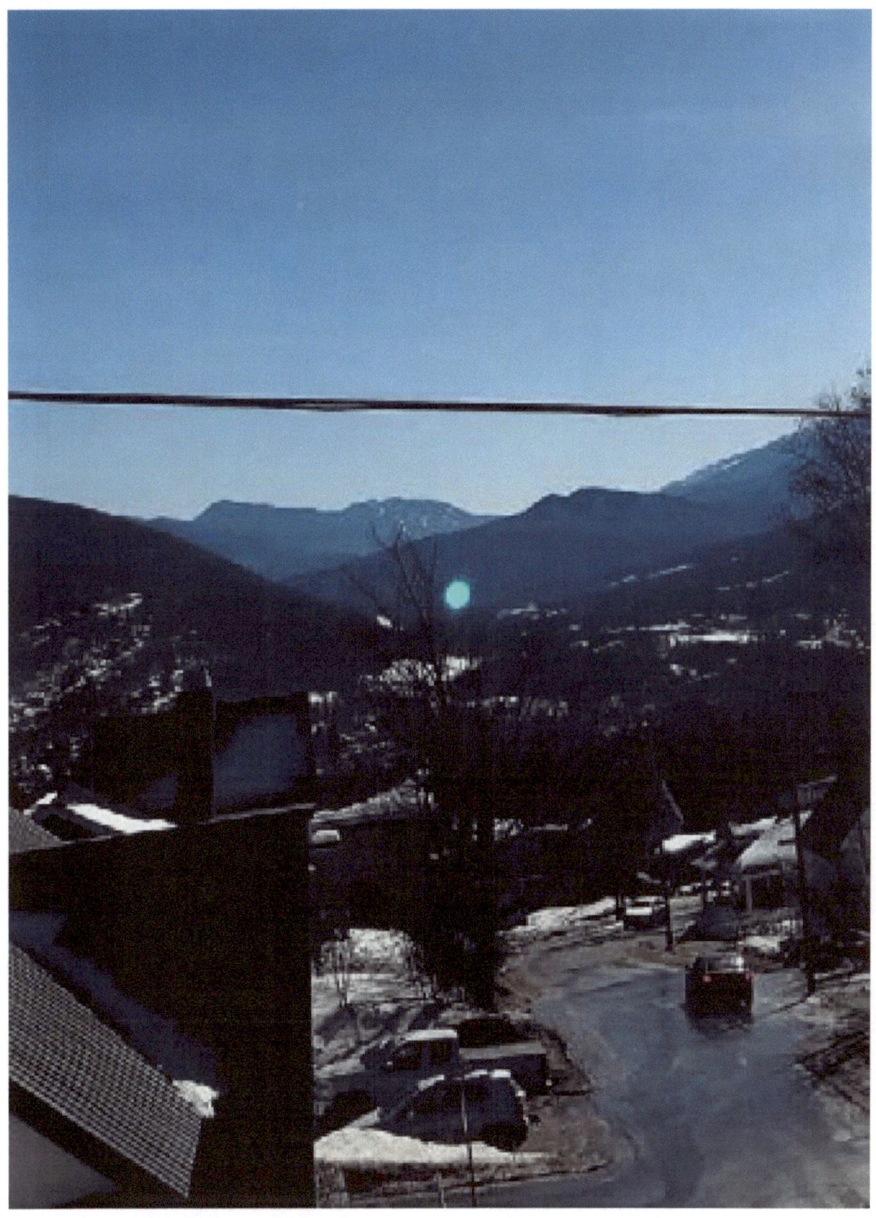

Picture of Green Energic UFO traveling down Cate's Hill Road in Berlin, New Hampshire, taken by the author. This appears to be the same kind of UFO craft Edward Teller and J. Robert Oppenheimer heard reports about, as these were spotted by "Manhattan Project" workers around Los Alamos, New Mexico and other nuclear bomb test sites in that area. These were referred to as "Green Fire-Balls" during the 1940s and 1950s.

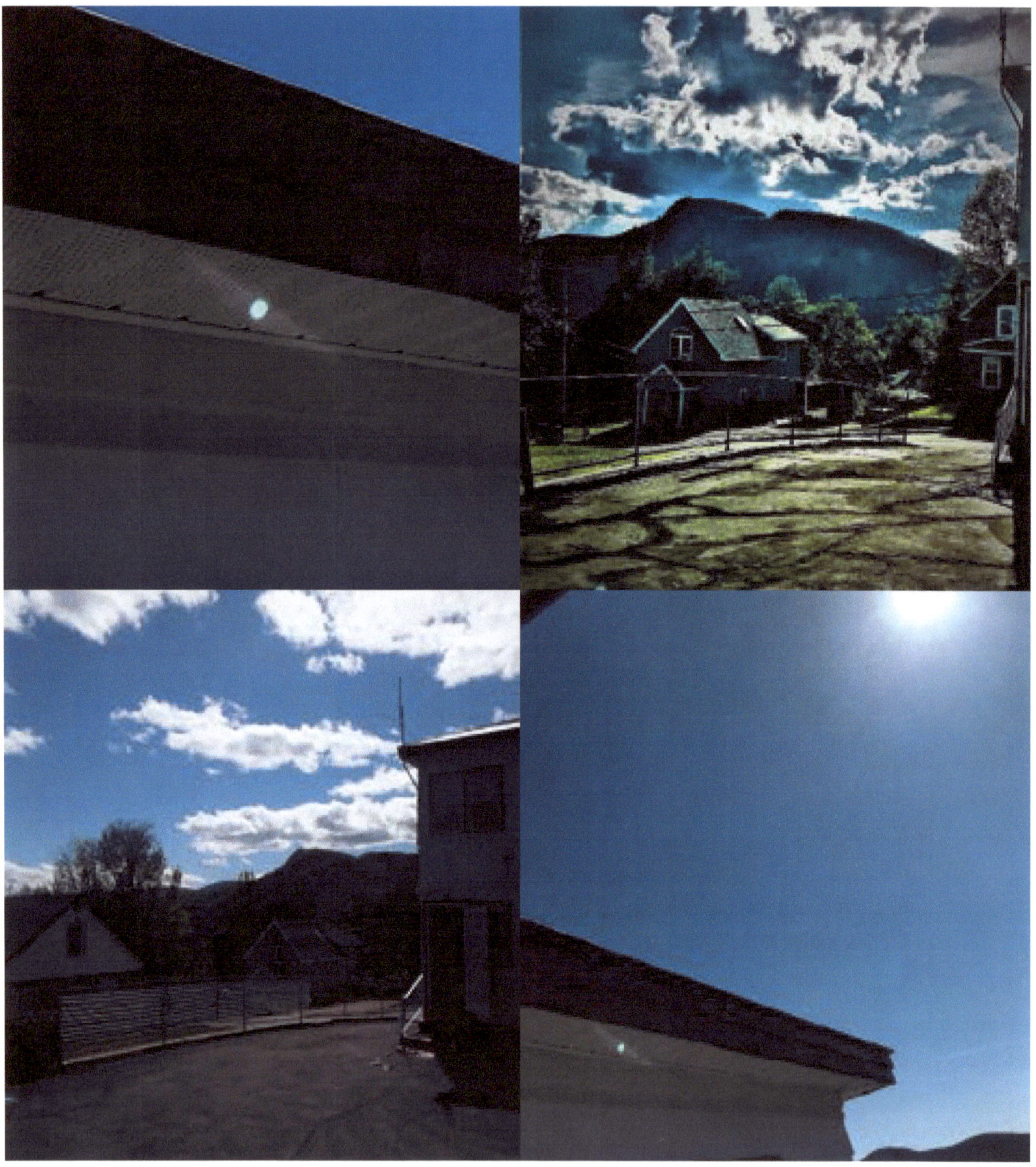

Small Neon Green Energic UFO, possibly an observation probe, which was right next to my wife and I on 10 March, 2020 when we were on our home's upstairs balcony taking photos of geoengineering jets' impact on the sky above us.

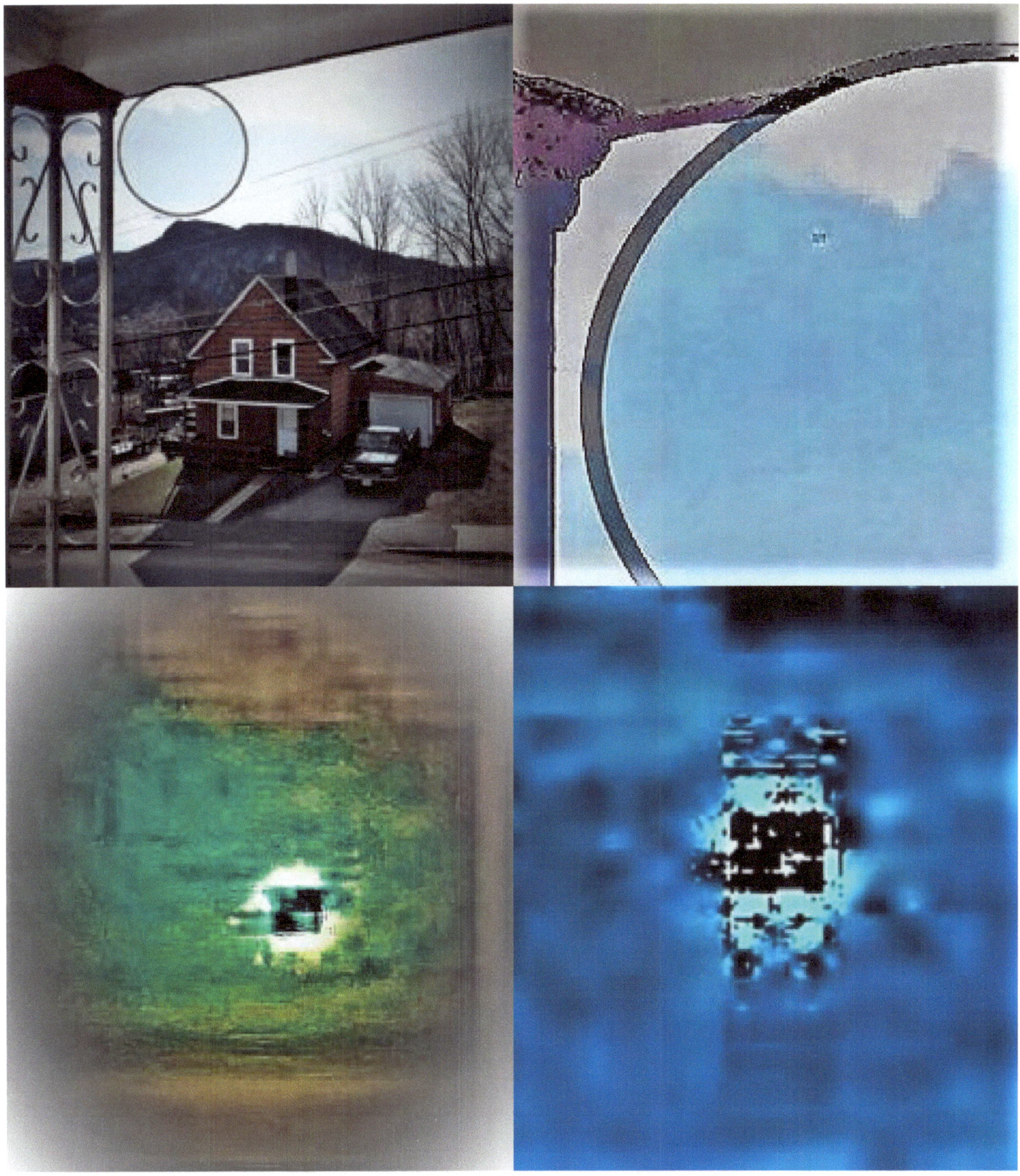

Spotted this large square-shaped UFO above Mount Forest with my binoculars.

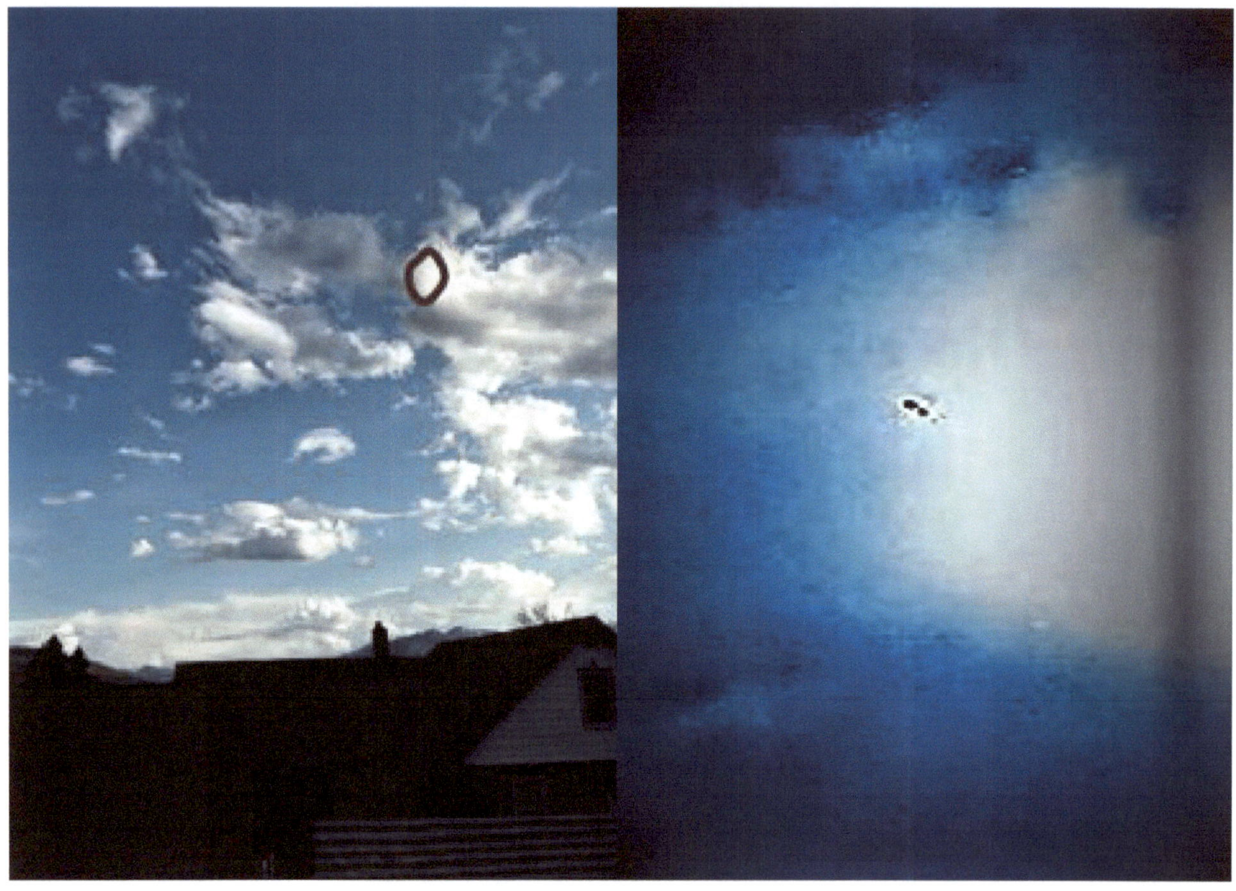

Another set taken from the author's back yard on Mount Jasper. Second photo shows the craft with the naked eye. The others are zoomed In with blue sapphire lens.

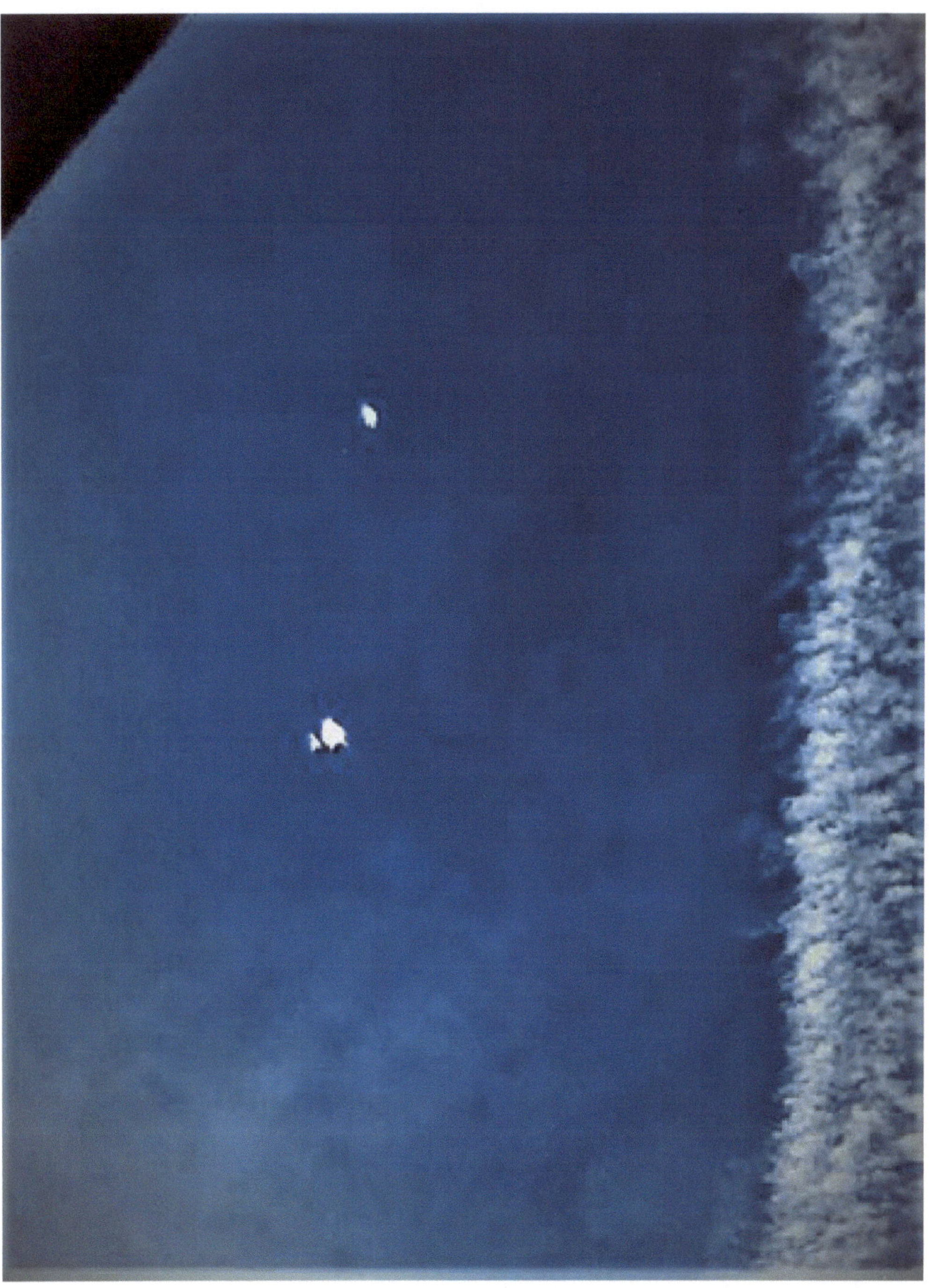

Jet-resembling UFOs. The reader can see the roof of my house to the upper left quadrant and the white cloudy aerosol stream from one of the geoengineering jets that went over our house to the right of the picture. The aerosol stream is already expanding horizontally and smogging up what had been a cobalt blue and clear sky.

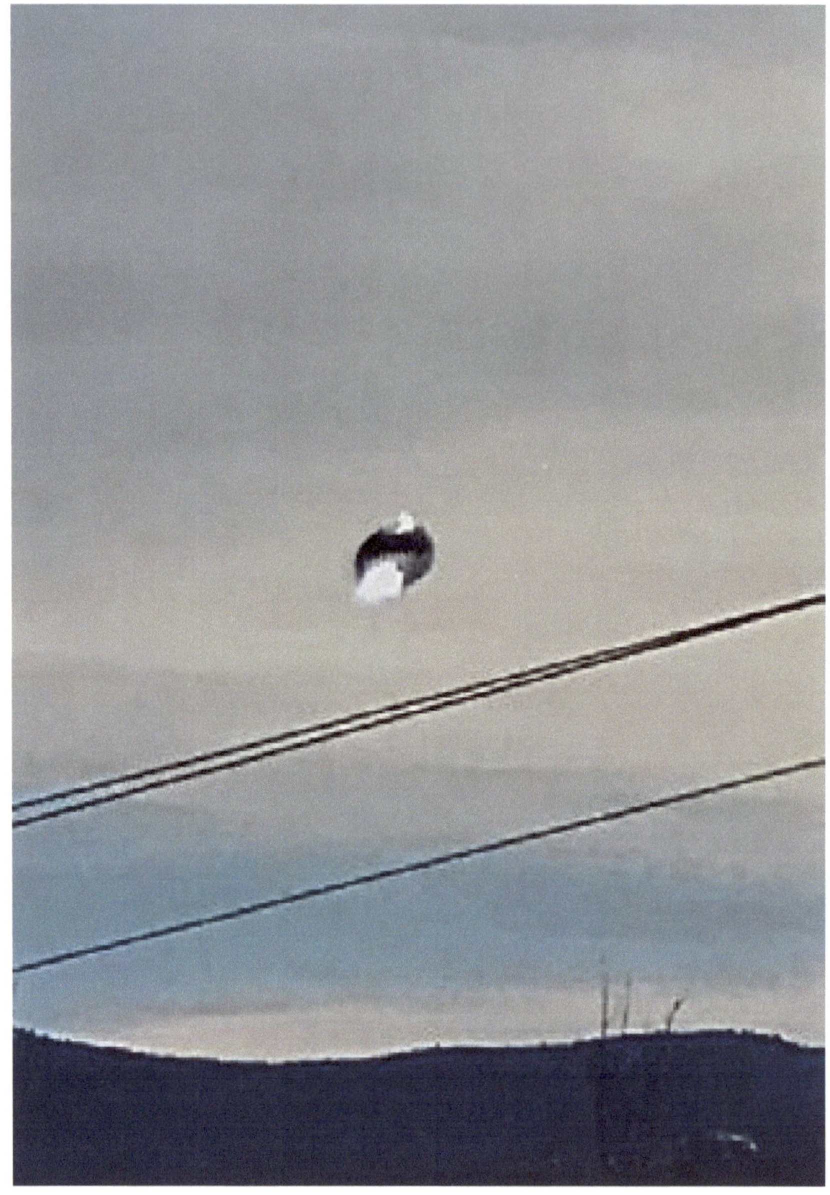

Silvery colored orb UFO craft with black-colored canopy on top, probably the bridge of the craft. This was one of the two leading crafts (of the two UFO formations) which had come down close to the author and his wife while we were taking "before and after" pictures of the sky after geo-engineering jets had passed overhead spraying aerosols.

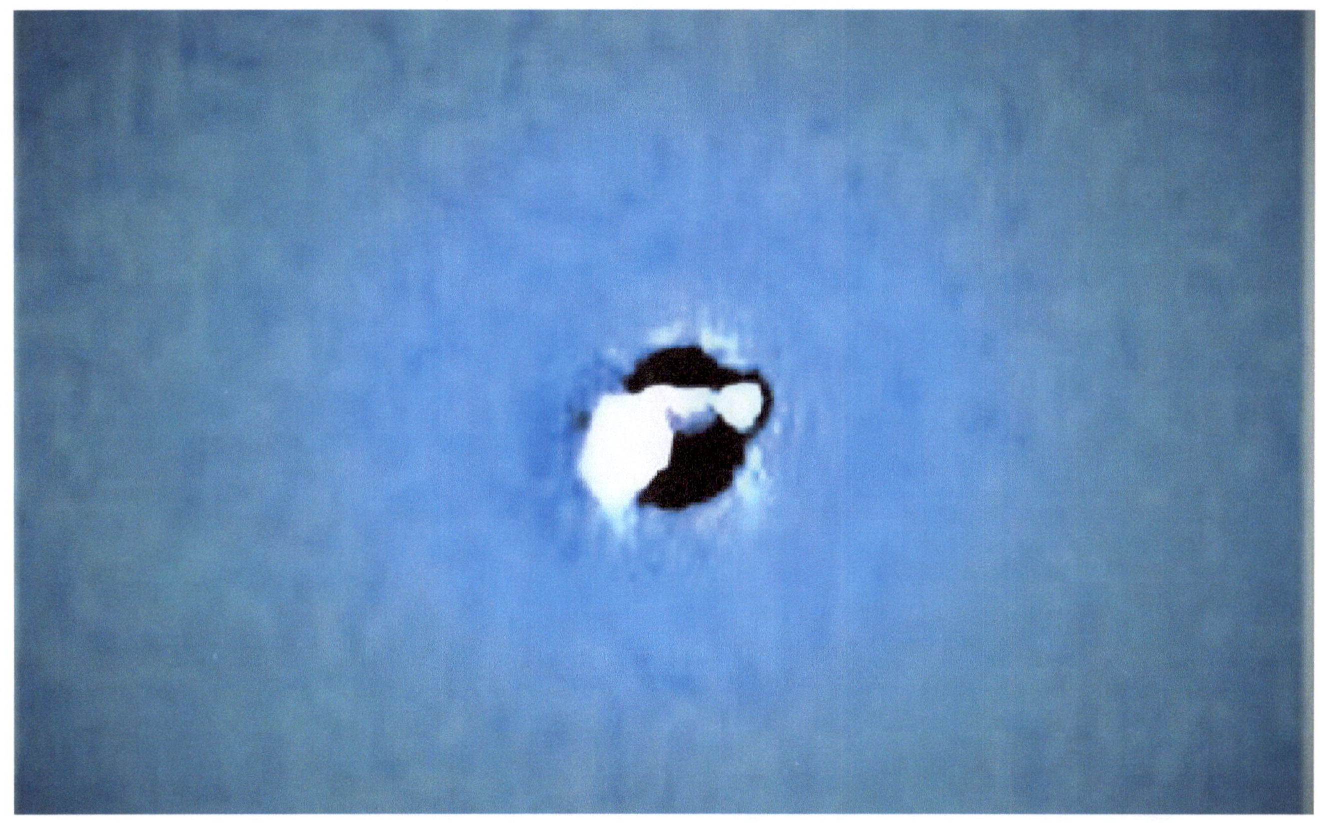

One of two orbs that descended from two UFO formations, all of the same type of craft. This was the leading ship.

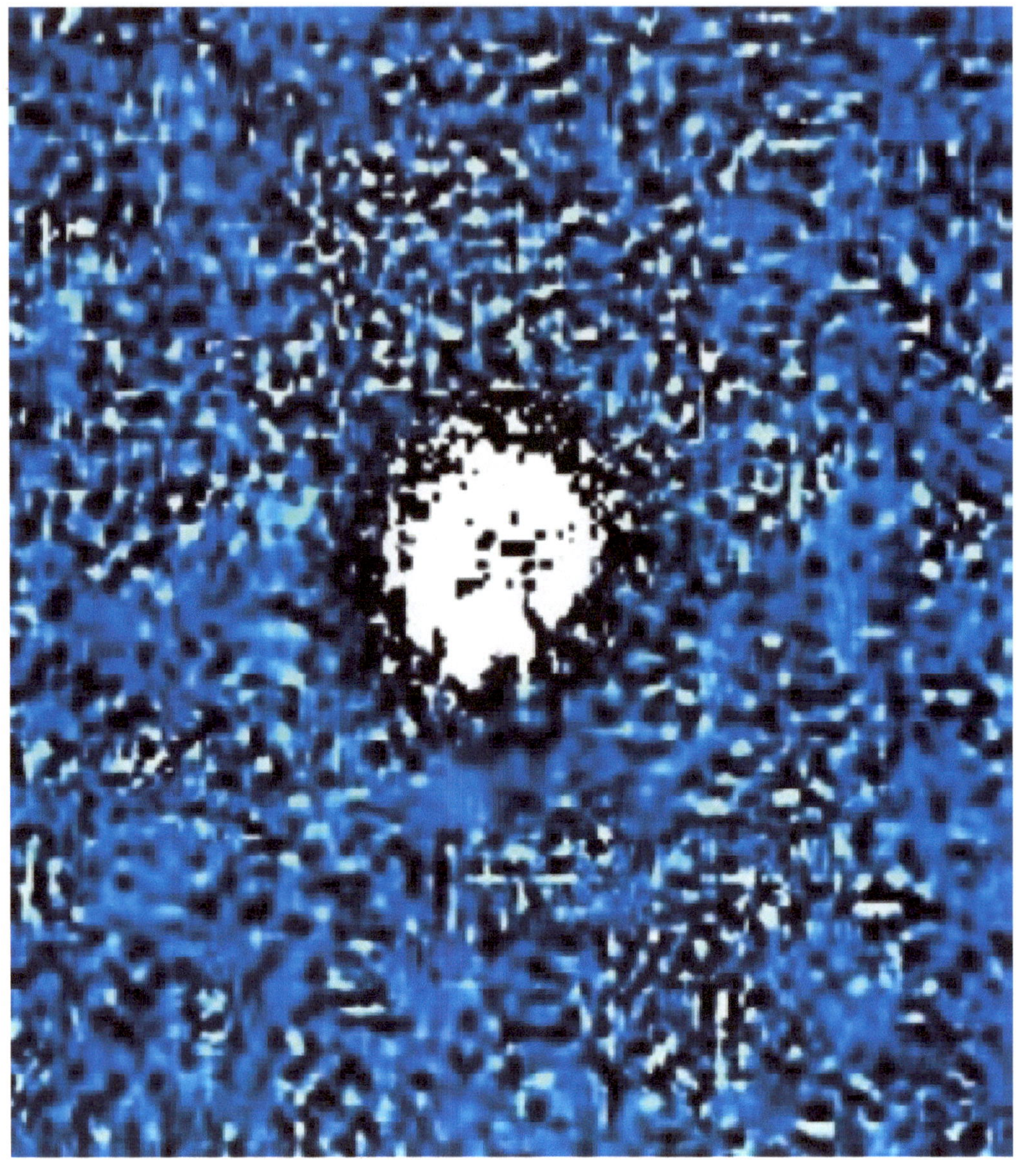

Picture author took of sky to the north from his house's top story balcony to record how blue and cloudless the sky was on March 10th, 2020. What is pictured is yet a different type of UFO leading the entire group of UFOs

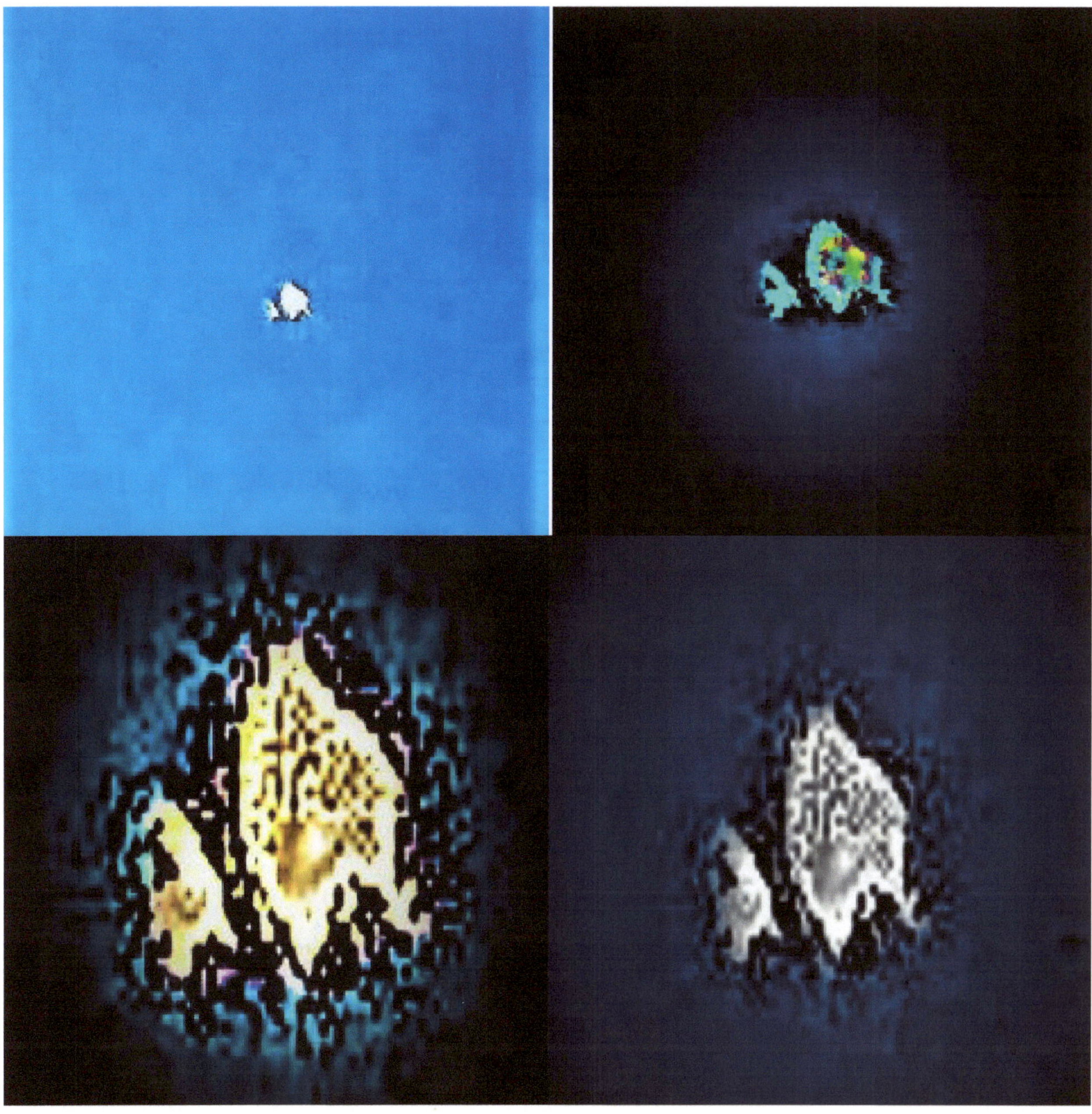

These four photos are of the other "two" UFOs close to the geo-engineering jets' aerosol trails, one of which is larger and in a chevron shape. Although they both resemble jets, the close-up photos reveal that what appears to be two UFOs are really comprised of many smaller UFO crafts that appear to have formed or are reconfiguring into a larger oval, or circular, UFO craft.

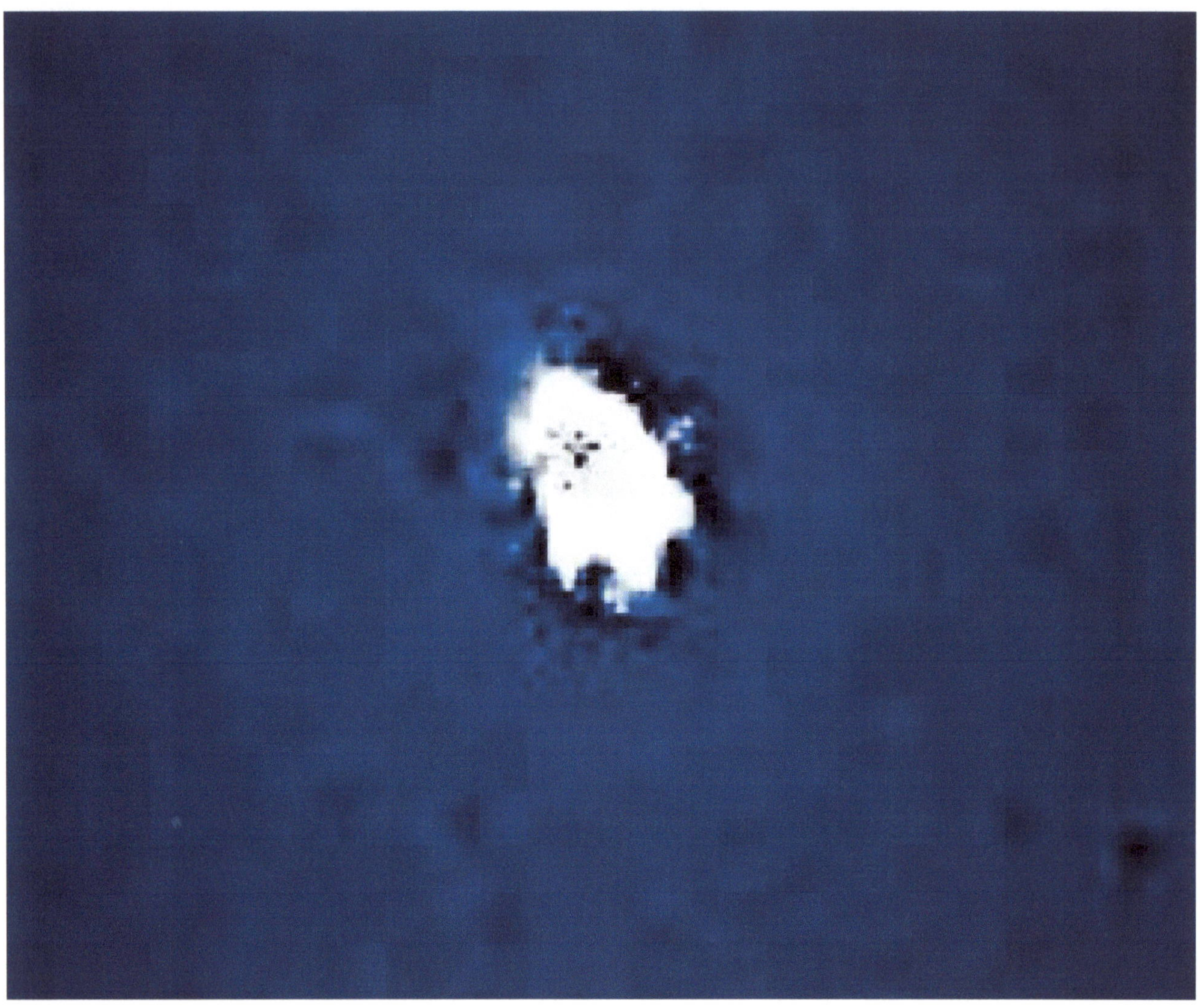

This is a close up of the highest UFO initially observed, which at a distance looks like some kind of Jet. Part of the anti-gravity array on the underside of the UFO Craft is observable. It is in reality a conglomerate of different UFOs, all combined and working together.

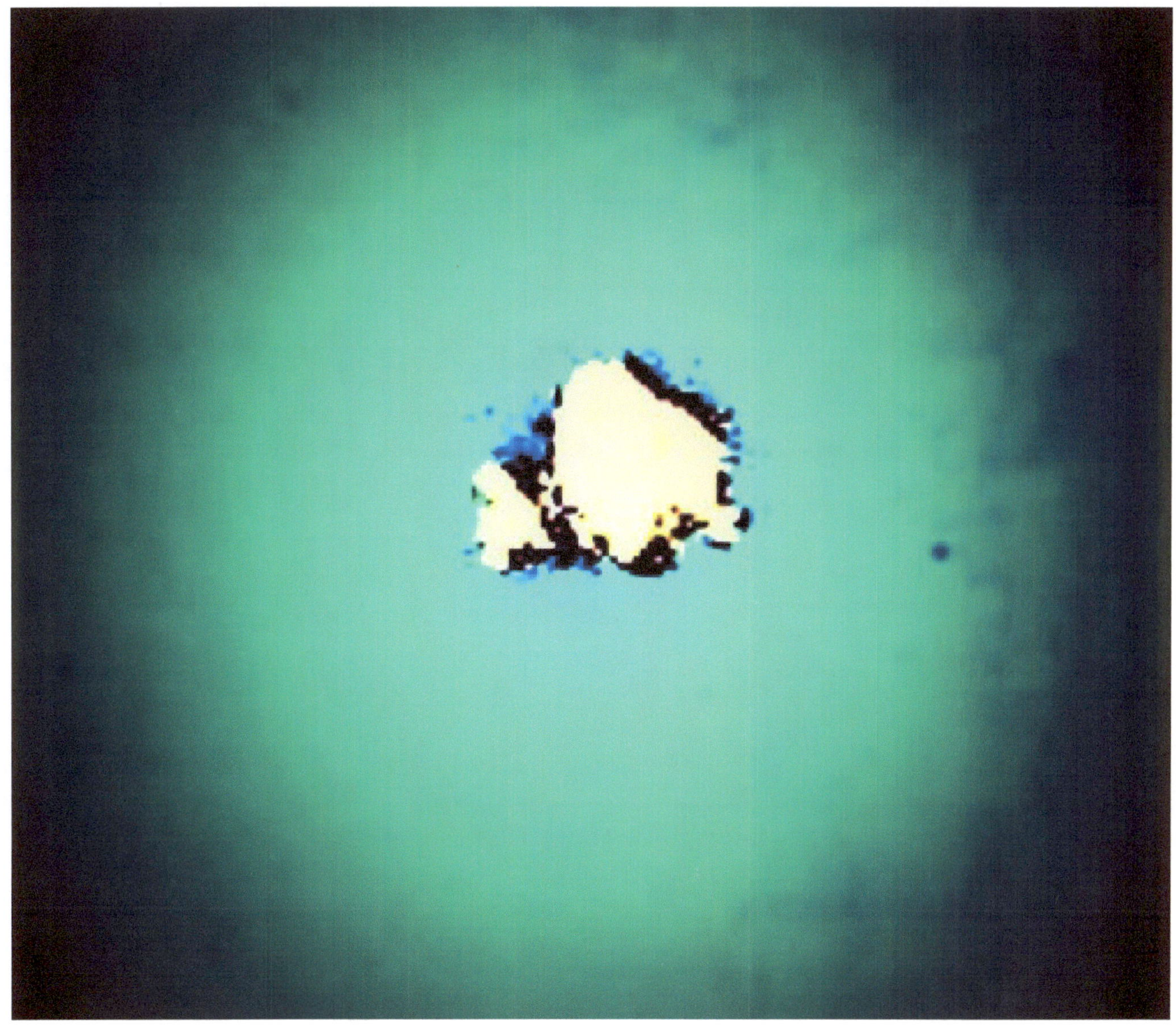

A closeup revealing a UFO platform that is a combination of starships and other UFO crafts.

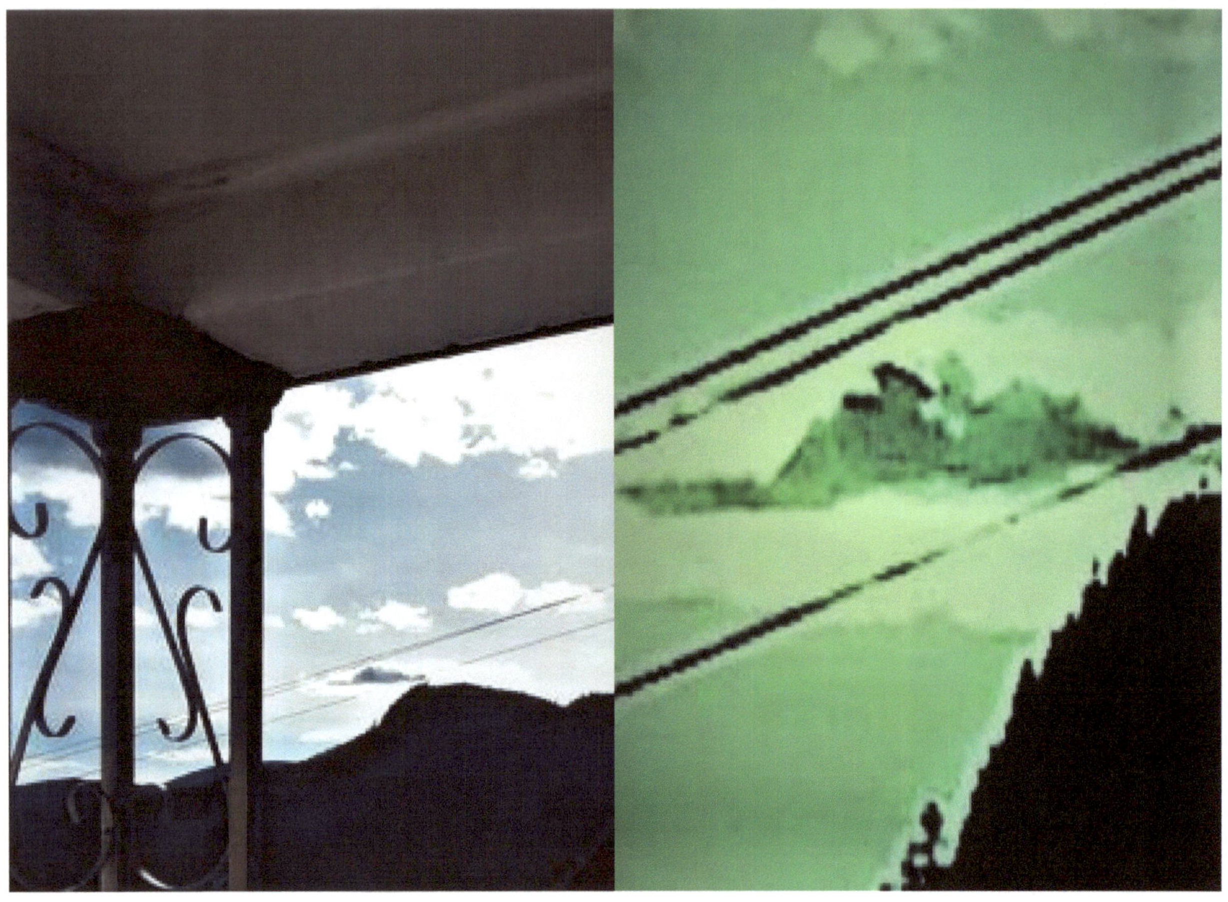

These are pictures of an alien "Bird of Prey" type of UFO. It is just to the left of Mount Forest (or Elephant Mountain) as it's called by locals in Berlin, New Hampshire. There are actually two Large UFO vessels there.

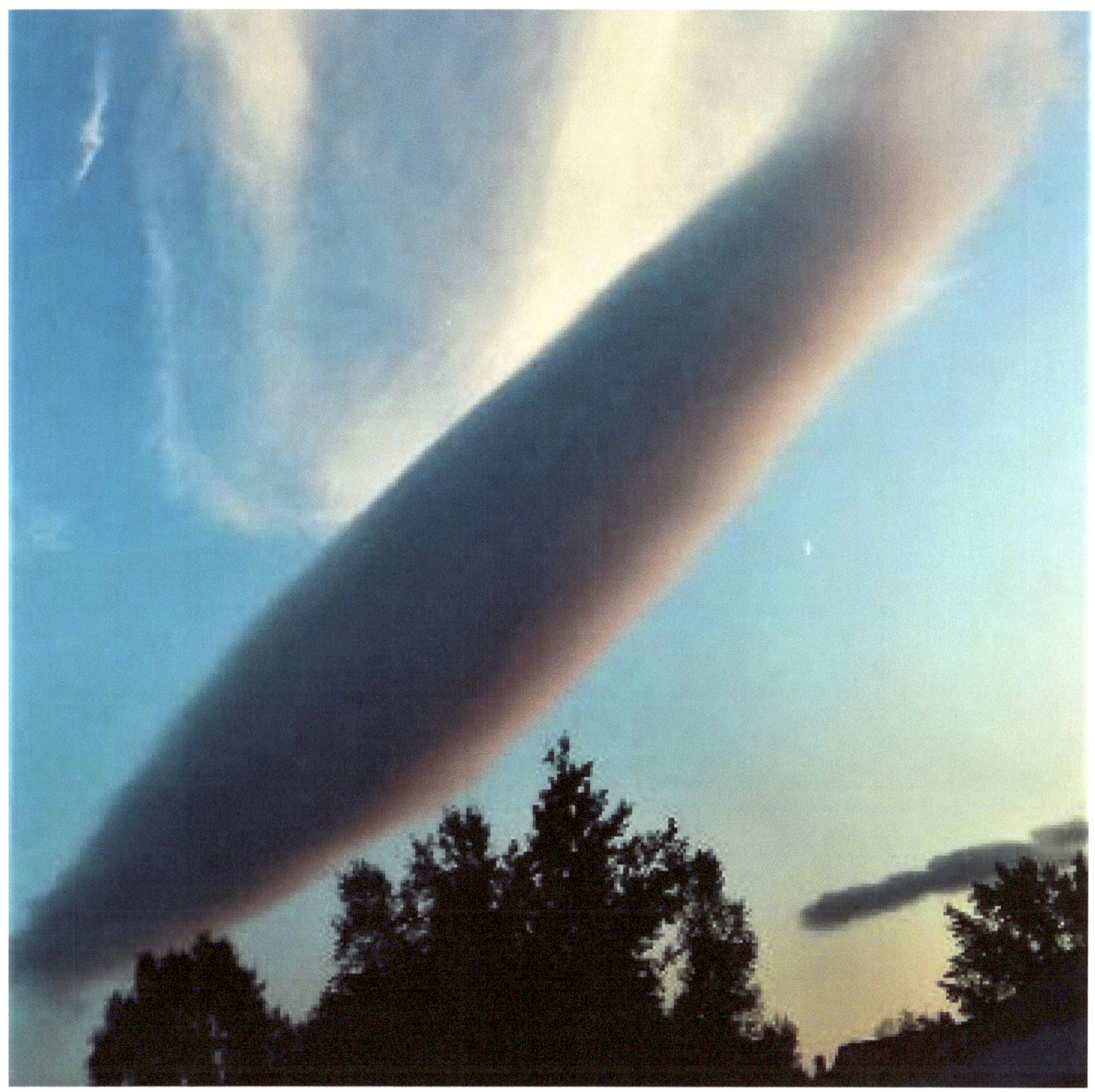

These unusual clouds immediately got my attention while hiking near Mount Washington. As a long-time scuba diver and fisherman, I tend to dig looking at squid and using them for fish-bait. What we are actually observing here are building-sized UFOs all entering a giant squid-like giant UFO transport. I speculate it being an intergalactic mass transport vehicle of some kind. You can see the smaller UFOs entering the giant squid-like craft and gathering inside of it. This is indica-tive that advanced civilizations are not only HERE in what must be large bases or settlements, but perhaps also work underground in major mining operations amidst the White Mountains of New Hampshire.

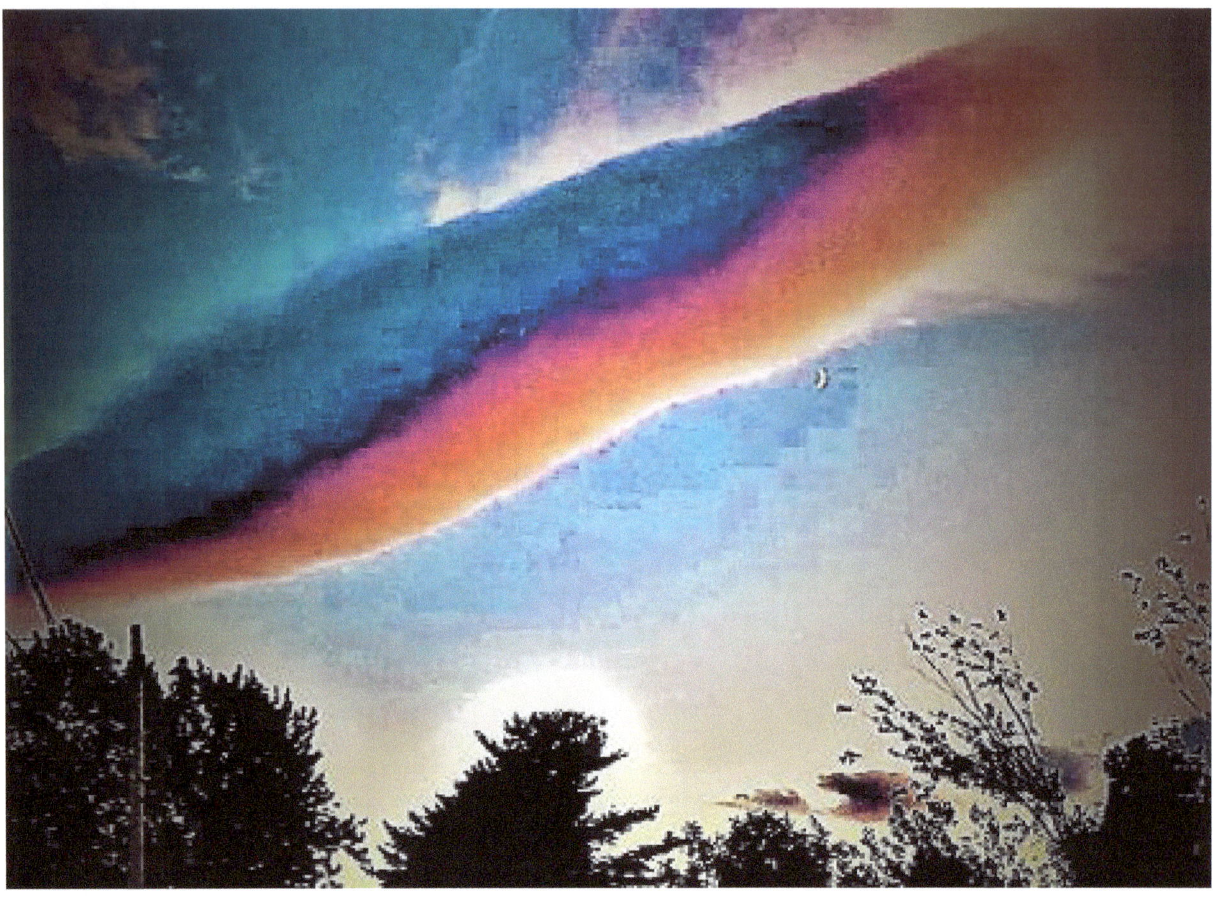

Another photo of the Squid-type UFO. These are a common type of UFO observable in the Mount Washington Valley.

Bibliography

Bisbee, Ernest E. (1946). *The White Mountain Scrap Book of Stories and Legends of the Crystal Hills or White Mountains of New Hampshire.*

de Bougainville, L. A. (n.d.). *The American Journals of Louis Antoine De Bougainville 1756-1760* [Review of *The American Journals of Louis Antoine De Bougainville 1756-1760*].

Boyer, P. (1994). *By the Bomb's Early Light: American Thought and Culture at the Dawn of the Atomic Age.* University of North Carolina Press.

Camerino, A. (2020, October 2). *"Mount Washington, NH: Home Of The World's Worst Weather."* https:snowbrains.com/author/alex-camerino/

Chisolm, Hugh J. (1887). *Chisholm's White Mountain Guide-book.* Chisholm + Brothers Portland.

Corso, P. J., & Birnes, W. J. (2017). *The day after Roswell.* Gallery Books.

David Michael Jacobs. (1998). *The Threat.* Simon & Schuster.

Drake, R. L. (1976). Environmental impact of stratospheric flight: Biological and climatic effects of aircraft emissions in the stratosphere. *Agricultural Meteorology, 17*(1), 55–56. https://doi.org/10.1016/0002-1571(76)90084-4

Edward Pierce Hamilton. (1964). *Fort Ticonderoga, Key to a Continent.* Little, Brown & Co.

Ellsberg, D. (2017). *The doomsday machine: confessions of a nuclear war planner.* Bloomsbury.

Erdoes, R., Ortiz, A., & Books, P. (2006). *American Indian myths and legends.* Pantheon Books, [Post], Cop.

Fuller, J. G. (1975). *Interrupted Journey.* Berkley.

Goebbels, J. (1948). *The Goebbels Diaries, 1942-1943.* Doubleday & Co.

Goodchild, P. (1980). J. ROBERT OPPENHEIMER: Shatterer of Worlds. In *British Broadcasting Corporation (BBC)*.

Good, T. (1988). *Above Top Secret*. William Morrow & Company.

Hamilton, E. P. (1962). *The French and Indian War*. Doubleday & Co., Inc.

Harvey Elliott White. (1959). *Physics, an Exact Science*. D. Van Nostrand Company, Inc.

Hellyer, P. (2016). *The money mafia: a world in crisis*. Trine Day Llc.

Henry Davenport Northrop. (1891). *Indian Horrors; Or, Massacres by the Red Men*.

Hoerlin, H. (1976). *United States high-altitude test experiences. A review emphasizing the impact on the environment. [Checkmate, Bluegill, Kingfish and Tightrope events]*. https://doi.org/10.2172/7122163

Icke, D. (2000). *The biggest secret*. Bridge Of Love.

Johnston, H. S. (1974). Photochemistry in the stratosphere—With applications to supersonic transports. *Acta Astronautica, 1*(1-2), 135–156. https://doi.org/10.1016/0094-5765(74)90013-7

J. Robert Oppenheimer. (2012). *Uncommon Sense*. Birkhäuser.

Manchester, W. (2008). *American Caesar: Douglas MacArthur, 1880-1964*. Back Bay Books.

McLuhan, M. (1964). *Understanding Media: the Extensions of Man*. Abacus.

Mount Washington Observatory (1934). "MWOBS: Mount Washington Observatory." New Hampshire State Parks.

Pretor-Pinney, G., Sanderson, B., & Cloud Appreciation Society. (2007). *The cloudspotter's guide: the science, history and culture of clouds*. Penguin Group.

Schneider, P. (Director). (1995). *UNDERGROUND BASES: Reptilians and the Battle for Humanity* [DVD]. The Phil Schneider Chronicles.

Smith, J. E. (1999). *HAARP: the ultimate weapon of the conspiracy*. Adventures Unlimited Press.

Sparks, J. (2006). *The Keepers*. Granite Pub Llc.

Stallings, J. (2015). The UFO Phenomenon (Mysteries of the Unknown) Free Download Book. In *Dailymotion*. https://www.dailymotion.com/video/x38pfhn

Toland, J. (1970). *Rising sun: the decline and fall of the japanese empire, 1936-1945. 1st ed.* Random House.

Vrooman, J. J. (1950). *Clarissa Putman of Tribes Hill*. The Baronet Titho Company.

Weart, S. R. (1988). *Nuclear fear: a history of images*. Harvard University Press.

Whitman, D. J. (2011). *CHEMTRAIL EVIDENCE: Stratospheric Aerosol Geoengineering (aka Chemtrails) Facts*. Arcrap.org.

Wight, D. B. (1967). *The Androscoggin River Valley, Gateway to the White Mountains*. Charles E. Tuttle Company, Inc.

John Sullivan, ATA, BA, and MA, is a former Enlisted Navy Hospital Corpsman (E-5) and Vietnam Era Veteran, former Reserve Naval Officer (0-4), and Psychiatric Nursing Supervisor who worked with criminally insane people in maximum security state prisons, forensic patients in state hospitals, acute care county mental health units, developmentally-disabled and psychotic residents in a state hospital, as well as private psychiatric asylums in his varied career. His U.S. Navy service has ranged from serving with the U.S. Marines to being a Division Officer on an aircraft carrier. He has traveled extensively through Western Europe, the Middle East, Cuba, North Africa, Latin America, and Asia both in the military and as a civilian. He enjoys kayaking, Harley motorcycle riding, and treasure hunting for old coins with metal detectors both on land, and under water (scuba diving), and of course photographing moose and UFOs. He is retired and lives in the White Mountains of New Hampshire with his wife Sydney and their black and tan dachshund, Angus.

www.ingramcontent.com/pod-product-compliance
Lightning Source LLC
Chambersburg PA
CBHW040130240726
48664CB00002B/433